The New Global Insecurity

The New Global Insecurity

How Terrorism, Environmental Collapse, Economic Inequalities, and Resource Shortages Are Changing Our World

Fathali M. Moghaddam

Praeger Security International

AN IMPRINT OF ABC-CLIO, LLC
Santa Barbara, California • Denver, Colorado • Oxford, England

Library of Congress Cataloging-in-Publication Data

Moghaddam, Fathali M.
   The new global insecurity : how terrorism, environmental collapse, economic inequalities, and resource shortages are changing our world / Fathali M. Moghaddam.
      p. cm.
   Includes bibliographical references and index.
   ISBN 978-0-313-36507-2 (hbk. : alk. paper) — ISBN 978-0-313-36508-9 (ebook)
1. Security, International—Social aspects. 2. Globalization—Social aspects. I. Title.
JZ5588.M64 2010
355'.033—dc22   2009046036

ISBN: 978-0-313-36507-2
EISBN: 978-0-313-36508-9

14 13 12 11 10   1 2 3 4 5

This book is also available on the World Wide Web as an eBook.
Visit www.abc-clio.com for details.

Praeger
An Imprint of ABC-CLIO, LLC

ABC-CLIO, LLC
130 Cremona Drive, P.O. Box 1911
Santa Barbara, California 93116-1911

This book is printed on acid-free paper (∞)

Manufactured in the United States of America

To Philip G. Zimbardo, scientist, activist, universal storyteller

Contents

Preface

The New Global Insecurity explores the profoundly new kind of insecurity arising from globalization that people around the world are experiencing in the twenty-first century. Threats to our security are coming from even the most remote and economically deprived parts of the world, and from new and unexpected sources. In addition to military hardware, food, health, environmental degradation, economic collapse, and other sources that are the focus of traditional "realist" and "human security" schools of thought, we must now give priority to identity, particularly collective identity. Threatened collective identities are integral to our feelings of insecurity in the first decades of the twenty-first century.

Globalized security translates to interconnected insecurity; a security threat in one part, even a seemingly peripheral part, of the world now necessarily threatens other parts. The new globalized security is impacting all of our lives, because we have all become actual or potential targets of security threats from terrorism to global warming to swift and unpredicted economic downturns. This new trend began with the development of biological weapons by the superpowers during the Cold War, when civilians became the potential targets for biological attacks in possible wars between the United States and the Soviet Union. This was a new kind of warfare in which biological agents would be used on a large scale against civilians to immobilize the enemy military. Fortunately for humankind, large scale biological warfare never actually took place. Although the Cold War has now ended, we are not safe because terrorists and other non-state actors have taken up the tactic of attacking civilians. In this new situation, attacks can come from anywhere, anytime; insecurity can arise from many sources, including sudden global economic shifts.

The traditional approaches to security are no longer adequate for dealing with the new interconnected global threats. The approach I am advocating is innovative and novel, and based on an exploration of "soft" and "hard" security capital, as well as the "dual-source theory" of security. In particular, I argue for a shift of focus from rational to irrational processes, from assuming that humans are rational creatures to accepting that our behavior is largely irrational, particularly in the domain of security. We must develop a far more effective policy for managing diversity and intergroup relations at national and global levels. This will enable us to more effectively prevent conflict and improve security. Thus, students of security must expand their horizons and also concern themselves more seriously with policies for conflict prevention. In this connection, I introduced the policy of omniculturalism, which I argue is superior to both multiculturalism and assimilation as a policy for managing diversity and preventing intergroup conflict.

I have adopted a writing style appropriate for the lay public, as well for as students and researchers interested in security studies, peace studies, conflict resolution, social psychology, human aggression, political psychology, cultural psychology, intergroup relations, war, interfaith relations, and terrorism, among others.

Acknowledgments

I am deeply indebted to an Italian and to a Scotsman, Phil Zimbardo and Jim Breckenridge, who generously invited me to join them on a "small project" some years ago. The project has continued, surprisingly managed to survive my participation, and afforded me the opportunity to learn much of value from Dr. Z and Jim, even a few things outside of wining, dining, and gender relations.

Rom Harré must also accept some responsibility for what you are about to read, particularly when he instructed me to: "Always study security in relation to risk." Rom holds so many different academic positions (it is difficult to understand how he manages to be in all those places at once!) that I will not even try to remember what lofty title he held when he lobbed this nugget my way—was it as Distinguished Research Professor at Georgetown, Director of a program at the London School of Economics, or something or other at Oxford? Rom recently gave me what he called "an ample part" of his Oxford house, a piece of stone that weighs almost 4 ounces. I wish he had warned me about the back-breaking taxes that come with this Oxford property. Despite the humongous costs and dangers, however, I have taken out second and third mortgages in the hope of building on this stone and passing on the property to future generations.

I continue to be deeply indebted to my students. Each year, they stride enthusiastically into my office eager to search for answers. Even though they seldom find answers, together we learn to ask more penetrating questions. Along this exhilarating journey, they come to see me as one of them, another wild-eyed soul struggling to discover how best to live.

For her support and advice throughout this project, I am deeply indebted to Debbie Carvalko, who is a great credit to the publishing world.

1

Insecurity and Globalization

Hard times bring hard questions. Calamitous wars, international terrorism, environmental degradation and global warming, interconnected global economic depression—the twenty-first century has given birth to hard times, and we now labor under hard questions. How will we manage a world severely challenged by shrinking resources, ballooning population, huge and increasing income inequalities, terrorism, torture, and environmental collapse? Is globalization leading us to a more peaceful world in which open borders and open societies flourish? Or is globalization resulting in greater economic and political instability, closed societies, and more violent conflicts? The questions explored in this book arise out of globalization and its consequences for *security*, the feeling of safety experienced by groups and individuals.[1]

Received wisdom presents us with two dramatically different pictures of the relationship between security and globalization. The first portrays globalization as leading to greater interdependence, openness, peace, and prosperity. Open borders, it is argued, will lead to the increasing trade of goods, services, and ideas. Nation states will become both more interdependent and, eventually, more democratic. Economic interdependence will mean that it will not be in the interests of countries to attack one other, because war against other nation states will mean war against one's own interests. In addition, the more democratic countries become, the less likely they will be to wage war against other democracies. Thus, this first perspective presents an idealistic view of globalization.

The second, less optimistic but equally compelling, picture portrays globalization as resulting in *greater insecurity*. As globalization unleashes unforeseen changes, some nation states prosper, invest in and strengthen their militaries, and inevitably attempt to expand their economic and political reach, while other nation states experience decline and wage wars to try to prevent competitors from taking over their threatened territories and resources. The shifting fortunes of nations will be associated with largely unforeseen military consequences and greater insecurity. This perspective dismisses the idea that democracies will not wage war against one another, and points to the exploitative and conflict-generating nature of economic interdependencies.

Also, it is not just changes in resource-rich and strategically located nations that have implications for the insecurity experienced by the rest of the world. The globalization of systems of electronic communications and transportation means that even a resource-poor country such as Afghanistan, which is geographically far away from North America, has come to pose a direct and high-level security threat to the United States. Consequently, following 9/11 we have had tens of thousands of American troops and thousands of contractors and North Atlantic Treaty Organization (NATO) personnel waging war on Afghan soil. Globalization means that security threats must be seen as potentially arising from every part of the world. Rather than being concentrated in particular "enemy" countries or easily identified and readily located actors, globalized security threats are scattered, multi-centered, and mobile. For example, as Al Qaeda is decapitated and its core is immobilized, its scattered ashes spark new flames and bring terrorist groups to life in remote parts of Indonesia and the Philippines.

Underlying these two contrasting perspectives is the acknowledgment that we have entered the age of *global insecurity,* meaning that in the twenty-first century we are experiencing a high and increasing level of interconnectedness between security threats and their impact in different parts of the world. Traditional security institutions, policies, and worldviews are struggling to adapt to these fast-changing global circumstances.[2] A threat to security in one part of the world can now have *fast-acting* and important implications for security in other parts of the world. For example, changes in security in the Middle East can directly and immediately impact security in Western societies.

Globalization has also brought identity threats to the fore. Indeed, the twenty-first century is proving to be the century of threatened identities, an era in which military conflict arises most often out of threats to identity. For example, major Islamic societies have been described as experiencing a "collective identity crisis,"[3] because the two alternatives open to them for identity development are both unsatisfactory. The first alternative involves copying the West and results in the "good copy problem."[4] After all, even the best copy is still only a copy, it lacks authenticity and genuineness—something not lost on the people in the situation. The second alternative is to take the Salafist path and "return to roots," but such a return to the sociopolitical system of 1,400 years ago has proved to be impractical for solving twenty-first century societal and personal challenges. Unfortunately, a combination of local dictators and U.S. support for certain (supposedly) pro-American Islamic dictatorships (e.g., Egypt, Saudi Arabia) has thwarted the development of a third secular alternative. Consequently, a number of major Islamic societies continue to experience a collective identity crisis, and this has given rise to radicalization and terrorism. Although globalized insecurity is associated with completely new trends, even those aspects of security that represent continuity have to be re-evaluated.

****

Fear, and the sight of the numbers of the conspirators, closed the mouths of the rest; or if any ventured to rise in opposition, he was presently put to death in some convenient way, and there was neither search for the murderers nor justice to be had against them if suspected; but the people remained motionless, being so thoroughly cowed that men thought themselves lucky to escape violence, even when they held their tongues.[5]

This is how the Greek historian Thucydides (c.460–c.400 BC) describes the atmosphere in Athens toward the end of the Peloponnesian War (431–404 BC). Athenians were gripped by fear and insecurity as the victorious Spartans maneuvered to snuff out Athenian democracy. In postulating how the war started, Thucydides again gives feelings of insecurity a central role: Sparta feared that its superiority in the region was being challenged by the rise of Athens. In modern terminology, Sparta waged war to return the international order to a desired balance of power. Received wisdom tells us that Thucydides is part of a *realist* tradition that continues to modern times[6] envisaging security as centered on rational and unitary state actors, seeking to maximize national interests, and giving highest priority to national security as reflected in military power.

But a closer reading of Thucydides clearly shows that he viewed security as much more than just military strength. Thucydides saw that citizens could feel insecure even when they lived in a powerful state (such as Sparta), because a powerful state can act as a double-edged sword, tyrannizing its own citizens within and waging wars against competitor states outside. Indeed, to this day, in some cases the leaders of powerful countries, such as the United States, have used the excuse of dangers posed by external enemies (such as communists and Islamic Jihadists) to crack down on freedom and liberty within their own societies. Thus, even within the realist tradition, there is room for viewing security as being broader than the mere military power of independent states. Since the Second World War, there have been new efforts to expand the concept of security, reflected by terms such as *global security, comprehensive security*, and *common security.*[7]

****

For most people, a feeling of insecurity arises more from worries about daily life than from the dread of cataclysmic world events. Will they and their families have enough to eat? Will they lose their jobs? Will their streets and neighborhoods be safe from crime? Will they be tortured by a repressive state? Will they become a victim of violence because of their gender? Will their religion or ethnic origin target them for persecution?[8]

The landmark United Nations *Human Development Report* of 1994, followed up by a report from the Commission on Human Security (2003), shifted the focus of security and insecurity from nation states to individuals, from military power to the struggles of ordinary people with everyday challenges—illness, poverty, unemployment, crime, political repression, and environmental pollution. Human security was now depicted as interconnected with human development. It was argued that just as national development must move away from a focus on roads, bridges, and "hard" economic factors to the development of human capital and widening the range of people's choices,[9] discussions of security must move away from military might to focus on human security, which is people-centered, universal, interdependent, proactive, and requires early prevention rather than later intervention.

Threats to human security were discussed under seven broad categories:

1. Economic security
2. Food security
3. Health security
4. Environmental security
5. Personal security
6. Community security
7. Political security

Although it omitted conventional aspects of security such as military and national security, the 1994 *Human Development Report* stated that "Human security is not a concern with weapons—it is a concern with human life and dignity."[10]

****

The mainstream approach to defining security and insecurity continues to be in terms of national interests, and specifically in relation to the threat of military attacks from other nations.[11] As one leading researcher succinctly noted, ". . . poor states are militarily weaker than rich states, and few poor societies can directly challenge the territory or autonomy of rich states."[12] Consequently, only rich and powerful competitor states could pose a serious security threat. The classic national security discussion is still very much influenced by the Cold War tradition, when two opposing powers, the United States and the Soviet Union, confronted one another, armed with both conventional military forces and nuclear missiles.[13] But enormous changes have taken place since the 1980s, and in the transformed world of the twenty-first century some security challenges have shifted to become far less important, while some others have suddenly erupted to become urgent priorities.

Whereas until the 1970s the threat of direct military confrontation between the United States and the Soviet Union was the greatest security threat facing both nations and the rest of the world, with enormous implications for the future of the planet, since the 1980s the importance of this threat has declined considerably. This is in large part because the Soviet Union suffered economic collapse, and a subsequent marked decline in political influence around the world, leaving the United States as the sole global superpower. The vacuum left by the disintegration of the Soviet communist empire has been quickly filled by the spread of capitalism, represented militarily by NATO. Not only has NATO expanded into what used to be strictly Soviet territory in Eastern Europe, but also most of the Eastern European members of the former Soviet block are now part of the EU, which has expanded to twenty-seven states. Russia now feels that in the twenty-first century it has to act aggressively to try to maintain influence over at least the weaker states immediately at its borders, such as Georgia (which Russia invaded in August 2008).

It could be argued that the decline of the threat of direct military confrontation between the United States and Russia is being replaced by the threat of direct economic and military competition between the United States and China, a communist giant that is rapidly rising in industrial and military strength and is predicted to become the largest economy in the world before 2030. However, China will probably not be able to continue juggling an open economy with a closed, dictatorial political system, and will experience major convulsions and disruptions (such as interethnic clashes that occurred in June and July of 2009), resulting in serious setbacks in the next few decades. Second, more generally, predictions that the twenty-first century will be the Asian century still seem premature. Just as the rise of Japan was exaggerated during the 1970s and 1980s, with slogans such as "Japan is number 1" proving to be misplaced, it is probable that the rise of China is being exaggerated, and by 2030 we will look back and wonder why we had imagined that China would become "number 1." (Japan and Russia are among a number of powerful countries that now face enormous economic, political, and cultural challenges because of their low birth rate and aging population. China also faces enormous challenges because of the huge burden about to be placed on an unusually small number of young Chinese, products of the "one child" policy having to support their aging parents.) Third, the economy of China is very closely tied to the economies of Western societies, with far closer ties than the Soviet economy had with the West, and such close economic ties limit (but do not preclude) the possibility of a direct military confrontation between China and the United States. A direct military confrontation between the United States and other major rising powers, such as the EU, India, and Brazil, seems even less likely in the next few decades.

It is unlikely, then, that United States national security will be seriously threatened by direct military confrontation with another national power in the next few decades. The security threats that have arisen in the twenty-first century are of a different kind.[14] These new threats are not located within a single competitor nation state (such as Russia or China), or restricted to the traditional "hard" (e.g., military) focus of security. Rather, the new security threats are dispersed globally and influenced by many different types of *security capital,* all the various "hard" and "soft" resources (discussed further in Chapter 4) that combine to determine the security level of a society.

Thus, another key feature of the new global insecurity is the dispersed nature of security threats. Unlike previous eras in which security threats tended to be more concentrated in the actions of one or a few "enemy" nation states, the new global insecurity arises from threats scattered around the globe. Indeed, we can describe a traditional security threat as uni-centered and fixed in geographical location, whereas a globalized security threat is more multi-centered and mobile.

****

The human security movement has been severely criticized by the more traditional security studies experts, and in some respects there is a large rift between the two camps. Human security seems to be based on vague and woolly ideas, with security defined broadly as something like "being free from fear." Traditional security studies experts focus clearly on military threats and national security, and believe that it is simply wrong and distracting to broaden the scope to include environmental, community, food, and other types of security. The human security approach, the critics argue, seems to include everything, and by including everything it tells us nothing of value about security.

On the other hand, supporters of the new human security approach are surely correct in arguing for a more expansive definition of security.

For example, surely food security is important to overall security?[15] Both sides, it seems, are making legitimate claims—but how can both sides be correct?

To sort through this controversy, it is useful to distinguish between what has traditionally been at the heart of security studies, military power, and national security, and their "enabling conditions." What factors enable a nation to have the ability to enjoy national security? My argument is that the extensive list of factors typically listed under human security actually serves as enabling conditions for what the traditional security studies experts regard as national security.

The enabling conditions are an essential platform for national security and freedom from military threat, particularly in the longer term. For example, consider "nation A" and "nation B," the first weak and the second strong in economic, food, health, environmental, personal, community, and political securities, and all other factors central to human security. The strengths of nation A in these areas that are central to human security enable nation A to develop and sustain a strong military and to have less fear of suffering a military attack. Nation B, on the other hand, is weak in human security, such as economic and food security, and as a consequence is not able to provide *long-term* support for a strong national security (we are reminded of Napoleon Bonaparte's saying that "an army marches on its stomach"). Thus, human security "enables" military security and other types of "realist" security.

Of course, there is interdependence between what I have termed *enabling conditions* and *traditional national security*. In other words, without the one, the other of these would *eventually* suffer serious decline. Traditional security based on military strength is needed for the long-term development of human security, just as human security is needed for the long-term survival of traditional security based on military strength.

The relationship between the traditional realist factors (focusing on military strength, defenses, and the like) and human security is characterized by what I term the *security cycle* (see Figure 1.1). During times of high military threat, the traditional realist factors come to have highest priority, and human security only becomes relevant as a support for traditional realist security. However, when military threat is perceived to be low, human security factors can take on the highest priority. Therefore during the Second World War and immediately after 9/11, traditional realist security took on the highest priority as the United States and its allies geared up to meet the external military threat. Efforts in all human security sectors, including agriculture, health, education, and so on, became subservient to the greater effort of military defense coupled with security.

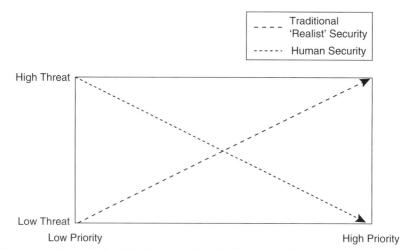

Figure 1.1 The relationship between level of perceived threat and the priority given to traditional realist security and human security

****

A neglected but important difference between traditional realist approaches to security and the more recent human security approach concerns the question: security for which group? Who is feeling insecure?

The traditional realist approach deals with threats that most directly concern the political, economic, religious, and military elite. A major attack from a determined enemy could bring about the downfall of a political order, and the downfall of a ruling elite. For example, the invasion of Iraq by U.S.-led forces in 2003 resulted in the downfall of Saddam Hussein and the collapse of his regime, together with the ruling elite that had controlled the political, economic, cultural, religious, and military levers of power. Similarly, the military defeat of Hitler and the collapse of the Nazi regime in 1945 resulted in changes in the ruling elite in Germany. Throughout history, military defeat has typically resulted in regime change, and this has meant a change in the status of the ruling elite.

Military defeat and regime change have not necessarily resulted in detrimental consequences for ordinary people. Indeed, often the removal of a ruling elite creates new opportunities for non-elite individuals to move up the political and economic hierarchy. For example, after the military defeat and removal of Saddam Hussein's regime, Iraqis (particularly Shiites and Kurds) who had previously not had the opportunity to vie for high political office now found their paths more open. Such Iraqis could make their way up the status hierarchy by collaborating with the American military and going along with American plans for Iraq. Thus, a security threat in the traditional realist sense of a military attack and possible regime change can result in better opportunities for members of the non-elite. It is the ruling elite who must be most concerned with traditional security threats.

On the other hand, human security is more directly of concern to ordinary people, the non-elite, who do not have access to political, economic, and military power. A threat to food or economic securities or other major domains of human security necessarily impacts ordinary people—the non-elite who have little or no reserve resources and live from hand-to-mouth. To once more return to the unfortunate case of Iraq, after the American-led invasion of Iraq a new ruling elite replaced the old ruling elite that constituted the regime of Saddam Hussein. The new ruling elite in post-Saddam Iraq has enjoyed access to superior food, housing, health care, and all the other elements of human security. However, the Iraqi non-elite have suffered a disastrous drop in their standard of living, including basics such as access to water, food, and energy.

IRRATIONALITY AND GLOBAL INSECURITY

The traditional realist perspective on security has combined an emphasis on military strength with an emphasis on national sovereignty. The adoption of the sovereign state as the unit of security is typically described as going back to the Peace of Westphalia, which brought an end to decades of bloody warfare in Europe in 1648.[16] The human security movement sought to shift the focus in debates about security, from military strength to education, health, and other humane criteria, as well as from the unit of the state to the unit of the individual person. However, what have now become the two major perspectives on security, *idealist* (human) and *realist* (materialist), both miss a foundational point: globalization has profound psychological consequences that can, and often does, shape what happens in economic, political, and other domains. Security is first and foremost a feeling experienced by groups and individuals, a feeling about how much they are at risk of being threatened and attacked, a feeling of insecurity.

Consequently, the debate in security studies should not be about the size of the unit—obviously *both* individuals and groups should be considered. A state (and all other collectives) can feel insecure, and an individual can feel insecure. The shift I am arguing for is from objectivity and rationality, to also include subjectivity and irrationality. The essential issue is the extent to which a collective (nation state, region, city, neighborhood, ethnic group, religious group, and so on) and individuals *feel* insecure. The feeling of insecurity that is the focus of attention here is often determined through irrational rather than rational processes.

- Samantha is a fifty-two-year-old accountant who, together with the rest of her accounting firm, was at work close to ground zero at the time of the 9/11 terrorist attacks, but she and her colleagues feel perfectly secure continuing to work in the New York City financial district. Meanwhile, thousands of miles away lives Jean, a middle-aged woman who works in a small pharmacy in the tiny town of Seaside, Oregon. Jean feels insecure because of what she and her family see as a serious threat of terrorist attacks—even in her isolated neighborhood on the Pacific ocean front.
- Richard is one of a group of managers who work at the headquarters of a major bank in Toronto. What worries the managers most at present is that computer hackers broke into the bank's computer system and gained access to the banking records of thousands of the bank's clients. This security breach and its consequences for management give Richard many sleepless nights.
- Since her birth eighty-nine years ago, Shuhan has lived in the same small town located about sixty miles outside Beijing, in an area always occupied by her ancestors. The survival of her neighborhood is threatened by new road construction and development schemes, and Shuhan and her neighbors now feel insecure and at the mercy of the new class of rich entrepreneurs in China, as well as corrupt government bureaucrats. Her one remaining wish is that she will be allowed to die in her ancestral home, but there are rumors that government-backed eviction orders will soon be handed to everyone in her neighborhood.
- Krishno is a farmer in southern India, and despite the severe flooding his village has suffered in recent years, he and the other villagers feel secure about their future. Krishno feels particularly secure because he believes his nine surviving children, seven boys and only two girls, guarantee a comfortable old age for him and his wife. "What bad thing can happen to me?" He says, "I have seven boys for protection."
- Susan is a thirty-two-year-old hair stylist living in Leeds, England, who saves money every week to buy new clothes. She experiences a wonderful sense of security walking into her closet full of new shoes and clothes. Just the scent of the luxurious leathers and fabrics that make up her wardrobe are a comfort to her and dispel the sense of insecurity she occasionally experiences.

- Maurice lives in the outskirts of Paris and feels extremely insecure. He is close to retirement age and believes his country is being taken over by "backward" Muslims, coming to France from the former French colonies of Algeria, Morocco, and Tunisia. He and his friends feel it is best to keep France for the French.
- Ahmed works as part of the morality police in Riyadh, Saudi Arabia. He and his family have a worrying sense of being overwhelmed by the Western values and goods flooding into their traditional homes. They feel anxious and insecure, and are determined to remain on guard to protect their way of life in this dangerous world, increasingly dominated by Western secularism.
- Thomas works in the oil industry in Nigeria. He is a devout Christian and attends church regularly. He feels moderately secure most of the time, but huge fluctuations in the price of oil in recent years have made life seem less predictable and far less secure for him and millions of others in oil-producing countries.
- Alf is a restaurant owner in Sweden. Initially he was very pleased about the thousands of third-world refugees who found their way to his region in Sweden, because it meant he could easily find cheap workers for his kitchen. But now he and his neighbors feel overwhelmed by the large numbers of Asian and African newcomers, and they feel less secure even in their own homes.
- Sarah's family have owned and operated their tobacco farm in Alabama since the early nineteenth century. However, they feel that the future of their family farm is insecure because of pressure from the anti-smoking groups.
- Janet is a two-year-old toddler living with her mother and father in the outskirts of Perth, Australia. She loves to accompany her mother when she goes shopping, but when she is outside her home Janet remains within an invisible circle about twenty feet in diameter with her mother at the center. Janet feels secure as long as she stays inside the invisible circle.
- Jeremiah is an African American who seldom comes out of his house since hurricane Katrina lambasted New Orleans in 2005, where he has lived all his life. Jeremiah did not suffer from the flooding directly, but was viciously attacked and robbed during the lawlessness that followed Katrina's landing. He is now disabled, constantly anxious, and feeling insecure.
- Dimitri is an officer in the Russian army. He is a strong Russian nationalist and he feels that the security of Russia is seriously threatened by NATO expansion into Eastern Europe. "We Russians are

being surrounded by American missiles; we must do whatever it takes to regain our security," he says.

• Mohammad is a traditional Muslim and sympathetic to the Taliban cause. His family has lived for generations in the region bordering Afghanistan and Pakistan, keeping to themselves and shunning foreigners. They feel deeply offended and threatened by the invasion of U.S.-led troops to their ancestral homeland.

THE MESSAGE AND PLAN OF THIS BOOK

Globalization has fundamentally transformed the nature of security, given birth to new security threats, and brought about serious feelings of insecurity. First, increasing interconnectedness has resulted in globalized security, so that changes in security in one part of the world impact security in other parts of the world. It is no longer possible for a nation, even a superpower, to isolate itself and remain immune to security threats in other parts of the world. John Donne's (1572–1631) admonition that "no man is an island, entire of itself . . ."[17] has come to fruition in the realm of security.

The interconnectedness of global security has resulted in what I term the *Ahmadinejad effect*, where minor actors on the world stage can rise to prominence and gain popularity at home by threatening the security of even distant lands. The threats made by Ahmadinejad, president of the Islamic Republic of Iran, against the United States, Israel, and other "distant" lands particularly in 2007 and 2008 only make sense in the context of globalized security. The new interconnectedness means that "local" radicals can threaten distant targets, garner world attention, and force the international community to take them seriously. This is because electronic communications, rapid long-distant transportation, and long-range missiles with the potential to carry nuclear warheads, allow local radicals to operate internationally. As 9/11 demonstrated, it does not take a lot of resources for local hotheads to inflict serious damage against distant targets that are much, much larger and more powerful than themselves.

A third feature of globalized security is that the main sources of insecurity are no longer concentrated in one or a few major "enemy states," characterized by military might and strength as defined in traditional realist terms, or indeed as defined according to the criteria of human security. Of course, there is still economic, political, cultural, and military rivalry between major powers. But such "traditional" interstate rivalries now pose only one form—often the less crucial and consequential form—of security threats. Non-state actors, often maneuvering between the spheres of influence of multiple states, now form the greatest sources of insecurity. Thus, globalized security threats are diffuse and scattered, rather than represented by one or a few nation states.

The fourth feature of globalized security is the transformation from static to mobile threats, from specific targets that can be geographically located to shifting targets that are difficult and sometimes impossible to physically pinpoint. Perhaps the best illustration of this is the continued search for Osama bin Laden. Despite what is probably the most extensive and elaborate manhunt in the history of the human world, involving both the most advanced technology and enormous personnel resources, the U.S. military still has not managed to find bin Laden. Modern electronic and communications systems, as well as biological and genetic research, have created the possibility for security threats to arise from sources that are mobile and extremely difficult to locate.

Along with the fluidity, dynamism, and ever-changing nature of globalized threat, threats to collective identity have become prominent—the fifth feature of globalization. In this "identity century," there are fierce battles over threats, actual or imagined, to collective identity. Threats to identity have come to the fore not because they are more important than material interests, such as land and mineral resources, but because they are seen to directly or indirectly *impact* material interests.

The centrality of identity in globalized security means that enemies do not need to have sophisticated military hardware to frighten or bully a target. The expansion of mass communications and transportation systems has created a situation in which just about everyone is now vulnerable to identity threats, even from the most distant lands and from militarily weak opponents. For example, the terrorist attacks of 9/11 damaged America materially, but the damage to the United States' identity as "the invincible superpower" was far greater. Similarly, the damage inflicted on America by mismanagement after the 2003 U.S.-led invasion of Iraq has been more moral and identity-based than material, but it has come back to negatively impact the material interests of the country.

Sixth, globalization is characterized by the tremendous speed with which change can take place, resulting in greater insecurity. This extraordinary speed is achieved because of a multiplier effect, brought about by the interconnected nature of the globalized world. Change in each country cascades into other countries, and change accelerates and becomes more widespread. For example, the economic downturn of 2008 suddenly accelerated and spread, because each country caught in the interconnected economic web moved other countries along the same path of economic depression. When individual countries, even those with large economies, attempted to reverse their own individual eco-nomic course of developments the general movement of other countries would not allow such a break. The tremendous speed of globalization is reflected in trends that do not directly threaten security at present, but could do so in the future, such as *globesity*,[18] the global epidemic of weight gain around the world. In a matter of decades, obesity has become an epidemic, with about a dozen countries (e.g., Germany and Greece) having a *higher* proportion of overweight adults than the United States.

In this new era of globalized interdependencies, with change taking place with tremendous speed and in an interconnected manner, there is an urgent need for greater coordination in economic policies of different regions and countries around the world. But so far this has proved impossible to achieve. Even in the case of the twenty-seven countries within the EU, in times of economic crisis there has been a strong tend-ency for each member state to return to protectionist measures and worry first and foremost about its own individual challenges, rather than to give primacy to the EU as a whole. This is in part because the new challenges emerging out of globalization, including the sheer speed of interconnected economic changes around the world, are unprece-dented, frightening, and more likely to lead to a closing up rather than an opening up of defensive and protective measures by individual member states rather than adventurous measures looking to strengthen and coordinate ties with the rest of the world.

The implication of globalized security is that we need to plan for a new era of insecurity and unpredictability. Indeed, we are on the brink of dangerously high, and potentially catastrophic, insecurity. What we can be certain of is the new uncertainty, and the unstable nature of glo-balized security. Some indications of this dangerous new trend of insta-bility are the rise of religious radicalization, terrorism, tribalism and balkanization, enormous resource disparities in association with rapidly rising expectations in the third world, environmental collapse, famine, and war. The emergence of about one billion (thousand million) new middle-class consumers[19] in China, India, Brazil and some other non-Western countries over the next two decades will magnify the chal-lenges ahead, because competition for scarce resources (oil, fresh water, food, etc.) will rapidly increase, as will environmental collapse.

Students of security studies must now pay far closer attention to the ways in which globalization is taking place. From a psychological per-spective, the most important feature of globalization is its "fractured" nature, leading individuals and groups to experience serious new contradictions and stresses. Some traditional communities (such as fun-damentalist Muslims) fear being overwhelmed by a secular Western culture that seems to be growing into a global culture. In the West, also, there are perceived threats about identity, both in the expanding EU (it is not at all clear what a European identity is) and in North America (e.g., as reflected by immigration debates in the United States and Canada). I have coined the term *fractured globalization* to capture the characteristics of twenty-first century globalization, which is associated with the new global insecurity.

Integral to fractured globalization are two apparently contradictory trends: on the one hand there is the well-known and often discussed trend of becoming a global village and melting into one world, and on the other hand the lesser-attended-to trend of communities withdrawing into themselves, reconstructing their past and "distinct" identities, and building higher walls around themselves, literally or figuratively. An indication of this latter trend is the decline of coverage of foreign news in major U.S. newspapers.[20] This seems counterintuitive, given the greater involvement of the United States in foreign countries, such as Iraq, Afghanistan, and Pakistan. Sixty-four percent of the newspapers reported cutting the space given to foreign news in the previous three years. About 50 percent of all papers reported that they had increased the coverage of local and particularly "hyper-local" news concerning the "small" community level. This return to the local is part of a larger trend of insecurity and resistance against melting into one global village with one overarching collective identity.

Book Plan

The nine chapters of this book are organized in three main parts. The three chapters in Part I of the book explore the idea of global insecurity in relation to risk, review "soft" and "hard" security capital, and put forward the dual-source theory of security. Chapter 2 focuses on the uneasy relationship between security and risk. In traditional security studies, the human experience of risk is often neglected, and this is folly because it is only when there is risk that there is insecurity. However, we seldom calculate risk objectively and rationally. How much risk we perceive is subjective and influenced by irrational factors. The main propositions of the dual-source theory of security are outlined in Chapter 3. This theory is designed to be integrative, incorporating both individual level and collective level processes—insecurity as experienced by individuals and groups.

A foundational claim in the dual-source theory of security is that individual security experiences are rooted in collective security experiences. When an infant arrives in this world, social constructions of security already exist at the collective level, and there are shared beliefs about security among the general population. The infant swims in this socially shared construction of security (within the family, the neighborhood, the nation, and so on), becomes immersed into it, and later climbs out with a personal sense of security. However, the root of the emergent personal sense of individual security is collective security. In an era of collective insecurity arising from fractured globalization, it is far more challenging to achieve personal security.

"Soft" and "hard" security capital is discussed in Chapter 4. "Soft" security capital serves as the enabling condition for hard security capital, and is made up of all the various social, cultural, historical, and psychological factors that impact security. These include trust, subjective justice, motivation for civil unrest, ideological fit, collective resilience, group cohesiveness, collective esteem, altruistic capital, leadership fit, and collective dynamism. "Hard" security capital consists of all the material resources and characteristics of a population, including the physical environment in which a society exists. Many of the resources considered by both realist and human security camps are part of hard security capital. I focus on military resources and economic resources in this discussion.

The deep global roots of the new international insecurity are examined in four chapters in Part II. Globalization is taking place in a fragmented manner, with identity central to this experience, which is the main theme of Chapter 5. Adopting a cultural evolution perspective, I argue that globalization is resulting in *sudden contact*, large-scale interactions between human groups without these groups being adequately prepared for the consequences. The result is decline and even extinction of some cultural and linguistic groups, and decreased cultural and linguistic diversity in the human population. These large-scale processes are associated with perceived threats to collective identities, particularly among minority groups (such as Islamic, Christian, and Jewish fundamentalists).

The focus of Chapter 6 is security threats associated with economic globalization. Of course, economic activity is closely related to resource availability, something that is being changed through population increases, environmental pollution, and global warming. The almost seven billion people living on earth are competing for resources in the context of a planet with a rapidly changing and seriously damaged natural environment. The continued collapse of the natural environment—deforestation, a shortage of fresh water, depletion of arable lands, disappearing fish supplies in the major bodies of water, global warming—is becoming more and more important as a source of human insecurity, and provides the context for considering economic globalization in Chapter 6. After all, the collapsing environment is the ultimate security threat and the collapse of the natural environment could well mean the end of human beings on earth.

Fractured globalization is resulting in enormous fluctuations, repeated booms and busts, in the now interlocked economy of the world. These fluctuations are associated with feelings of insecurity, social unrest in various shapes, and potential dangers of further inter-group conflict. Within this boom-and-bust economic context, religious belief systems take on a more important role and relations with people from other religious can also result in perceived collective threats. The experience of religious insecurity is further explored in Chapter 7. Although religious insecurity is an important source of violence and terrorism, in Chapter 8 I argue that there is a need to delve deeper and to go beyond the surface explanation of terrorism.

The issues explored in Chapters 5, 6, and 7, including threatened collective identities, economic booms and busts, and religious insecurity, provide the setting for examining terrorism and torture. The main reason I discuss terrorism and torture together is because, although they have obvious surface-level differences, at a deeper level the motivations for implementing terrorism and torture are highly similar. Indeed, I claim that torture is terrorism carried out by the state.

This analysis leads to an exploration of important commonalities in terrorism and torture. On the surface, terrorism and torture are intended to inflict material damage or to gather resources (such as information). At a deeper level, however, terrorism and torture are not directly about material resources, such as information, but about creating feelings of collective humiliation, shame, and helplessness among the members of a target population. Through such tactics, the goal is to instill fear and to control a target population.

Having set out the main characteristics of globalized security in Part I, and explored the global roots of the new insecurity in Part II, in Part III I critically re-assess the main overarching challenge confronting human societies in the age of fractured globalization. The heart of this challenge is how we can manage intergroup relations in a context in which people from diverse cultural, religious, ethnic, linguistic, and other backgrounds are interacting with others from different backgrounds, with very little preparation. At the global level, I argue that there is a need to re-think our policies for managing cultural and linguistic diversity within states and around the world. This rethinking is needed because of the failure of what have become the two traditional policies for managing diversity, assimilation, and multiculturalism. Both of these traditional policies are based on psychological assumptions, a number of which are invalid and contrary to available empirical evidence. As an alternative to assimilation and multiculturalism, I put forward the alternative policy of *omniculturalism*, which begins by high-lighting important human universals in thought and action (stage one) and during a second stage introduces the idea of group-based differences.

There is an urgent need to develop a world development plan for managing diversity and intergroup relations. Such a plan has become essential because of high and increasing economic, cultural, technological, and even political interdependence in the world.

CONCLUDING COMMENT

An assumption implicit in much of the work in security studies is that any threat to security is necessarily bad, and should be opposed. Of course, this is an invalid assumption, because there are certain sociopolitical orders that are blatantly unjust and to defend the security of such sociopolitical orders is to support injustice. For example, as I revise this section of the book, people in Iran are being denied the right to protest what they perceive to be a fraudulent presidential election. Peaceful protesters in Tehran and other Iranian cities have been violently attacked, killed, and injured, because the protests against the 2009 presidential election results are being seen as breaches of security. As is clear from this and other similar examples where citizens are not allowed freedom of expression, freedom of assembly, and other such basic rights, it is not always the case that threats to security are detrimental to the common good.

Part I

Key Elements of
Global Insecurity

*. . . the most complicated achievements of thought are possible without
the assistance of consciousness.*

Sigmund Freud (1856–1939)[1]

What are the factors that influence feelings of insecurity experienced by
individuals and groups? In addressing this broad question, the three
chapters in Part I push aside and move beyond received wisdom in a
number of ways.

First, risk is given high importance (Chapter 2), because risk has to
be present for there to be a perceived threat to security. However, our
perception of risk is not always, or even often, rational. We tend to mis-
perceive risks, without always being aware of the misperception, and
also without being aware of the real motives behind our own misperception of risk. Thus, irrationality rather than rationality characterizes
our perceptions of risk. As discussed by Freud (1856–1939), even the
most complicated kinds of thinking, including about risk, come about
without conscious awareness.

Irrationality rather than rationality is also integral to the dual-source
theory of security (Chapter 3). This theory incorporates five main propositions, starting with the proposition that humans have an inherent
need for both collective and individual security. However, in everyday
life "security" is what is subjectively experienced, which can be
divorced from "real" material factors (proposition two). For example, I
might be much better armed than my enemy, but still feel a greater
sense of insecurity, because I sense that my enemy is eager to sacrifice
his life in the fight against me.

The particular sense of security experienced by adults is viewed as
having two main sources (proposition three): first, temperament and
early socialization experiences; second, culture and collective processes.

The nature of culture and collective processes is changing, because globalization is resulting in greater and greater interdependency in security around the world (proposition four). As a result, the insecurity experienced by individuals is routinely and directly impacted by events in distant places; the members of a family living in Texas can feel their security threatened by events in Baluchestan, just as the members of a family living in Baluchestan can feel threatened by events in Texas.

The rapidly increasing interconnectedness and interdependence brought about by globalization will initially result in greater insecurity (proposition five). This is because enormous re-adjustments have to be made in the economic, cultural, political, social, and psychological orientations of different communities and nation states to cope with changes, the sheer speed of these interconnected changes being new and unprecedented (proposition six). These adjustments will often be painful and initially will have negative consequences in the everyday lives of people in many parts of the world. The tremendous speed of the economic downturn starting in 2008 gives a hint of the global experiences we must expect and plan for.

The collective and personal insecurity experienced by a society and individuals in that society is associated with the characteristics of the security capital available in that society. Traditionally, the focus has been on hard security capital, which includes military, economic, and other such resources. In this discussion, I also focus on various kinds of soft security capital, which serve as the enabling condition for military security and other forms of realist security.

2

The Risk-Security Dynamic: An Uneasy Marriage

. . . humans, unlike squirrels, can recognize through rational reflection that violence can have positive payoffs. With that, there is considerable risk for nastiness. . . .

Jesse Prinz[1]

. . . in postmodern militaries, threats are generally seen to stem from subnational actors. In earlier eras, threats of enemy invasion and nuclear war were the main concern; nowadays, threats to a state and its people are more likely to be terrorism and ethnic violence.

Jean Callaghan and Franz Kernic[2]

Risk intelligence refers to an individual's or an organization's ability to weigh risks effectively. It involves classifying, characterizing, and calculating threats; perceiving relationships; learning quickly; storing, retrieving, and acting upon relevant information; communicating effectively; and adjusting to new circumstances.

David Apgar, 2008[3]

Security and risk are intimately connected; so much so that it is meaningless to consider security without also considering risk. Feelings of insecurity can only come about when an individual or group perceives there to be a risk of directly or indirectly coming under attack. If there is no risk, then there is no threat to security. When we see an individual, organization, or country as a security threat to us, the implication is that there is a risk that the individual, organization, or country will attack us. People and organizations that more accurately assess risks can be said to have higher risk intelligence. However, in practice risk intelligence involves a great deal more than rational information processing and logical decision making.

In traditional security studies, the risk has been associated with the possibility of military attacks, of being invaded or even suffering a nuclear attack. The response to such a perceived risk has involved a combination of military build-up, investment in research to develop more efficient military weapons, and strategic regional and international alliances. In more recent years, particularly since the tragedy of 9/11, risk has also been associated with terrorist attacks and with intergroup conflicts (involving ethnic, religious, social class, and other groups) at home. The response to this perceived risk has been anti-terrorist measures and a re-organization of security apparatus at home (such as through the creation of the Department of Homeland Security in the United States), as well as greater efforts to coordinate anti-terrorism activities internationally (in part through NATO and existing institutional frameworks, but also by creating new international anti-terrorism networks).

RATIONALITY AND RISK ASSESSMENT

Risk assessment has mushroomed into an enormous industry, dealing with risk in just about every domain of life, from the insurance of houses and cars, to the possibility of civil war in different countries (particularly non-Western ones), to the risk of environmental hazards, and on and on. Security risk assessment is a sub-branch of this bourgeoning field, with its own sub-specialties.[4] On the one hand, there is risk associated with the possibility of major international conflicts. On the other hand, risks are also associated with possible smaller-scale attacks, for example against transportation and communications systems, embassies and cultural centers, political leaders, and the like.

Risk assessment, whether from a financial, political, or military perspective, can be organized as a series of logical steps, each step involving a probabilistic calculation. First, the probability of an event occurring. For example, how likely is it that an earthquake, terrorist attack, fire, or major military attack will take place against a certain target? Is it a once-in-a-hundred-years event, or once-in-a-decade event, or perhaps even a once-a-year event? The likelihood of such events varies a great deal across time and across situations. For example, the likelihood of terrorist attacks against NATO forces is very high in Afghanistan in 2010, but relatively low in Western Europe.

Second, what is the expected loss from this event? Risk always has costs (military, financial, political, and so on) and the cost of each event can be estimated. If it is likely that the event will be repeated, the cost of an event multiplied by the number of expected occurrences in a year yields the total estimated annual cost. However, this estimate is complicated by the probable decrease in (1) costs over repeated attacks, because of eventual increases in efficiency to recover from attacks, and (2) the possibility that increased attacks might weaken the target to such an extent that it becomes impossible to recover fully.

Third, a target is made prone to attack by various vulnerabilities. For example, unguarded coastlines represent vulnerability for a sovereign state. Each vulnerability influences the risk of attack. For example, unguarded ports increase the risk of a terrorist attack. Vulnerabilities can be dealt with by detecting and preventing attacks, by limiting the impact of an attack, by deterring attacks (for example, through the threat of counter-attacks against enemy targets). However, dealing with vulnerabilities involves financial, military, political, and other types of costs.

Risk can never be reduced to zero; consequently, security is never 100 percent. The critical question, then, becomes one of "acceptable" levels of risk. How much risk can be tolerated and at what cost? "Acceptable loss" is far easier to estimate if we assume that human beings are rational creatures who seek to maximize their "rewards" (defined broadly). Thus, in traditional risk assessment exercises, humans are seen as capable of rationally working out the path of action that will achieve for them maximum rewards and minimum negative consequences.

Another key feature of the rational model is the assumption that human beings respond rationally to changes in circumstances. For example, a rational model leads us to assume that when we invest in strengthening our defenses and decrease our vulnerabilities so that attackers are more likely to be killed, then potential attackers will recognize this change and be less likely to launch attacks. This is because they recognize that the costs of launching an attack have become too high.

A more subtle assumption of the rational model is that the process of decision taking with respect to risk takes place within self-contained individuals. Each person is treated as a kind of independent thinking machine. Data are fed into the thinking machines, and each item independently computes the risk-loss probability in different situations. The estimation made by a collective is seen as the sum of individual estimations. The tendency to view risk assessment in this reductionist, rational manner, assuming step-by-step logical problem-solving to be the norm, is magnified by the increasing use of computers, robots, and machinery in conflicts. As we become "wired for war,"[5] we more readily fall into the trap of reductionism and rationality. Of course, this approach is challenged by those who believe that "the whole is more than the sum of its parts," that the decision-making process and outcome of a group is in important ways different from the sum of decisions made by individuals.[6] But if this is the case, are we justified in studying risk taking at the level of the individual and generalizing our findings to the level of the collective? I believe that in the vast majority of cases we are not justified, but as we see below, this dilemma continues to haunt a major body of both research and policy in the domain of risk and security.

Risk and the Gaming Research Tradition

There is a long tradition of scholars undertaking "thought experiments" to explore risk taking and security (broadly defined). For example, in his writings on inequality, Jean Jacques Rousseau (1712–1778) discussed the example of a stag hunt, which requires the cooperation of hunters.[7] Each hunter must contribute to the group effort, but runs the risk of the hunt failing. When a rabbit crosses the path of a hunter, should the hunter take the surer path of catching the rabbit but risk being excluded from the spoils of the stag hunt, if it is successful? Cooperating with others to hunt the stag involves greater risk, but going it alone results in a smaller prize.[8]

David Hume (1711–1776) explored a similar theme through the cases of two men rowing in a boat, and also two neighbors faced with the task of draining a meadow.[9] In each case, individuals face the risk of investing their resources in a collective effort and accurately estimating how little they can invest but still gain returns. For example, each of the two rowers would be better off if the other rower did most of the work, but at the same time if both of the rowers do not make an effort the boat might move in circles. Similarly, each neighbor would be personally better off if the meadow was drained by the other neighbor, but the risk is that each neighbor will wait for the other to take action and the meadow will remain undrained and unusable.

The most powerful metaphor illuminating the nature of risk in the modern era was introduced by Garrett Hardin (1915–2003):[10] consider a group of people who own cattle and have the right to graze their animals in *the commons*, land owned by the community. Each individual stands to gain by putting more animals out to graze on the commons, even though more and more grazing animals will eventually destroy the commons and diminish the benefits to the entire community. But the gains made by individuals who put more animals to graze on the commons can be greater than the losses these particular individuals suffer as a member of the larger community experiencing the loss of the commons. Hardin's "tragedy of the commons" highlights the different risks faced by individuals versus the communities to which those individuals belong, and points to tensions between individual and collective interests.[11]

Hardin's "tragedy of the commons" metaphor is appropriate for illuminating the plight of individuals and communities confronting limited and sometimes shrinking resources. A fable with even greater influence on the gaming tradition is about the so-called "prisoner's dilemma" (see Figure 2.1). Imagine two recently captured prisoners who are being cross-examined by the police. The prisoners will soon face criminal trial and each faces a grave choice, of cooperating with the authorities and "spilling the beans," or keeping quiet and refusing to tell what happened. If one of them keeps quiet and the other informs, the one who keeps quiet will receive a lengthy prison sentence and the informer will be set free. If both of them keep quiet, they both receive light sentences. If both inform, they both receive lengthier sentences. Because the prisoners are forced to decide on a course of action without communicating with the other, each of them has to take a risk. The best outcome for each is to be set free, but if both of them talk, instead of being set free they will both receive heavy sentences.

Based on this situation, a so-called Prisoner's Dilemma Game (PDG) has been repeatedly adapted and used as the framework for thousands of studies,[12] with some variation in the payoff matrix that determines what outcomes or rewards result from the different choices made by the two prisoners. In games with a zero-sum reward structure, each player necessarily wins at the expense of the other. This corresponds to a real-world situation where resources are strictly limited and if one person gains a resource, then somebody else necessarily loses the same resource. For example, if Group A gains land, then Group B must necessarily lose land. In a non-zero-sum game, the wins and losses of one

		Prisoner 2 (P2)	
		'Spill the beans'	Keep quiet
	'Spill the beans'	Both receive heavy sentences	P1 receives light sentence P2 receives heavy sentence
Prisoner 1 (P1)	Keep quiet	P2 receives light sentence P1 receives heavy sentence	Both set free

Figure 2.1 The reward matrix for the two prisoners in the Prisoner's Dilemma situation

individual do not impact the outcomes of others. How much each individual wins or loses depends on his or her own choices. Whereas in a zero-sum game the wins and losses of all the players must add up to zero (what I lose is your gain), in a non-zero-sum game, the fortunes of the different players are completely independent from one another, so that both can gain (and both can lose, or one can gain at the same time that the other loses).

In the typical PDG, the focus is on the decision-making strategies of individuals working independently over repeated trails. These games are *mixed motive*, meaning that each individual can decide to behave competitively or cooperatively. It is assumed that cooperative behavior results in a best possible solution,[13] on the basis of a *minimax* principle, intended to maximize rewards and minimize losses for everyone.

Although the PDG has typically involved individual decision making, the results of this research continues to be used to extrapolate to the intergroup level. In particular, the risk-taking behavior of individuals in the PDG has been extended to discussions of risk taking by nations caught in the international arms race. Consider the multitude of different risks faced by national leaders in their relationships with rival countries. It might appear that they only have two choices: they can increase arms expenditure and continue to build up their militaries, or they can allow rival powers to move ahead of them in the "arms race" and ultimately fall under the military domination of competitors. Because of the secrecy with which military research is undertaken, decisions regarding whether or not to build up the military even further have to be considered as risky. Consequently, even decades after the end of the Cold War, the PDG continues to influence both research and practice in the broad area of security.[14]

The classic Cold War scenario involves direct competition between the United States and the Soviet Union, two giant powers with a lot of information about one another. In the post-Cold War situation, the main danger lies not so much in the possibility of a confrontation between America and Russia, but with the far less predictable actions of actual or would-be rogue nuclear states, as well as the actions of terrorists and other non-state actors who might gain access to weapons of mass destruction. Thus, despite the end of the Cold War, we continue to face a danger, and perhaps an even greater one now, of conflicts spinning out of control because of unknown and unpredictable rogue state and non-state actors. The behavior of these rogue state and non-state actors is actually less predictable and involves higher risk than the behavior of the former Soviet Union.

The PDG and gaming research more broadly have traditionally faced two related challenges: how to better explore collective processes and how to give more importance to *irrational* behavior, thoughts and actions influenced by factors that we are not aware of. The vast majority of studies in the gaming tradition focuses on the decision making of individuals rather than groups, and assumes a rational model of humans. As I argue in the next section, this individualistic rationalist approach has serious shortcomings. An approach that focuses on collective processes and gives adequate attention to human irrationality is far more realistic and fruitful.

RISK, IRRATIONALITY, AND SECURITY

> *In an era when military thinking was dominated by nuclear weapons or guerilla warfare, the Iran-Iraq War recalled the trench battles of an earlier age . . . After eight years of maneuvers and confrontations up and down the winding 700-mile boundary between the two countries, the battle lines returned almost exactly to their original borders. Like Britain, France, and Germany in 1918, Iran and Iraq lost a generation of their best young men.*
>
> John Stoessinger, 2008, p. 293 [15]

I was working in Iran for the first three years of the bloody Iran-Iraq war (1980–1988), and I accompanied three United Nations missions to the war front. This war resulted in the death of well over a million people, the serious injury of many more millions, and the utter devastation of the economies of both nations. Absolutely nothing was gained by either side, and yet both sides declared themselves victors, and of course both sides insisted "God is on our side." It is remarkable and tragic that over the last 15,000 years or so, since humans developed agriculture, achieved a consistent surplus, and built stable settlements, our tendency to engage in collective violent conflict has persisted. The role of organized religion in supporting and justifying wars has been especially tragic.

But disappointment with the role of organized religion in promoting rather than preventing violent conflict does not mean that science and technology have been any more successful than has religion at ending violent conflicts. Clearly, our expansive scientific and technological advances since the Renaissance have not been accompanied by a demise of our collective aggression. On the contrary, science and technology continue to be used to achieve a more effective military, to make war more efficient, rather than to achieve a sustained peace.

Also, the empirical research that we have undertaken on conflict resolution for the most part is hampered by the erroneous assumption that human beings are rational thinkers and take action on the basis of rational decision making as independent individuals. This is exemplified by research in the gaming tradition, as discussed earlier in this chapter particularly using the example of the PDG. We are still crippled by the illusion that human beings are rational, and we are motivated to see ourselves "in control" even when a course of events is clearly out of our control and the risks have become too high.[16]

Irrespective of whether we adopt a psychodynamic approach based on qualitative and case study evidence[17] or if our perspective is more based on quantitative research,[18] evidence suggests that human beings are in large part irrational rather than rational. This does not mean that we are not able to rationalize. The subtle but important difference between behaving rationally and rationalizing behavior has to be kept in mind when we consider risk and security. It is instructive to study the rationalization that takes place when human beings take the risk of engaging in violent conflict. Wars are rationalized through claims such as "we are fighting to spread freedom and democracy" or "we are fighting for peace" or "we are fighting for justice" or, as in the case of rhetoric at the start of the First World War (1914–1918), we are going to war to "end all wars." Such rationalization does not really mean that people are aware of the factors that are leading them to go to war; only that people can provide explanations that seem rational, on the surface at least.

There seems no limit to our ability to construct rationalizations for human actions—actions that are often folly. It seems that whatever form of action we decide to take, whatever form of social order and social relationships we choose to bring to life and make the norm, we are able to manufacture a reasonable account to fully justify, at least to ourselves, the choices we have made. Thus, for example, we witness the enormous variations in religious beliefs and practices, all of them fully justified by the various groups of faithful practicing each religion.[19] The risk of conflict is relatively low as long as those who believe in each rationalization interact only or mostly with others who share their rationalization. However, the risk of conflict dramatically increases when the religious faithful come across others who firmly believe in competing rationalizations (this issue is further explored in Chapter 8).

In practice, people tend to base decisions on highly flawed risk assessments, without being conscious of the various biases influencing them, and the role of emotions in their apparently rational decisions.[20] This includes everyday decisions, such as the decision to drive a car rather than to travel by air—the notorious example here being the decision by hundreds of thousands of people to travel by car rather than by plane in the months immediately after 9/11, which resulted in many more deaths because of car accidents.[21] The odds of being killed in a car accident is about one in 7,000, whereas even if one plane per month were attacked by terrorists, at normal rates of air travel the odds of air travelers meeting up with terrorists would be one in every 500,000.[22] The odds of dying from cancer in any given year is about one in 600, yet millions of people continue to engage in high-risk behavior, such as smoking. Clearly, our decisions tend to be irrational.

The old newspaper business slogan that "bad news sells" is based on an important psychological truth: negative information is more memorable and moving, relative to positive information. This is well-known in politics (at least in democratic countries), where negative information about a candidate often proves to have more impact on voters than positive information, and it is easier to bring about distrust than to create trust.[23] This *negativity bias*[24] is one of a number of examples of heuristics[25]—mental shortcuts that help us to quickly make decisions in the context of vast amounts of information. The problem is that such decisions are often seriously flawed.

Judgments in the domain of risk and security are profoundly influenced by the *availability heuristic*, the cognitive strategy for assuming that how easily one can bring to mind a phenomenon correctly tells us how common it is. Consider the kinds of information that are most widely publicized and readily available to us. Our various sources of information, from personal sources (e.g., family and friends) to the mass media, tend to highlight the spectacular and the negative, particularly what seems threatening. For example, a plane crash or a terrorist attack is widely publicized, whereas car crashes and all the hundreds of thousands of plane flights that run smoothly are not publicized—news about aircrafts landing safely does not sell newspapers or attract viewers to television stations. Consequently, we tend to overestimate the risk of terrorist attacks and air travel.

Our assessments of risk are further influenced by a *confirmation bias*, the tendency to look for evidence to support our prior expectations instead of being open to other possibilities.[26] For example, one reason why the 9/11 terrorist attacks were not thwarted is because the security community was not expecting an attack using such methods and on such a scale. Not imagining such an attack meant that data pointing to the attack were not given attention.

Styles of Risk and Threat Assessment across Individuals and Societies

Individuals and groups do not all see risk and threat in the same way. At the level of the individual, research has shown that those who score higher on measures of authoritarianism as a personality trait tend to focus more on risks and threats.[27] Authoritarian individuals, in general, tend to be submissive to authority figures, but punitive toward minorities and those with less power. The original personality instrument developed to measure authoritarianism was labeled the F-Scale, because it was designed to identify individuals with pro-fascist tendencies. These individuals provided strong support for Hitler in Germany and Mussolini in Italy, presumably today support dictators and an end to freedom in various countries, and tend to be intolerant of ambiguity and distrust those who do not think or look the same as they do.

Another line of research suggests that individuals who score higher on measures of Machiavellianism also see the world as more threatening and involving greater risks.[28] The "high Mach" personality believes that you have to hit before you get hit, you have to cut corners to get ahead, and basically the world is a risky and threatening place in which you have to keep up your guard and distrust others. Another facet of Machiavellianism is *Machiavellian intelligence*, the ability to manipulate others in social relationships. Some researchers argue that selection for social manipulation played an important part in humans achieving huge leaps in thinking ability, and that the roots of Machiavellian intelligence are also found in animals, particularly monkeys and apes.[29] Part of Machiavellian intelligence involves the ability to recognize threats and risks.

Authoritarianism and Machiavellianism have been measured as the personality characteristics of individuals, but from the perspective of those concerned with security it is more useful to focus on behavioral styles of collectives rather than individuals. Certain societies are dominated by cultural norms and values that emphasize and strengthen perceptions of the world as threatening, potentially unstable, and full of dangerous risks. These societies tend to be more *ethnocentric*, meaning that they are inward-looking, unquestioningly see their own ways as necessarily the best way, and try to keep a distance between themselves and out-groups.[30] In modern times, these societies tend to be dictatorships, with a high level of censorship and lack of openness to the outside world.

CONCLUDING COMMENT

Perceptions of risk are at the heart of feelings of insecurity, because it is only when there is perceived risk that security is seen to be threatened. This foundational point indicates important ways in which irrationality can influence behavior that bears on security, specifically through irrational estimations of risk. Our irrationality often leads us to exaggerate or deny risk, and in one way or another fails to gage the true nature of the security threat we are facing. Some individuals and some societies are extreme in their irrational accounts of risks related to security, and authoritarian individuals and regimes are particularly susceptible to exaggerating security threats.

3

The Dual-Source Theory of Security: Why Tomorrow Is Different, and Far More Dangerous

Modern science is characterized by increasing specialization, which brings with it important advantages.[1] Among these advantages are opportunities for teams of researchers to probe deeper into a subject, to develop expertise in narrow areas, and to precisely test out specific questions. For example, security studies are now an established specialized discipline, with some sub-specialties also evolving.[2] The question of how a personal sense of security evolves is also studied in developmental science by specialists focused on child development. Researchers interested in psychological well-being, influenced particularly by a Freudian tradition that emphasizes the importance of early socialization experiences and personality development, also explore the childhood roots of security and insecurity associated with particular psychopathologies. Progressing ever deeper along narrow research lines, such groups of scholars are able to make new discoveries—a trend that has led to substantially improved efficiencies in many new avenues, including health treatment.

But increasing specialization also has some serious disadvantages, such as groups of experts tackling a topic from different perspectives but never communicating across their specialized lines of research. For example, a person's security experiences have been examined from many different specialized perspectives, taking into account macro-level factors such as military strength and economic resources, and also micro-level factors associated with how infants develop bonds with their caretakers and grow up to experience security in particular ways.

Still other groups of researchers have expanded the horizon by exploring security from the lens of factors such as natural resources,[3] justice,[4] and global poverty.[5] But so far, these different groups of specialists have not made serious efforts to communicate with one another to nurture a holistic perspective on security. As a consequence, each specialized group presents us with a picture of security that is narrow, incomplete, and flawed in major ways.

In this chapter I present the broad outline of a comprehensive theory of security. This theory is comprehensive in the sense that it incorporates all of the major macro-level and micro-level factors that influence the experience of collective and personal security in a population. The theory begins with the assumption that primacy must be given to the subjective and often irrational experience of security, people's feelings about their level of security, and the factors that shape their feelings. This subjective and often irrational experience is shaped by infancy and early childhood development and by the factors that are influential in the lives of adults. Because of this distinction between sources that influence early experiences of infants and children and those sources that influence later experiences of people as adults, the theory is termed the "dual-source theory of security."

Before discussing the main propositions of the dual-source theory of security, it is useful to clarify and distinguish between the following basic terms.

- *Subjective versus objective criteria for assessing security*: Valid objective criteria exist that can be used to assess threats to security. For example, security resources can be objectively assessed in terms of the size of the military. Although an enemy may succeed in some deception and camouflage, resulting in a level of inaccuracy, estimates of security resources will in general be fairly accurate. However, in practice, far more important than objective assessments is what people subjectively feel security threats to be, often based on exaggerations or minimizations of security threats.
- *Personal versus collective threat target*: Does the individual perceive himself or herself personally to be the main target of the threat? Or does he or she believe the collective to be the primary target of threat? For example, does Jane feel threatened because she feels she personally is the target of potential attack, or does she feel that all Americans are under attack and her national group is the primary target?

The discussion begins with the development of a sense of personal security in infancy and childhood. The main propositions of the dual-source theory of security are then set out and briefly explained. The chapters that follow reflect back on these propositions and elaborate on them.

THE DEVELOPMENT OF A SENSE OF PERSONAL SECURITY

Directly relevant to how we develop a sense of personal security is developmental science research that has focused on *attachment*, an observed bonding between the young of many species and their primary caregivers.[6] This research demonstrates that feelings of personal security in adulthood are influenced by early socialization experiences and *temperament*, an inborn level of energy and style of coping with the environment.[7] As suggested by Charles Darwin's (1809–1882) theory of evolution,[8] attachment is a functional behavior that improves survival chances. For example, the research of Konrad Lorenz (1903–1989) on newly hatched ducklings demonstrated the vital functional role of *imprinting*, a learned and stable attachment formed at a critical period in early development. Lorenz showed that about ten hours after birth, a newly hatched duckling is able to walk, will follow, and become imprinted on the first moving object it encounters.[9] Of course, this "moving object" is typically its mother, and the ability to stay close to the mother in important ways determines survival chances.

Other animal researchers have demonstrated that the role of the mother is far more expansive than that of "food provider." For example, Harry Harlow (1905–1981) studied rhesus monkeys raised in isolation with two surrogate stationary mothers, a "wire" mother and a cloth-covered, cuddly mother.[10] Infant monkeys preferred to be with the cuddly mother, particularly when they were frightened by unfamiliar noises or objects, even when milk was only dispensed from the wire mother. An implication is that attachment arises from a deep-rooted need to feel secure, and in some conditions the need for security can overpower the need for food.

The research on attachment in humans has been shaped in large part by the ideas of the British psychiatrist John Bowlby (1907–1990), who gained valuable insights by studying the experiences of schoolchildren during the Second World War.[11] Hundreds of thousands of children were separated from their parents during the war, mostly because children were evacuated from major cities to live in rural areas so as to escape enemy bombing. Many children also lost one or both parents in the violence of war. Bowlby studied the impact on children of becoming separated from their parents, and he emphasized the evolutionary function of children developing emotional ties to caretakers and developing trust in others through this foundational relationship. The research of

Bowlby, Harlow, and others has led us to see attachment as being based on emotional rather than just physiological needs.

Bowlby eventually developed a four-phase model of attachment that has had considerable influence on subsequent research.

1. *Preattachment (birth to about 6 to 8 weeks)*: Even in the first few weeks of life, infants prefer the smell of their mother's milk over the milk of another woman and they can imitate and engage with another person in joint action (such as by gazing in the same direction as another). Despite these abilities and despite being able to differentiate between and communicate with other people in the first two months of life, they do not react strongly when left alone with a stranger.
2. *Beginning of attachment (6 to 8 weeks to about 6 to 8 months)*: Infants gradually develop better discriminatory ability to differentiate between faces, as well as to show preferences for familiar faces. This has a functional basis: the familiar is safer; novelty can have benefits but also involves greater risk. The group can gain by having risk-taking members who explore the larger world, but the risk takers are also more prone to injury and death.
3. *Clear-cut attachment (6 to 8 months to 2 to 3 years)*: at around 6 to 8 months, most infants start to crawl and by the end of the third year of life, toddler legs are able to move fast (many young parents find they need to be fit to catch the little sprinters). Now that both infant and mother are able to move, potential hazards increase. Infants can run into all kinds of dangers as they wander away to explore their surroundings. From a functional perspective, it makes sense that infants experience separation anxiety and cry out if they become separated from their mothers for too long.
4. *Mother-infant partnership (2 to 3 years and older)*: Through cooperation with one another, mother and toddler gradually negotiate the use of space and "safe distances" from one another. An invisible circle, a kind of "safety zone" evolves, with the mother at the center, within which the toddler feels secure to wander around.

Research methodology developed by Mary Ainsworth has been used to explore Bowlby's ideas on attachment.[12] In the so-called *strange situation* research procedure, a mother and infant enter a room and the infant settles down to play with toys.[13] They are by themselves at first, but a stranger joins them a little later. The mother temporarily leaves her infant in a room with the stranger and then returns after a brief absence. Of particular interest to researchers is the reaction of the infant to the return of the mother. Some infants demonstrate *secure attachment*: they react positively to the return of the mother and quickly overcome their initial anxiety caused by the absence of the mother. A second group of infants shows *anxious/avoidant attachment*: their reactions are not strong to the mother leaving or returning, and they do not seek to get closer to the mother when she returns. A third group shows *anxious/resistant attachment*: they are anxious even in the presence of the mother, become upset when she leaves, and resist the mother's efforts to comfort them after she returns.

How can we ensure that infants achieve secure attachment, rather than anxious/avoidant or anxious/resistant attachment? To some degree the change we can bring about in type of attachment is limited because of temperament. For example, some individuals are predisposed to be energetic and higher risk takers; as infants they are more inclined to move away from their caretaker and explore the environment. Activity level and risk-taking behavior can be shaped to some degree through training, but differences in temperament mean that individuals begin life with different tendencies in activity level and risk taking. The research of Stephen Suomi demonstrates consistency in this trend in animals and humans, suggesting strong evolutionary roots to temperament.[14]

The question of infant attachment is important because our early experiences have a profound impact on our characteristics as adults.[15] From traditional Freudian psychologists to modern neuroscientists, researchers agree that the kind of attachment achieved in infancy influences in important ways subjective security and relationships in adulthood. This does not mean that early experiences predetermine adult experiences in a fixed, absolute manner. Rather, early experiences predispose individuals to certain feelings of personal security and certain kinds of relationships. The influence is probabilistic rather than absolute, as is the case with almost all human thoughts and actions.

Cultural context plays an important role in shaping the kind of attachment individuals achieve, as well as their experiences of personal security. Since the 1990s there has been a greater focus on *resilience*, the ability to quickly overcome adverse environmental conditions and negative experiences. Unlike temperament, resilience can be reshaped to a considerable degree by training, and this point has important implications for security: individuals can be trained to feel more secure even in environmental conditions that typically induce feelings of insecurity. But it would be a grave mistake to interpret the role of resilience by giving priority to the individual rather than the collective as the unit of analysis, just as in exploring subjective experiences of security we must keep in mind that the source of personal security is *collective*.

In practice, there is an association between micro-level and macro-level factors influencing the experience of personal security. For example, macro-level factors such as the military strength and economic resources of a society influence socialization practices and the style of training the young receive. In turn, socialization practices influence how adults experience personal security, and how adult behavior relates to military and economic performance.

Clearly, micro- and macro-level factors are inter-related in complex and often indirect ways. This is in large part because at the center of both personal and collective security is subjective experience, even when the issue of security concerns macro-level changes. How secure do Americans feel after the terrorist attacks of September 11, 2001? How has the establishment of the Department of Homeland Security significantly increased how secure Americans feel? Has the weapon development program of Iran changed feelings of security among Europeans? Are the Japanese feeling less secure because of the economic and military rise of China? Do Russians feel less secure because of the expansion of NATO into Eastern Europe? What steps would India and Pakistan have to take to make their respective populations feel more secure? These questions lead us to think about security as subjective experience—how secure individuals and groups *feel* in a given situation, even when the target of threat is collective (e.g., Americans, Westerners).

A key characteristic of security as subjectively experienced is that for the most part it is irrational rather than rational, meaning that people tend not to accurately recognize the nature and sources of their own feelings of security. In many situations, people tend to be mistaken about how and why they came to experience a certain kind and level of security. At the same time, the claim that security is subjective does not mean that experiences of security are private and isolated from the rest of collective life. Indeed, the source of subjective experiences is collective experiences, just as the source of individual consciousness is collective consciousness.[16] People experience a certain type and level of security by making a wide range of social comparisons.[17] The comparison targets they select include (but are not exclusive to) the following:

- Others in their group.
- Their group, as they believe it could be in a security situation that is better and feasible.
- Themselves personally, as they believe they could be in a security situation that is better and feasible.

Bowlby's model is concerned with individual experiences with security, and how individual children cope with separation anxiety, but the dual-source theory of security extends the discussion to collective reactions to a perceived security threat. Through this switch to the collective level, the question becomes: How does the group interpret and cope with perceived security threat?

AN OUTLINE OF THE DUAL-SOURCE THEORY OF SECURITY

The dual-source theory of security consists of six major propositions. Proposition three is particularly important because it involves the two hypothesized sources of subjective security: temperament and early socialization experiences on the one hand and macro societal factors shaping individual experience on the other hand.

Proposition One

People have an inherent need for security both at the individual and group levels. When individuals or groups lack a minimal sense of security, they feel anxious and strive to overcome their anxiety by changing their actual situation, or their interpretation of the situation they are in, or both, so as to feel adequately secure.

The need for security has been recognized by psychologists such as Abraham Maslow[18] (1908–1970) and Clayton Alderfer[19] as being foundational. Maslow put forward a hierarchical model of human needs, with physiological needs (such as a need for food) as the most basic level, and the need for self-actualization as the highest level. The second most basic need recognized by Maslow is the need for security. Maslow's assumption was that the activation of needs is stepwise and hierarchical, so that each need will not become activated to influence behavior until and unless the preceding need has been satisfied. A different approach is adopted by Alderfer's model, according to which two or more different needs can be activated simultaneously. For example, the need to satisfy hunger can be activated at the same time as esteem needs are activated. Despite their differences, both models of needs put forward by these researchers give central importance to the need for security.

The need for security has played a vital role in our evolutionary history. Human infants are born helpless, unable to look after themselves, and utterly dependent on caretakers for survival. It is thus functional for young human beings to develop a sense of attachment to caretakers, and to experience anxiety when separated from caretakers. There is also an advantage to having some individuals who show independence and rebellion; they will become the future explorers and adventurers. Risk takers and rebels will blaze new paths—if they survive the many haz-ardous pitfalls they face as they grow up. However, these are the minority; most individuals prefer to remain in more familiar situations where they feel secure. Of course, this does not mean that people avoid exciting places such as circuses and ski slopes, but the need to feel secure guides people to adopt safeguards. Even Formula One race car drivers wear seat belts.

Perhaps the most important but neglected aspect of the need for security is the primacy of the group. The need for security has been discussed by Maslow, Alderfer, and most other researchers with a focus on the individual as the unit of analysis. However, individual security is dependent on group security. Because of the social nature of human beings and the dependence of individuals on the larger society for survival, a collapse of collective security inevitably means a collapse of individual level security. Consequently, the "need for security" is a need for collective security first and foremost.

Proposition Two

Part A: The subjective experience of security is the primary force that shapes behavior. This subjective experience of security does not always correspond with objective conditions. An individual might feel com-pletely secure in the middle of a battlefield, but the same individual might feel utterly insecure sitting at home far away from actual violent conflict.

Part B: How secure a group feels takes primacy over, and tends to shape, how secure individual group members feel. In situations of collective insecurity, most individuals will feel personally insecure. How secure a person feels arises from social processes involving social comparisons that result in relativistic estimates.

The claim that subjective experience shapes behavior is supported by considerable research evidence generated through psychological science over the past century or so, particularly research on *conformity*, changes in behavior that arise from real or imagined group pressure. The impli-cation of this proposition is not that we each live in our separate, private, subjective worlds, independent from one another. We do not experience security in such an individualistic, idiosyncratic way. Rather, our subjective experiences are interconnected through, and dependent on, the normative system of our particular cultures. Consequently, it is the collectively constructed and collaboratively upheld normative sys-tem that influences our actions and thoughts.

A central component of a normative system is *norms*—prescriptions for correct behavior in given settings. Although norms regulate our lives, they are often arbitrary and far from being based on objective criteria. This point was brilliantly demonstrated by Muzafer Sherif[20] (1906–1988) in a series of groundbreaking experiments using the *autokinetic effect*, the apparent movement of a tiny spot of light seen against a dark background. Sherif asked participants to estimate the amount of movement of a single spot of light against a dark background. When participants made their estimates in the company of other people, they arrived at a group norm for the amount of perceived movement. After the group was disbanded and the participants were brought back to make individual estimates, they were still influenced by the group norm. If participants had made estimates working by themselves before joining the group, then the group norm still had an impact on them, but less so than in the condition where they started in the group. When Sherif introduced an extremist confederate into the group, the group became influenced by the extreme estimates of the confederate, and participants continued to be influenced by the original extremist estimate even when the confederate had left the group.

A key point about Sherif's norm formation studies is that the norms were arbitrary and the group was always wrong when it gave estimates of how much the spot of light moved, because the spot of light never actually moved (of course, it is not impossible for a group to make a correct estimation by declaring that the light does not move). The influence of arbitrary norms was also demonstrated through experimental studies by Solomon Asch[21] (1907–1996), who examined the power of a majority to pressure a minority to conform. Asch placed individuals in situations where they could clearly see the correct answer in tasks involving length of line comparisons, but they also heard the majority of other people in their experimental condition identify the wrong line as similar in length to the comparison line. The research question was, having heard others (confederates of the Experimenter) give the wrong answer, would the (naive) participant conform and also give the wrong answer? Despite clearly recognizing the correct answer, about one-third of the participants, highly intelligent, healthy young individuals with normal eyesight, conformed to the rest of the group and gave the incorrect answer. The French researcher Serge Moscovici[22] demonstrated that under certain conditions in an Asch-type experimental situation, even a minority can influence a majority to give the wrong answers.

In our everyday lives, there are many instances when arbitrary norms influence our behavior. For example, consider norms that regulate clothing in the early twenty-first century: women rather than men wear skirts and have long hair, and men rather than women wear neck ties and have short hair. Most people in the West conform to these norms, even though there is no objective reason to do so. In Iran,

Saudi Arabia, and a number of other Islamic countries, women but not men are obligated by law to wear a veil. Again, there is no objective reason for this policy. Norms and conformity to norms are determined by group power. For example, in Iran and Saudi Arabia, women are forced to wear the traditional veil, but men are not forced to wear traditional clothes because men have more power to choose how they dress.

In most cases, arbitrary norms, such as those regulating dress and hair styles, evolve naturally in the course of social life to regulate behavior among people who share a culture, without being made explicit. However, problems can arise when attempts are made to explicitly portray arbitrary norms as objective. For example, consider the widespread public confusion and criticism that has arisen as a result of the federal government's color-coded terrorist alert system (formally known as the Homeland Security Advising System). This consists of labels for five levels of perceived threat: red (severe), orange (high), yellow (elevated), blue (guarded), and green (low). These threat levels have been perceived by the public as confusing and arbitrary, rather than useful and objective. The major problem is that, on the one hand these threat levels are not based on the subjective experiences of the public, and on the other hand the public has not been persuaded to view these threat levels as based on objective criteria.

Proposition Three

The feelings of security experienced by adults in society have two main sources. The first source is temperament and early socialization; the second source is culture and all the factors that influence cultural interpretations of security (including military and economic strength, population resources, and so on).

Source One: Temperament and early socialization experiences, particularly the nature of attachment achieved, result in a predisposition for individuals to experience security in particular ways. For example, because of temperament and early socialization, some individuals are more predisposed than other individuals to experience feelings of insecurity in the same situation.

Source Two: Culture and collective processes serve to shape individual level predispositions, and to lead individuals to interpret their personal experiences of security. In this way, individuals predisposed to experience security differently in the same situation come to share a collective and common experience of security (or lack thereof). The feeling of security experienced by a society is different from the sum of all the experiences of the individuals in that society.

The A, B, C of Reactions to Insecurity

The second source of security experiences also regulates the style of collective reactions to feelings of insecurity. When a group, including a nation state, perceives its security to be threatened, its reaction is characterized by one or a number of the following behavioral styles (what I term the *A, B, C of security threat reactions*):

- **Aggression**: Take aggressive action against the perceived source of threat.
- **Barter**: Engage in a "give and take" to negotiate the best deal possible for itself, given its own strengths and weaknesses and those of the threat source.
- **Coalition**: Enter into coalitions to thwart the threat more effectively.

The developmental science research on attachment, discussed earlier in this chapter, clearly shows that both dispositional and contextual factors play an important role in the shaping of a sense of security in individuals. However, in situations of greater threat to collective security, the role of contextual factors increases. To better appreciate this tendency, it is useful to consider the concept of degrees of freedom.

Contexts vary with respect to the degrees of freedom they afford individuals. In situations of high degrees of freedom, individuals enjoy a wide range of possibilities with respect to how they behave; however, in situations of low degrees of freedom, individuals have relatively limited behavioral options. An example of a situation with high degrees of freedom is a casual party, when a group of friends get together, eat, drink, and have fun. A lot of spontaneity and creativity can come into social life at a party. However, consider the context of a law court. The judge, the jury, the lawyers, the law clerks, trial witnesses, all have to conform to strict guidelines for what to say and do. There is a low degree of freedom in the law court.

In a situation where there is a low threat to collective security, people enjoy high degrees of freedom. For example, when a country enjoys peace and there is little or no threat from external enemies, then there is less pressure on people to conform to norms, rules, values, and so on, reflecting values such as nationalism. In such a situation, critics and even radicals can be active within a country, and feel little pressure to conform. Also, in such a situation there is great opportunity for individual differences in the experience of security to manifest themselves. Even when there are high degrees of freedom, some individuals will experience greater threats to security.

However, when there is a perceived serious threat to collective security, then the degrees of freedom decrease and can become extremely low. For example, when a country faces a serious threat from an external enemy, as when the perceived threat of the Soviet Union was heightened in the United States during the 1950s and when the threat of Islamic fundamentalism was highlighted after 9/11, then pressure increases for people to conform to nationalistic stereotypes and to "rally around the flag." In such situations, human security factors (e.g., food, health, education) take a back seat to realist security factors (e.g., military strength).

Because of the tendency for conformity and obedience to increase when there is a high security threat, leaders in power tend to exaggerate risks, particularly risks associated with external threats. This tendency increases with the dictatorial inclinations of the leadership, so that it is extremely high in countries such as Russia and Iran. Within democratic countries, this tendency to exaggerate risks also varies across administrations; for example, it was high during the presidency of George W. Bush (2000–2008).

Proposition Four

Globalization is resulting in increasing interdependency in feelings of insecurity experienced by people in different societies around the world. Even the United States, the sole superpower on the world stage, is now far more exposed to the negative impact of events in other parts of the world, including natural disasters, wars, and famines.

Increased security interdependence is integral to the globalization process. The feelings of insecurity experienced by people in different parts of the world are becoming increasingly dependent on events outside their own societies. This is most obvious in the areas of (1) news and the mass media, (2) terrorism, (3) cyber space, (4) the economy, and (5) the environment.

To a great degree, messages in the media and what is manufactured and presented as "news" shape subjective security—how safe people feel. After all, what ends up being presented is only one tiny part of the vast amount of information available about events and people around the world. News is socially constructed[23] just as societal problems are manufactured. For example, are drug addiction, gun violence, jail breaks, illegal immigration, or crime major problems in American cities?[24] Resource mobilization theory[25] is among a number of orientations that argue it is possible to socially construct any of these as major social/political problems, provided one has the necessary access to global media networks and outlets. The globalization of the media means that (1) news manufactured in the context of one society is more likely to be transmitted to other parts of the world, and (2) the same issues are being presented as serious problems throughout the world. To better appreciate this point, we need to consider security broadly, as relating to activities such as eating, for example.

Consider the social construction of weight as a major hazard, and the media spotlight on the serious dangers of eating disorders.[26] On the one hand, the intricately interconnected global mass media is spreading the image of the "slim is sexy" Western body ideals throughout different Western and non-Western societies. The glossy magazines and popular television shows of different countries are promoting the same super-slim body image as ideal. On the other hand, the same global media is socially constructing eating disorders, particularly anorexia nervosa and bulimia, as major problems. The other side of the same coin is the central role of the global media in selling a fast-food lifestyle around the world, at the same time that the global media spotlights obesity as a major hazard with grave health risks. In this way, eating disorders are globally presented as a danger faced by everyone around the world.

The interconnectedness of feelings of insecurity has also been reinforced and amplified through the spotlight on terrorism. We all know about the enormous global impact of terrorism both on macro-level policies and micro-level behavior, particularly since 9/11: the so-called global "war on terror," the disastrous situation in post-invasion Iraq and now Afghanistan, the increased radicalization of Muslims in many parts of the world, the spread of Al Qaeda into Afghanistan and Pakistan, the constant security checks people undergo . . . the list seems endless. What we are apt to treat as routine, and gradually as normal, is the impact of terrorism on the everyday lives of ordinary people around the world.

The greatest impact of acts of terrorism, particularly the attacks of 9/11, has been on the sense of vulnerability people feel in relation to *distant* sources of attacks. Before 9/11, most Americans had not heard of the Taliban, or even of Afghanistan. Suddenly, what happens in madressehs (Islamic schools) in remote parts of Afghanistan and Pakistan has come to influence the sense of security experienced by Americans in New York; Washington, DC; and elsewhere. This connection is now made much stronger by the wars in Iraq and Afghanistan, respectively Bush's war and Obama's war (or rather, Obama's Vietnam). The U.S-led war in Afghanistan could well prove to be a bigger and longer-running disaster than the U.S-led war in Iraq. This is in part because, once again, the American media has failed to ask the tough critical questions in a timely manner.

Terrorism has also impacted the routine, everyday activities of ordinary people around the world, and in this way made us more interconnected. For example, consider what happens every time a person wants to travel, particularly by air transportation. Think of the hundreds of millions of people who each week spend hours waiting to be searched as they go through security check points at airports, train stations, or other transportation centers. Enormous resources are being dedicated to achieve tighter security, resources that could have been allocated to education, health, and other needy sectors of human security (this links back to my early claim that at times of "real" material threat to security, there is less importance given to human security).

Most importantly, there is now an implicitly accepted uniformity to security screening as a result of the global war on terror, a uniformity that makes the behavior of people in democracies and dictatorships rather similar. In democratic societies where previously citizens would not have accepted being routinely searched, photographed, and investigated in multiple different ways, the passive response of citizens to intrusions in their personal lives is now no different from the response of citizens living in dictatorships. The perceived need for security has dampened opposition to government oversight in all aspects of everyday life, so that privacy has become in practice far more limited than it was during the 1960s and 1970s.

But just as the war on terror has increased the vulnerability of ordinary people to greater scrutiny and control by government agents, computer technology has made government and non-governmental organizations vulnerable to attacks from various groups around the world, from individual hackers and small groups of cyber terrorists to well-organized groups with extensive resources, often located abroad and sometimes backed by foreign governments.[27] The computer systems of United States government agencies, particularly security and military agencies, are probed almost countless times every day, mostly by sources located in Russia, China, and other counties.[28] In this way, cyberspace has made security even more of a global issue.

When ordinary people talk about perceiving a threat to security, the economy has a central part in their discourse. The dramatically increased interconnectedness of the global economy is another important factor that has made people's sense of security more global. In industrialized societies, the sense of economic security has become more global through job outsourcing and the perception that companies are now moving to those countries that have the cheapest labor markets— all of these being non-Western countries. Thus, job loss and job outsourcing is the subject of the day in conversations among ordinary people in Western societies. On the other hand, people in non-Western societies feel vulnerable because increasingly the available jobs depend on sustained consumer demand from Western societies; even a slight change in the economy of Western societies translates into hundreds of thousands of jobs lost in non-Western societies.

The sense of security experienced by human beings is also now far more interconnected around the globe because of threats posed by environmental pollution and global warming. The challenge we face is probably best discussed through a materialist perspective: planet earth has finite resources, being overused by a continually growing human population that is also experiencing rapidly rising expectations. Put simply, there are now a lot more of us, and more of us expect to consume greater resources. No doubt scientific breakthroughs and production increases can meet some of this rising demand, but the cost to the environment might be too great and our survival could be in danger. So far, our attempts to bring environmental pollution and global warming under control, such as through the so-called *Kyoto Protocol* (1992) which is supposed to reduce greenhouse gases, have fallen well short of what is needed to reverse environmental degradation.

The human abuse of environmental resources seems the perfect example of what Garrett Hardin meant by *The Tragedy of the Commons*[29] (discussed in Chapter 2). The tragedy Hardin identified has been the concern of many thinkers focused on the consequences of over-population, particularly Thomas Malthus[30] (1766–1834). Whereas Malthus explored the cycles of boom and bust, feast and famine arising out of population growth being faster than food supply growth (he argued that population growth is geometric—2, 4, 8, 16, and so on, whereas food supply increases arithmetically—1, 2, 3, 4, and so on), Hardin discussed the consequences of rational individuals maximizing personal profits by overusing and ultimately destroying common resources.[31] Through the example of a group of herdsman using a common land to graze their animals, Hardin argued that it would be to the benefit of each individual to have as many of their own animals as possible grazing on common land, because the profit from their animals would come to them individually whereas degradation costs of the commons would be shared by everyone. To extend the analogy to global warming, it would be beneficial for each country to spend as little as possible on saving the planet and concentrate on making profits for themselves, because the costs of their pollution is shared by all the world. Of course, if everyone follows this rational line of thinking, the result would be the tragedy of the commons and possible human extinction.

Proposition Five

Increased global interdependency will initially result in greater feelings of insecurity over a period of adjustment, during which time there will be enormous economic, political, social, cultural, and other changes, including increased intergroup competition and violent conflict, in many different parts of the world.

Globalization would move ahead far more smoothly if the different nation states and regions of the world were more similar economically, technologically, politically, and culturally. However, the enormous differences between nations and regions in key sectors means that increased interconnectedness is moving ahead with massive disruptions and difficulties. Consider, for example, just the disruptions associated with the cost of manufacturing production differences between nations. Because labor costs are far lower in some countries (for example, labor costs in China and India continue to be about less than half of labor costs in the United States in the manufacturing sector), increased interconnectedness and open markets result in jobs being moved from countries with higher labor costs to countries with lower labor costs.[32] The result is rapid economic shifts, with production and jobs moving from higher-cost countries to lower-cost countries. For example, the manufacturing of televisions, washing machines, refrigerators, telephones, computers, automobiles, and trucks, among many other products, has moved from the United States and other higher-cost Western countries to China and India, with associated increases in competition for energy resources around the world.[33] But this is not the end of the story, because as the standard of living of workers in China and India improves, so does production costs in these countries. Consequently, by the second decade of the twenty-first century there is already a movement of some jobs from China and India to relatively lower-cost countries, such as Vietnam and the Philippines.

The movement of production and jobs from one country to another is not new; we can find some examples of this trend certainly as far back as the Roman Empire. What is new is the tremendous speed with which production and jobs now move from place to place; for example, in the first decade of the twenty-first century millions of manufacturing jobs have vanished from the United States and the profile of the American labor market has changed. Just as dramatically, tens of millions of manufacturing jobs are created in China and India in the first decade of the twenty-first century, with entire new industries being born and maturing at a pace that was unimaginable just a few decades ago. These shifts have direct relevance for security, as demonstrated by the popular anger and revolt associated with disruptions in United States labor and financial markets at the dawn of the twenty-first century.[34]

According to the micro-macro rule of change,[35] the maximum speed of change at the micro level of psychological processes and social relationships is slower than the maximum speed of change at macro economic, technological, and political levels. Thus rule is directly applicable to the disruptions associated with globalization. For example, shifts in jobs from high-cost to lower-cost countries can take place rapidly relative to the slow rate of adjustments that take place in individual functioning and social relationships. Of course, countries that rapidly gain jobs also face huge challenges, particularly because workers could experience rising expectations that prove impossible to satisfy and result in feelings of relative deprivation. A combination of rising expectations and relative deprivation is a formula for collective insecurity, violence, and even revolution.

Proposition Six

Globalization has brought about dramatic increases in the speed of major economic, technological, and social shifts around the world. The interconnectedness of societies around the world has important consequences, particularly for the speed with which change takes place in economic and cultural spheres. The globalization of trade and modern communications systems means that, for example, youth clothing fashions, movies, and music move around the world at tremendous speed.

The political leadership of countries such as China, Russia, Iran, Egypt, and other dictatorships has been able to prevent the spread of open political systems. Each of these dictatorships has resisted the pull of openness, under the guise of protecting the people from capitalism, or protecting Islam, or protecting nationalism, or some other such "divine" cause. However, they have not succeeded in cutting off their countries from being connected to the global economy. For example, the economies of Russia and Iran are heavily dependent on income from oil exports, and an international drop in demand for oil immediately and detrimentally impacts them. Similarly, China's export-driven economy is dependent on high global demand, leaving China exposed to influence from global economic trends.

The rapid spread of youth culture has been even more difficult to prevent, even by Islamic dictatorships that have both political and religious organizations at their disposal to try to control the cultural changes. Because young people are relatively more in tune with new electronic communications systems (e-mail, blogs, Facebook, Twitter, and so on), and because they are generally open to new fashion trends, even the most stringent government efforts fail to stop the spreading of new styles of music, clothing, and so on. It is not clear, however, to what extent such cultural trends will translate to political change in closed societies.

The most important new feature of this situation is that interconnectedness has resulted in a multiplier effect that speeds up economic and cultural trends around the world. Changes in one part of the world, particularly in large Western societies that serve as centers of innovation in entrepreneurship, ideas, arts, and fashion, quickly cascade into other societies. This sets off a multiplier effect, so that a change initiated in country A impacts countries B, C, D, and E, and subsequently changes in B, C, D, and E cascade back into country A and add to the strength of the original change trend. These trends have been dramatically speeded up by globalization, so that policies at the level of national governments are even less effective. Increasingly, there is need for regional and global development policies. National five-year development plans have become less meaningful in a situation where such powerful and rapid global trends overwhelm national trends, as took place in the global depression starting in 2008.

CONCLUDING COMMENT

The dual-source theory presents a holistic account of security, stressing the primacy of the subjective experience of collective insecurity. When individuals arrive in this world, the group into which they are born already has a certain sense of collective security. Individuals become socialized to adopt the worldview of security prevailing in their group. In some groups, individuals are led to adopt vastly exaggerated estimates of risk, a trend that works to "rally people around the flag." But in other cases, people are led by the cultural worldview of their group to deny security risks, and this is often the case with respect to risks associated with globalization. The dual-source theory proposes that the sudden economic and cultural shifts associated with globalization pose serious security threats. Moreover, security threats will increase with globalization in a transitory period, during which nation states are attempting to adjust to the often uncomfortable interdependencies in which they find themselves.

Paradoxically, the interdependence arising out of globalization will in the initial period result in feelings of *greater insecurity*, a return to isolationism, and a greater reliance on the nation state as a defender of security—particularly economic security. This transitory period will last for at least decades and be associated with a dangerously high level of hypernationalism.

4

"Soft" and "Hard"
Security Capital

We saw in Chapter 1 that there has been a serious re-thinking of security in the last few decades. During an earlier phase, analysts focused mainly and sometimes solely on military resources and rational processes, but there is now a movement toward focusing also on non-military factors.[1] Indeed, this movement away from considering security in terms of military factors seems to have gone so far as to focus on everything except military factors,[2] which is obviously too far for the pendulum to swing. An approach is needed that is balanced, encompassing both military and non-military factors,[3] *and* with adequate attention given to irrational processes.

The dual-source theory of security adopts a holistic approach, and the main propositions of this theory were outlined in Chapter 3. In particular, the discussion focused on the first source of personal security: temperament, early socialization, and attachment. The main topic of this chapter is a foundationally important source of collective security: *security capital.*

I begin by distinguishing between two types of security capital. *Hard security capital* consists of all the physical factors, particularly those concerning military resources and economic resources, that impact on the security of a group. (It also includes natural resources, population resources, science and technology resources, health and medical resources, agricultural resources, and transportation and communications resources, but they are not discussed here due to space limitations.) The security of a group is also influenced in important ways by *soft security capital*, what I described earlier in this book as part of the *enabling conditions* for military security and other types of hard security. The enabling conditions include trust, ideology, cohesion, collective resilience, collective dynamism, and the like. These are factors that have been neglected, but which I regard as of primary importance and consequently give priority in this discussion.

TYPES OF SOFT SECURITY CAPITAL

Soft security capital comprises all the social, cultural, historical, and psychological characteristics of a people that serve as the enabling conditions for military security and hard security more broadly. These characteristics, particularly trust and subjective justice, reside within individuals, but it would be a mistake to focus on the individual as the only or even the main unit of analysis in this discussion. Mental processes and higher psychological experiences are located within individuals, but they start in the larger social world and are imbedded in social relationships.[4] For example, a certain type and level of trust already exists within society when a child is born. Collectively constructed concepts of trust, and representations of how, when, and who to trust in everyday life (including which foreign nations and governments can be trusted) are already present in the larger society as the child is socialized and grows up to become an adult. From these societal sources, and through personal experiences (which are always necessarily in social context), the individual takes on a "sense of trust."

Trust

Trust involves assumptions about predictability and fulfillment of expectations. For example, I trust my bank with my money, because I believe my bank will return my money if I were to need it. I trust my friend with my car on the expectation that he will drive it with care. I trust my doctor and take the medication he prescribes on the expectation that it will make me feel better. Of course, in most cases my trust in others goes beyond the evidence immediately available to me. I do not know all the details of my bank's financial history, or my friend's driving record, or the chemical composition of the medication prescribed to me. My trust is to some degree based on "blind faith."

The kind of trust most common across societies is *particularized trust*, limited to one's in-group (family, tribe, ethnicity, and so on).[5] Most people in most societies tend to have more trust for in-group members, and in some societies trust is limited to the family and other close in-groups. Nepotism thrives in conditions where particularized trust is high, but there is a lack of *generalized trust*, involving trust for strangers. Generalized trust serves as the basis for making interconnections in modern complex societies, with enormous institutions involving millions of strangers collaborating on the basis of some trust.

Trust plays a role in the effective working of all societies, but has an essential role in democracies.[6] Dictatorships function by nurturing distrust among the general population, so as to prevent political mobilization. For example, a government tactic in dictatorships is to encourage rumors about the enormous scale and reach of the clandestine security forces, so that the population will be cowed into subservience and will distrust each other.[7] In such contexts, even particularized trust is weakened, so that family members might come to suspect one another of "working for the other side."

Subjective Justice

Do people feel that they are living in a just society, and that they are being treated fairly? This question is different from asking if there are just laws "on the books," because *black letter law*, the formal law that is found in print, can be very different from how fairly people feel they are being treated.[8] The law on the books could allow for all kinds of *rights*, a demand placed on others by the person who possesses it, such as free speech and freedom of assembly, but citizens could find that in practice they are unable to exercise their rights as they exist in black letter law. Correspondingly, people might find that authorities have obliged them to take on unwanted *duties*, obligations to fulfill the needs, commands, and expectations of others[9]—duties that are against the formal laws on the books. For example, in some countries the norm is for authorities, including judges, to receive bribes from the public. In such contexts, it becomes the unwritten duty of individuals to pay bribes to receive services from the courts, taxation offices, the police, and so on.

In societies where people feel they are treated fairly, their sense of security is greater. The feeling of being treated fairly is enhanced when everyone is treated equally before the law, even when the laws on the books are not progressive. Independent of how progressive or backward the laws on the books are, it is better that the law be applied equally to everyone, irrespective of their power and status in society.

Research suggests that another important factor that enhances the sense of fairness is the participation of people in decision-making processes. The assumption had been that the sense of fairness would be determined by outcome and *distributive justice*; for example, by how much money a person receives, or the guilty or not-guilty verdict given at the end of a legal trial. But there is now strong empirical evidence to show that in many contexts an even more important factor in shaping subjective fairness is *procedural justice*, the processes through which resources are allocated (rather than *distributive justice*, the end result of the resource allocation procedure).[10] For example, the extent to which John feels he has been treated fairly by the police officers who stopped his car does not just depend on whether or not they punish him with a fine (distributive justice), but also, and perhaps more importantly, on the extent to which John feels the police have treated him respectfully and listened to his side of the story (for example, about the pedestrian who jumped out onto the road and forced him to sharply turn and run over a neighbor's dog).

Motivation for Civil Unrest

From the perspective of the status quo, there is an inverse relationship between the motivation for civil unrest and security: As the motivation for civil unrest increases, security declines. The question arises: To what extent are people motivated to instigate and to support civil unrest, intended to change the sociopolitical system? This question has been explored by an enormous variety of researchers, including many inspired by Marxist historical-materialism. Modern research has focused on the tendency for people to prefer individual routs to social mobility, rather than collective action to try to bring about social change. For example, in a study I conducted with several colleagues,[11] North American participants showed a strong preference for individual mobility over taking collective action. The tendency to want to make it on one's own seems to be socialized very strongly in North American culture.

This tendency for individualistic rather than collective reactions to perceived injustice has been interpreted by some as reflecting *false consciousness*, the inability of people to recognize which social class they objectively belong to and the contradictions between the interests of their social class and other social classes. As a broad generalization, the following statement serves as a guide to students of security: agents interested to ferment social unrest and changes in the intergroup power structure must focus on bringing about collective mobilization and intergroup conflict; agents interested in preventing social unrest and maintaining the intergroup power structure must focus on strengthening individual mobility, and limiting group-based movements, as the favored path to making progress in society. Individualism serves to protect existing group-based power relationships; collective mobilization challenges existing group-based power relationships.[12]

False consciousness and related concepts indicate the important role of psychological factors in the motivation for civil unrest. Factors such as the availability of cognitive alternatives to the present sociopolitical order (can people imagine a realistic alternative to the present conditions?) and the perceived stability-instability of the present order (do people see it as possible to change the current conditions?) play a central role in the motivation to instigate or participate in civil unrest.

Of course, material conditions are also important, but there is *not* a direct and simple relationship between economic inequality and

motivation for civil unrest: greater economic inequality does not necessarily result in people desiring civil unrest. For example, in the United
States, the objective indicators show an increase in the difference
between those with the most and those with the least economic resources. Between 1972 and 2001, the income of the poorest 10 percent of
Americans rose only 1 percent while the income of the richest 1 percent
rose by 87 percent.[13] The plight of the poor in America has been well-
documented and publicized in books such as *Nickel and Dimed: On (Not)
Getting on in America.*[14] The astronomical incomes of the rich is also
well-publicized. For example, during the economic meltdown of the
early twenty-first century, the worst economic decline since the 1930s,
The Washington Post reported that the total compensation for the ten top
earning business executives in 2007 alone came to about 1,362 million
dollars, with the highest compensation being about 350 million dollars
(which went to the Chairman and CEO of the Blackstone Group).[15]
These income inequality excesses, coming in the midst of the economic
downturn starting in 2008, brought about a backlash from the public
and forced a government intervention in the form of new rules to regulate the financial market.

Ideological Fit

In order for a political system to survive, it must be supported by an
appropriate ideology, one that is a good fit with the political system.
Ideology encompasses all the worldview of a population, including
beliefs, values, norms, rules, and so on.[16] *Ideological fit* is the appropri-
ateness of an ideology for the task of supporting a political order with
its particular group-based inequalities. Security is higher when there is
a better fit between the dominant ideology in society and the sociopolitical order of that society.

  A lack of ideological fit means that security is threatened and there is
a possibility of societal collapse. This can come about when social, cultural, and political changes take place among a population, bringing
about shifts in their ideologies away from what is needed to support
the existing sociopolitical order. This shift is often associated with revolutions. For example, during the 1960s and 1970s hundreds of thousands of Iranians went abroad to study at universities in the United
States, the United Kingdom, and other Western democracies, and
returned to Iran to work in society ruled by a hereditary (and incompe-
tent) monarch. These hundreds of thousands of students brought Western political ideas back to Iran. Over time, imported Western ideals
of "the rights of the people" became coupled with the aspirations of
revolutionary Islamic thinkers, such as Ayatollah Ruhollah Khomeini

(1900–1989), so that by the mid-1970s there was a lack of ideological fit in Iran. That is, the ideologies dominant in society did not support the continuation of a hereditary monarchy.[17] The political explosion that followed eventually resulted in the birth of the Islamic Republic of Iran, which by the twenty-first century had abandoned the "republic" part of the description and simply become an "Islamic dictatorship."

A related debate concerns the fit between different ideologies and human nature. Underlying the ideology of capitalism and free enterprise is the assumption that human beings are more productive and happy when they are able to work and live in a free society: government should be small and should not interfere in the lives of people. Under such free enterprise conditions, it is assumed that the entrepreneurial spirit will allow some talented individuals (e.g., Ford, Rockefeller, and Gates) to create enormous wealth for their own families, but that everyone will benefit because "the rising tide will lift all boats." As expounded by right wing groups, such as Libertarians, the capitalist ideology calls for insignificant or no government at all. This happens to correspond, as concerns the role of government at least, with the ideal end point in historical development as conceived by Marxists: the society without government.

But from a Marxist perspective, the debate about human nature is moot because the capitalism ideology implies that human nature is fixed and unchanging, which it is not. What we assume to be human nature is the product of certain material-historical conditions; when these conditions change, then what we take to be human nature will also change. According to this Marxist perspective, human beings are not yet shaped to live in a society with very limited government oversight. Greed and self-interest still dominate human behavior, so a lack of government oversight will inevitably result in corruption, monopolies, inefficiencies, and a boom-and-bust economic cycle as experienced by the major economies at the start of the twenty-first century, for example. Strong government intervention is needed to bring about changes in human thoughts and actions toward people acting on the basis of the conviction that the interests of the larger society and the interests of the self are synonymous. In such a situation, people will not need to be rewarded individually and they will not need to personally own things, because everyone will own everything and private property will become redundant. Human consciousness will reach a point where there are no social classes, and this means that a central government is not needed, because according to Marxist ideology the real function of a central government in a class-based society is to protect the interests of the capitalist class and to use coercion, guile, and force keep the lower classes "in their place."

So far, the idealistic ideologies of both capitalism and Marxism remain very far removed from capitalism and Marxism as practiced. In the United States, the most powerful capitalist country in the world, the twenty-first century has began with the federal government buying up huge parts of the private sector; in a policy summed up as privatizing profits and nationalizing debts. In China, the major remaining communist state, the Chinese central government has allowed considerable freedom in the marketplace, so that the entrepreneurial spirit has as much room to show itself in this communist state as it has in the "capitalist West."

Collective Resilience

Resilience, the ability to overcome obstacles, is traditionally treated as the characteristic of individuals.[18] Of course there are differences between individuals with respect to the ability to overcome obstacles: from among the hundreds of people at the scene of a terrorist attack, many will emerge traumatized, a few will suffer long-term post traumatic stress disorder (PTSD), but a small number will walk away as if nothing had happened. The individuals who are more resilient can play an important role in strengthening societal reactions to serious threats. However, even more important than individual resilience is *collective resilience*, the ability of a group to overcome obstacles.

Collective resilience is more than the sum of the individual resilience of group members. For example, consider the case of a college basketball team. At the start of the basketball season, the team suffers a number of unfortunate incidents and ends up losing all of the first ten games against the teams of rival colleges. Can the team recover? Factors such as school spirit, leadership, and group cohesion—none of which is dependent on separate individuals but arise out of the group as a whole—will determine how effectively the group can recover. In this sense, collective resilience abides by the Gestalt motto, "the whole is more than the sum of its parts."

At the more macro level, clearly there are differences in collective resilience across societies. For example, consider the recovery of Germany and Japan after their defeat in the Second World War. After only a quarter of a century, both countries had re-established themselves as competitive industrial forces, and after only half a century both had emerged as among the world's leading economies. Collective resilience accounts for this transformation, from total defeat to societal resurgence. (Of course, another vitally important factor was the economic and political support given to United States allies under the *Marshall Plan*.[19])

Group Cohesiveness

Cohesiveness is the forces that push group members closer together. As a general rule, there are important advantages enjoyed by more cohesive groups, particularly in contexts where a group has to achieve specific tasks (as in work groups, sports teams, and the like).[20] For example, the members of more cohesive groups tend to feel greater pride in and loyalty to the group, and be more engaged in group activities.[21] Social contexts in which people are interdependent are more likely to lead to greater cohesiveness.[22] This underlines the importance of successfully introducing *superordinate goals*, those goals that are desired by most people or everyone, but can be achieved only through collaboration (rather than individuals or groups working independently).[23] For example, when national security is threatened, a high priority superordinate goal for society would be "defending the nation using maximum effort and resources," a goal that can be achieved only if everyone pulls in the same direction. At the global level, a superordinate goal should be "saving the environment." Obviously this cannot be achieved by one country alone, because it requires that all nation states reduce their carbon footprints.

Groups that are more cohesive are more effective in meeting challenges such as threats from external enemies. Perhaps because of this advantage enjoyed by cohesive groups, human beings have evolved to become more cohesive when there is a threat from outgroups.[24] For example, the most immediate impact of the 9/11 attacks on U.S. domestic politics was a huge increase in support for President George W. Bush, as Americans rallied around the flag and the country became more cohesive to protect the homeland. Of course, politicians in power, knowing that an external threat results in such support, regularly attempt to invoke external threats as a means of increasing support for themselves.

But group cohesiveness also has potential disadvantages. An important example of such disadvantages is demonstrated by research on *groupthink*,[25] the tendency for people in a group to converge on unwise courses of action that they would have avoided if they were making the decision individually. Groupthink results in a group making poor decisions that are much worse than would have been taken by each individual group member working independently. There are numerous examples of disastrous national policy-making decisions that have been made by highly educated and intelligent groups. Decision-making groups that resulted in fiascos, from the Bay of Pigs invasion during the time of the short-lived John F. Kennedy administration (1961–1963), to the nonexistent Weapons of Mass Destruction and the mismanagement of post-war Iraq during the George W. Bush administration (2000–2008), to the continuation of the ill-fated Afghanistan invasion policy in Afghanistan and Western Pakistan during the Obama administration.

Altruistic Capital

The survival of society relies on a minimal level of *altruism*, the willingness of people to do things for others without expecting a direct reward. *Altruistic capital* is the general willingness of the members of a society to behave unselfishly in regard to others. This willingness is integral to individuals and there are individual differences in how altruistic people are in a society, as well as how altruism is interpreted cross-culturally.[26] However, there are also differences across societies in altruistic capital. In some societies, the general level of altruism is higher than in some other societies.

Altruism involves immediate sacrifice on the part of an individual or group, and as a general rule security is best safeguarded when altruistic capital is higher in society. For example, higher altruistic capital means that in the face of an attack from external forces, the population will be ready to make greater sacrifices to defend the homeland. In societies with a higher level of altruistic capital, people are more prone to carry out *supererogatory duties* (what a person is not obligated to carry out, but is applauded for carrying out) and *supererogatory rights* (what a person is owed by others, but is willing to forego for the sake of the greater collective good). But the question arises: why should people behave altruistically? A wide range of theories have been put forward to address this question, but most of them assume that altruism does not really exist, and that people do things for others because of motives that are ultimately self-serving.

Arguing from evolutionary perspectives, groups of researchers working under titles such as "sociobiologists" and "evolutionary psychologists" have been particularly influential through the thesis that altruism is ultimately about improving the survival chances of one's gene pool against competing gene pools. This argument is profoundly influenced by the *Selfish Gene* thesis of the British researcher Richard Dawkins,[27] whose ideas have revolutionized evolutionary theory. From this new perspective, the most important competition in evolution is that between gene pools. Humans are conceived as convenient vehicles for genes, as they compete for survival. Thus, John steps forward to sacrifice his life for the homeland because those around him share more of his genes than do the attackers from outside the homeland. This is not because John is conscious of the role that genetic similarity-dissimilarity plays in his thought and actions; rather, inbuilt tendencies unbeknown to John, a kind of "whispering within," move him to behave as he does.

This kind of gene-based explanation seems far too simplistic to deal with the complexities of contemporary societies. For example, multi-racial societies such as the United States have multi-racial military forces that fight very effectively, despite the fact that genetic differences within their militaries are at least as large as genetic differences between their militaries and those of enemy forces.[28]

Leadership Fit

Security is enhanced when there is a better fit between leadership style and the population of a society. The better the fit, the more effectively will the leader be able to mobilize defenses and inspire collective sacrifice on the part of the population.

Leadership style must be considered in relation to the characteristics of a population. Effective leadership style enhances security, but the same leadership style will not necessarily be effective across two different societies or even across time in the same society. For example, consider leadership in two countries with roughly the same population size: the Islamic Republic of Iran and the United Kingdom (U.K.). If the current Supreme Leader of Iran was transplanted to London, and the U.K. prime minister was transplanted to Tehran, they would find their leadership style unsuitable for their "new" populations.

The idea of "leadership fit" raises certain ethical questions. One interpretation of leadership fit could be that all leadership styles are of equal value, what matters is how effective they are in relation to a particular population. For example, it could be argued that there is nothing inherently good or bad about a dictatorial leadership style; what matters is whether a particular population is effectively managed by a leader using this style. An alternative view, which I endorse, is that some leadership styles are of higher value, because they allow the people greater choices, as well as more participation and influence in decision making. On this basis, a democratic leadership style is preferable to a dictatorial one. But this does not mean that a society with a tradition of rule by successive dictators can be speedily given democratic leadership. Many revolutions have succeeded in overthrowing dictatorships in the hope of transforming a closed society to an open one, only to find that after the revolution there is a slide backward to dictatorship, but now under a new name, new ideology, and new leadership.

The so-called *paradox of revolution* refers to this tragic and often repeated tendency for societies to sink back into despotism after a revolution has overthrown the last despot. One important factor resulting in this repeated trend is the extreme difficulty of changing the thoughts and actions of a population that results in a certain *follower style*, the tendency for a population to behave in ways that support one leadership style rather than another. Leaders and followers tend to develop behavioral styles that reciprocally support one another, and in large societies with long histories such mutually supportive behavior can evolve over long time periods, sometimes centuries, and require a long time to change. Consequently, when a dictator is suddenly overthrown through a revolution (as in Iran in 1978) or foreign intervention (as in Iraq in 2003), even the strongest democratic aspirations do not result in fast or smooth transitions to democracy. Indeed, in many cases there is a strong tendency to slip back, in some respects at least, to dictatorial leader–follower relationships.

It is in this way that the persistence of a particular "follower style" results in patterns of leadership style to be repeated, despite revolutions and power changing hands. In this way, the tsar was followed by Lenin, Stalin, and their "strongman" successors in Russia, Mao and other "new emperors" followed the ancient emperors in China, just as Napoleon had become emperor in the tradition of old kings in France, and Khomeini and other "Supreme Leaders" followed the "strongman rule" of the shahs in Iran.[29]

Collective Dynamism

Collective dynamism consists of all the features of a society that generate constructive growth. This includes *collective esteem* (a sense of worth of one's ingroup), space and encouragement for innovation, and openness to new ideas and influences external to the group. Each of these characteristics is an essential component of collective dynamism.

High collective esteem allows the group to have the confidence needed to be open to new ideas and to explore new paths. However, *high collective esteem* should not be confused with what critics have called *inflated, unstable* esteem.[30] For example, if group X believes that they are the most talented and productive group in the world, but their estimation is wrong and grossly inflated, it will also prove to be unstable because when faced with real competition from other groups they will be shown to be low in talent and productivity. There is a danger that groups suffering from inflated, unstable collective esteem will react violently to any perceived internal or external threats.

Groups with genuine high collective esteem enjoy the confidence to allow room for critical self-reflection. Such groups are open rather than closed, and at the societal level they are characterized by freedom of speech and assembly, open borders, and strong support for research in the sciences, humanities, and the arts. Obviously this rules out dictator-ships of various kinds, including those based on religious (e.g., Iran, Saudi Arabia) and political (China, Russia) dogmas.

An essential component of collective dynamism is openness to new ideas and innovation. In all societies there are certain limitations to change. For example, the United States Constitution, the Bill of Rights, and other foundational documents serve to limit the extent to which American society can change. Thus, even in the largest free market sys-tem in the world, there are severe limits to change. However, at least in most cultural, artistic, economic, and scientific domains, the American system remains relatively open. Moreover, well over a million immi-grants arrive in the United States each year, and this serves as another vitally important source of innovation and renewal in the American system.

Basic evolutionary principles suggest that groups that continue to change to adapt to transformations in surrounding conditions are more likely to survive. This suggests that over the long term, societies higher in collective dynamism, which happen to be democratic, will win in the competition against societies that are closed and rigid, which are dicta-torships. However, the short-term developments might be very differ-ent. A determined group of dictatorships might well wage war and defeat democracies. It would be utterly foolish and irresponsible for open societies to disregard this possibility and to drop their guard.

Soft security capital is essential particularly because it creates the en-abling conditions in which military security and other types of hard security capital can be realized, as discussed next.

"HARD" SECURITY CAPITAL

Hard security capital encompasses the material characteristics of a popu-lation, its various material possessions, and the physical properties of the environment it has under its direct control. This includes the size, age distribution, and physical health of a population, as well as the geo-logical resources of the land it directly controls. In this discussion, I only consider the two major types of hard security capital: military resources and economic resources.

Military Resources

Discussions of military resources and strategies have been at the heart of traditional approaches to security. Security studies as a specialized discipline continues to be dominated by the military mindset, and a rationalist approach to war (although Handel points out that "Despite its normative emphasis on waging war as rationally as possible, the classical strategic paradigm recognizes that many factors can limit the rationality of the calculations made"[31]). The role of military resources in intergroup conflicts, and security more broadly, has been transformed by a number of new trends in the twenty-first century.

A first trend is the acceleration of technological advances, which has given industrialized countries such as the United States enormous advantages, particularly in weapons. In 1066, when the Normans invaded England, the two warring sides were not very different in terms of technical knowhow and weapons. At that time, the swords, spears, shields, axes, armor, bows and arrows, and other weapons available to the armies were comparable. Although some armies were better equipped than others, they were all roughly in the same league.

A thousand years later in the twenty-first century, the situation has completely changed. Iran and Iraq had access to similar levels of weapons, and they fought an eight-year war (1980–1988) to an utter standstill. It took the United States and its allies only about two weeks in 2003 to break the back of the Iraqi military and overthrow Saddam Hussein's government. The superior military resources of the United States and other industrialized countries give them huge advantages when fighting against traditional armies that do not have access to military drone planes, robots, and other technically superior weapons. Advances in robotics will no doubt further increase this difference: the United States military will undoubtedly rely more on unmanned crafts in the air and robots on the ground to fight future wars.

Although technologically less sophisticated societies do not have access to the most advanced military hardware, their military capability has been increased by another change that has come about: the rise of ideologies that make available suicide bombers, the "poor army's guided missile."

Economic Resources

> . . . _economic failure abroad raises the risk of state failure as well. When foreign states malfunction (in the sense that they fail to provide basic public goods for their populations), their societies are likely to experience steeply escalating problems that spill over to the rest of the world, including the United States. Failed states are seedbeds of violence, terrorism, international criminality, mass migration and refugee movement, drug trafficking, and disease._
>
> Sachs (2003)[32]

Fractured globalization means that it is not sufficient for a country to achieve economic prosperity on its own, because economic success as an independent state can be jeopardized by the failure of surrounding states. The new economic interdependency means that failed states even in Asia, Africa, and Latin America, can detrimentally impact economic growth in the United States and other "advanced" industrialized countries.

Since the 1980s the global financial community that has developed a vitally important new feature: an extraordinary high level of interdependency. A major weakness in this new system is the complete lack of global regulation. The only possible mechanism for regulating this new global interdependent system is the International Monetary Fund (IMF), but the IMF has not been given the power and authority needed to regulate. As a consequence, there is not an effective mechanism through which the greed in the market could be transformed from vice to virtue.

The exact way in which greed is managed in the market is absolutely essential to the good workings of the economy. Imagine a continuum with *Completely Free Market* at one extreme and *Complete State Control* at the other extreme (Figure 4.1).

In order for greed to be transformed from vice to virtue, the right balance must be achieved between "free market" and "state control." On the one hand, the market must be free enough to allow for entrepreneurial creativity and innovation, so that change and progress are not stifled. The profit incentive must be large enough (in relation to the characteristics of the psychological citizen) to allow for this. On the other hand, limits must be placed on what people can do in the marketplace, so that the profit motive does not result in greed overwhelming common sense and resulting in the kind of financial meltdown that occurred starting in 2008.

The new interdependencies in the global financial market mean that it is even more difficult in the short term to manage greed and prevent vice. Asia is now also a major driving force—some would say "the engine" (although this will prove to be an exaggeration)—in the global economy. The emergence of Asia as a global power further complicates the task of regulating greed and achieving a constructive balance between free market and intervention. In the competition for economic success, a great deal will depend on how economies meet the challenge of resource limitations. As Roberts has noted,

> *In countries like China and India, lack of energy security is clearly inseparable from the larger economic problems . . . Yet we should not imagine that lack of*

Completely Free Market -------------------------------- Complete State Control

Figure 4.1 The 'free market–state control' continuum

energy security is a problem of the poor alone: even . . . the United States is having serious trouble shifting its energy economy to gas. Worse, these difficulties are spreading rapidly throughout the industrial economies, disrupting energy markets and delaying the emergence of the gas economy that is supposed to serve as a bridge to the energy economy of the future.[33]

CONCLUDING COMMENT

Security capital is an essential part of collective security, for all groups but particularly for nation states. Both "soft" and "hard" forms of security capital are important, but in this discussion I have focused primarily on the enabling conditions, soft security capital, and limited my discussion to the main two types of hard security capital. Of course, hard and soft security capital are interdependent and each would be dysfunctional without the other. For example military security capital would be seriously impaired without adequate strength in collective resilience and leadership fit. But sovereign states are not able to survive and thrive on the basis of soft security capital alone. A state that invests only in soft security capital and neglects hard security capital would soon find that competitors and enemies are crashing through its gates. Consequently, those concerned with strengthening security capital need to attend in a balanced manner to all of the major types of hard and soft security capital.

Part II

The Global Roots of Insecurity

. . . this is a paradigmatic case of cultural evolution in technology out-pacing cultural evolution in the ethics of human relations.

P. R. Ehrlich and A. H. Ehrlich [1]

. . . we have created a global culture of consumption that will come undone, perhaps in a few decades, perhaps a bit later. We are at risk of being engulfed in a flood of barbarism magnified by the ecologists' night-mare of overpopulation, resource scarcity, biotic impoverishment, famine, rampant disease, pollution, and climate change. The only response that does credit to our self-proclaimed status as Homo sapiens is to rechart our course.

D. W. Orr[2]

Now economic liberty is under attack and capitalism, the system which embodies it, is at bay.

Capitalism at Bay[3]

We saw in the introductory chapters that security in the twenty-first century is different from anything experienced by humankind in previous eras, in part because the new insecurity is globalized. The global-ized nature of the emerging insecurity has been underlined by the devastating economic meltdown that swept across the world starting in 2008. The interconnected nature of the global economy meant that what began as a major problem in the United States housing sector, spread to the banking sector of America and then to Europe, Japan, Australia, Canada, and almost all of the rest of the world. The slowdown in eco-nomic activity resulted in lower demand for oil, a sharp drop in oil prices from an all-time high of around $147 a barrel to around $70 a barrel in October 2008, to even dip below $40 in 2009. The result was a steep economic slowdown in oil-producing countries, including Russia and most of the members of the Organization of Oil Exporting Coun-tries (OPEC).

Another important feature of the new global insecurity is that it is multidimensional, meaning that in addition to being based on economic ties, it also involves many other types of ties, including psychological, social, political, and cultural ones (as discussed in Chapter 1). This means that in the twenty-first century, people are as likely to feel that their security is threatened as a result of attacks against a host of "soft" targets, such as their collective identity, social relations, cultural heritage, or sacred values, as much as they are as a result of actual military attacks or economic disasters.

The perceived threats to security have been heightened by a mismatch between the maximum speed of change at the macro level of politics, economics, and technology, and change at the micro level of everyday thought and action.[4] Macro-level change can come about very quickly. A government with new policies can come to power through elections or a bloody revolution and new technologies can transform entire industries (as the computer and the World Wide Web have done in the last few decades). Transformations in technologies and medical sciences, together with economic and organizational efficiencies, have enabled us to increase our own population size and dramatically increase the rate at which we utilize the resources of planet earth. On the other hand, our everyday thinking and behaving have not changed in ways necessary to allow us to conserve and limit our negative environmental impact.

We are depleting the resources of planet earth at a very rapid rate. Many of the resources we are using, such as fossil fuels, are not renewable. A great many of the other resources, such as land and fresh water, are in very limited supply in relation to the ballooning world population, which has already reached around 7 billion. At the same time that severe resource limitations, environmental degradation, and global warming are looming as problems for humankind, the capitalist system that was supposed to save humanity seems to have faltered. The capitalist countries, with the United States as their center, continue to experience cycles of boom and bust. But even if we disregard these cycles, a major shortcoming of the American-style free market system is that it has resulted in increased gulfs between the richest and the poorest. This can become a security threat, not just because the poor might see it as unjust and react violently, but also because the poor might lose motivation to compete and try to move up the social hierarchy. A loss of dynamism and increasing learned helplessness among the poor, rather than the Marxist formula of a "proletariat revolution," poses the greatest long-term threat to free market democracies.

5

Fractured Globalization, Identity, and Insecurity

Nasrudin decided that he could benefit by learning something new.
He went to see a master musician. "How much do you charge to teach lute-playing?"
"Three silver pieces for the first month; and after that, one silver piece a month."
"Excellent!" said Nasrudin. "I shall begin with the second month."

I. Shah[1]

Sufi stories, such as the one above, are intended to teach us to better understand ourselves, often through humor. Mulla Nasrudin,[2] the central character in numerous Sufi tales, wants to skip the first month of lute lessons and jump straight to the second and subsequent months, which involve lower input from him—both in terms of payment to the teacher, and also presumably in terms of his efforts as a beginner. In a sense, this sort of "jump" is just what we would like to do with globalization; we would like to skip the painful first month and get to the easier parts. Unfortunately, the process of globalization has very painful periods, and although how we go through globalization is not predetermined, our present path is taking us directly toward a very bumpy patch of ground.

In *Song of Myself*, the American poet Walt Whitman (1819–1891) wrote, "I launch all men and women with me into the unknown,"[3] and in one important sense the path of globalization is launching all of us into the unknown. The globalization experience is proving to be extremely problematic, particularly for those billions of people who have less power and resources. On the one hand, globalization seems to promise political unity, economic improvement for all, and peaceful relationships. On the other hand, the globalization process has in practice so far been associated with enormous friction between international and regional rivals, the relative impoverishment of billions of people, and wars involving both Western industrial powers and non-Western, economically poor nations. Globalization is taking place, at best, in a fractured manner, with insecurity as one of the main underlying themes.

I have identified seven main characteristics of fractured globalization, reflecting the particular globalization path we are following. The first two characteristics center on the issue of identity, the other five characteristics center on perceptions in relation to globalization changes. Fractured globalization demands the attention of those seriously interested in global and national security.

IDENTITY-BASED CHARACTERISTICS

Identity Threats

"We will not let America shame us. We will not let America change who we are." These words were not spoken in anger, or by an illiterate religious fanatic. Rather, the person speaking was a mild-mannered electrical engineer. True, the context in which these words were spoken was radicalized: I was researching in Tehran in 1980, and the speaker was an Iranian male being interviewed by me outside the walls of the American Embassy at the time of the hostage crisis. Iranian extremists invaded the United States embassy in Tehran, Iran, on November 4, 1979, and held fifty-two American diplomats as hostages for 444 days, finally releasing them on January 20, 1981. But the words of the mild-mannered electrical engineer might have been spoken by tens of millions of other Iranians at the time. Indeed, the sentiment he expressed came to be shared by hundreds of millions of non-Westerners as the pace and scope of globalization increased.

The intense mood of anti-Americanism that has swept around the world in the last few decades (with a temporary halt to this trend in the initial period of the Obama administration) is in part arising because many people outside the United States see globalization as synonymous with Americanization. There is no doubt that the largest single influence particularly on the content of globalization is American culture. For example, through its monopoly of youth cultural products, including popular films, music, clothing, computers, and electronic hardware and software generally, the United States has become the most powerful influence on young people around the world. A second timely example is in the area of higher education. The "American model" of higher education has been adopted widely in non-Western societies, so that universities have generally modeled themselves after the American credit-based, free market, and cafeteria-style higher education system. Even the old university system of Western Europe is changing direction and becoming "Americanized." For example, the elitist higher education system of England, which allowed only a small percentage of 18-year-olds to enter university, has given way to a far more open system with more than 35 percent of 18-year-olds now entering university.

American global influence can be threatening, even for other Western societies. For example, I have often heard European researchers complain bitterly that researchers in the United States pay little attention to research outside their national borders. There is a lot of truth to this; less so in the "hard" sciences such as physics and chemistry, but more so in "soft" sciences, such as psychology and security studies, and the humanities. But the insularity of American researchers becomes more understandable when we consider that in areas such as security studies and psychology research productivity in the United States is amazingly high, and just keeping up with what is published in one part of the United States is a full-time occupation. Of course, American researchers in most research areas would improve the quality of their work if they did open up and took notice more of what is going on in the rest of the world, but the volume of activities inside the United States makes this a difficult task, one that has yet to be achieved. For American researchers, globalization continues to mean the exportation of research knowledge, whereas for most other countries globalization has brought a continual avalanche of imported research knowledge (mostly from the United States).

The impact of globalization was being felt very strongly in Iran in the 1960s and 1970s. The Shah, Mohammad Reza Pahlavi (1919–1980), had lost power in the early 1950s through a democratic-nationalist movement in Iran, but he had been brought back to power in 1953 through a coup famously engineered by the Central Intelligence Agency. Throughout the 1960s and 1970s, the Shah used oil revenues to push through a Westernization program in Iran. Unfortunately, in part because the Shah's system was characterized by corruption and mismanagement from the very top, even the positive aspects of his modernization program failed to gain the support of most Iranian people. For example, the most promising aspects of this program concerned changes in the role of women in society. Specifically, women gained access to the expanded higher education system, and family law was reformed to give women greater rights, particularly in marriage. Family planning programs were implemented to help women plan pregnancy. Despite these changes in favor of women, the despotic, corrupt, and inefficient nature of the Shah's regime meant that millions of women actively supported the revolution that toppled the monarchy and sent the Shah fleeing abroad for the second[4] and last time in his life.

But the Shah's modernization program was opposed not only because his regime was dictatorial, corrupt, and inefficient, but for the deeper reason—particularly among traditionalist and fundamentalist Muslims—of the Shah's perceived frontal assault on the collective identity of Iran as an Islamic nation.

In most non-Western countries, globalization is perceived as a threat to collective identity, to how people perceive themselves as a group and want to be viewed by the rest of the world. Of course globalization is also a threat in Western societies, but in a very different way. In the West, when people talk about the threat of globalization, they usually have in mind job outsourcing, the flood of cheap goods from Asia, and other such trends that seem to threaten jobs and the standard of living of people in the West. Westerners see China specifically, and Asia more broadly, as an economic threat, not a cultural threat; it is Chinese and Asian goods that are flooding Western markets, not Chinese and Asian culture. The situation is very different in most non-Western countries, where they see their cultures and collective identities under assault.

Psychological evidence suggests that human beings have a need to achieve and defend an identity that is both positive and distinct.[5] The experimental evidence for this derives from studies demonstrating that people show bias in favor of their own group and differentiate between their in-group and other out-groups, even when the groups are formed on the basis of trivial criteria (such as the number of dots individuals see on a screen or the flip of a coin), and they do not know the other members of their group or the group to which they do not belong, and they will not receive any of the points they allocate. It seems that even the flimsiest excuse will lead us to show bias in favor of our group; in defending the group identity, we are defending our personal identity.

Well before the advent of modern experimental psychology, a number of writers pointed out that humans can form groups and fight great battles on the most trivial excuses. For example, in Shakespeare's play *Hamlet*, we witness an army on the march to fight a battle in which thousands will probably die, presumably over some great cause (Act IV, scene 4). But when Hamlet asks an army captain why he is marching to war, the captain tells him that it is to fight over ". . . a little patch of ground/That hath no profit in it but the name" (lines 18–19). How can so many men die over a worthless patch of ground? Shakespeare speaks to this question through Hamlet:

> Rightly to be great
> Is not to stir without great argument,
> But greatly to find quarrel in a straw
> When honour's at the stake.[6]

From this viewpoint, being "great" does not mean that one is only moved by great causes; rather, it means being ready to defend one's honor even for the sake of "a straw," something worthless.

The tendency for humans to use even trivial differences as a basis for building up their group identities, and perceiving out-groups as inferior, is satirically highlighted in Jonathan Swift's (1667–1749) *Gulliver's Travels*. On arrival in Lilliput, the land of the little people where he is a giant, the hero Gulliver learns that there are two competing parties, distinguished by the "high and low heels on their shoes."[7] So intense is the conflict between the high and the low heels that they "will neither eat nor drink, nor talk with each other."[8] But there are also conflicts between Lilliput and a rival empire, Blefuscu. A Lilliputian nobleman describes for Gulliver the roots of the bloody war between the empires,

> It began upon the following occasion. It is allowed on all hands, that the primitive way of breaking eggs before we eat them, was upon the larger end: but his present Majesty's grandfather, while he was a boy, going to eat an egg, and breaking it according to the ancient practice, happened to cut one of his fingers. Whereupon the Emperor his father published an edict, commanding all his subjects, upon great penalties, to break the smaller end of their eggs. The people so highly resented this law, that our histories tell us there have been six rebellions raised on that account; wherein one emperor lost his life, and another his crown. . . . It is computed, that eleven thousand persons have, at several times, suffered death, rather than submit to break their eggs at the smaller end . . . Now the Big-Endian exiles have found so much credit in the Emperor of Blefuscu's court, and so much private assistance and encouragement from their party here at home, that a bloody war hath been carried on between the two empires . . . during which time we have lost forty capital ships, and a much greater number of smaller vessels, together with thirty thousand of our best seamen and soldiers; and the damage received by the enemy is reckoned to be somewhat greater than ours.[9]

Thus, we see that the basis on which we often form groups, differentiate between ourselves and others, and even go to bloody wars, can be objectively trivial. Clearly, the psychological need to uphold a positive and distinct identity can lead us to use the flimsiest excuse to violently defend our honor.

Local Identities—Global Economies

> Where, how and when could this young countess, who had had a French *émigrée* for governess, have imbibed from the Russian air she breathed the spirit of that dance? Where had she picked up that manner which the *pas de châle*, one might have supposed, would have effaced long ago? But the spirit and movements were the very ones—inimitable, unteachable,

Russian—which "Uncle" had expected of her . . . Her performance was so perfect, so absolutely perfect, that Anisya Fiodorovna, who had at once handed her the kerchief she needed for the dance, had tears in her eyes, though she laughed as she watched the slender, graceful countess, reared in silks and velvets, in another world than hers, who was yet able to understand all that was in Anisya and in Anisya's father and mother and aunt, and in every Russian man and woman."[10]

In Leo Tolstoy's (1828–1910) monumental novel *War and Peace* (1865–1868), the "little countess" Natasha gets an opportunity to dance in traditional Russian style when she is out in the countryside with a hunting party, and surprises everyone with her ability to connect with the peasant culture surrounding them. Natasha had never been taught to dance in this "Russian" way, but her intimate connection with the land and air of Russia gave her this natural ability.

Our identities are formed first and foremost in relation to the air, land, nature, people, culture, and society we directly experience as we grow up. It is what we go through most intimately and closely, particularly the family[11] and the landscape we grow up in,[12] that influences how we think and act. The experiences we have in the small groups we grow up in, and in connection with the landscape we come to know, result in us having strong associations with the local—both in terms of social life and physical space.

This intimate connection with the local and with small groups contrasts sharply with the push of globalization toward larger and larger units, both in terms of social relationships and physical spaces. Globalization is unidirectional, moving us from smaller to larger, from including only the near to including what is distant, from seeing the world as involving those who are close at hand to seeing the world as including people in faraway lands we might never visit. The "little countess" in *War and Peace* spontaneously danced in a traditional Russian manner, but what would it mean to dance in a traditional human manner? The scale of "the world" and "humanity" seems far too large for individuals to connect to, at least as we are socialized at present.

CHANGING PERCEPTIONS AND GLOBALIZATION

Rising Expectations

His specialty is the ritual called a puja, in which he spreads the munificence of the god Lord Ganesh upon a parade of newly purchased vehicles—cars, trucks, SUVs, motorcycles, and auto rickshaws, along with the occasional bicycle or bullock cart—whose owners wouldn't think of hitting the road without the blessings of a happy, four-armed god with the head of an elephant who brings prosperity and good fortune, particularly to machines and those setting out on something new.[13]

The above description of a slice of social life in India in the early twentieth century reflects the coming together of new and old worlds, of technological innovation meeting traditional values and practices. The new modes of transportation such as SUVs are being used along with more traditional transportation modes such as bullock carts, but not without first getting the blessing of a god through the services of a traditional holy man. There are now hundreds of millions of "new consumers" in India, people who feel they need to have televisions and cars and washing machines and all kinds of modern appliances, and can afford a middle-class consumer lifestyle.

Perhaps the most important and often neglected aspect of globalization is the changes being brought about in the expectations of people in non-Western societies. The tremendous global reach of modern advertising and media has meant that information about new consumer goods and services are reaching the farthest corners of the globe. There really is no escape from messages about consumer products: across distant oceans and lands, mountains and valleys, even in distant skies, the messages of advertisers for consumer goods are getting there. The jet plane flying over a village in the remote regions of rural Africa or Latin America or Asia is advertising to the villagers, telling them of the consumer urban world they could join, tugging at them to abandon their farms and move to the big cities.

Messages about consumer goods often reach the non-Western world in subtle, indirect ways. For example, the most powerful messages about consumer products reach the non-Western world not through direct advertising, but through television programs and Hollywood movies that portray the consumer lifestyle and the products and services involved in this lifestyle. A television program such as *Orange County*, which depicts the life of a group of young people in an affluent California suburb, does an enormous amount to convey messages about the lifestyle young people around the world should aspire to achieve. I am not referring here only to the products that are intentionally inserted into the program and treated as "advertising." When the glamorous boys and girls on the television screen jump into cars and race to the beach, the particular brand of designer clothes they are wearing and the particular type of cars they are driving are less important than their expressed way of thinking and their worldview.

Images of the consumer lifestyle are changing expectations in non-Western societies, and the direction of this change is clear: happiness means consumption; more consumption means greater happiness. This trend is associated with rising expectations, and the homogenization of expectations around the world. Ideas about the "good life" as consumerism have become global well before consumerism itself has become global. This trend likely will lead to particularly detrimental health consequences in societies with larger wealth disparities.

Research on health and relative deprivation suggests that greater wealth disparities in society are associated with poorer health among lower status people.[14] This intriguing research literature suggests that it is not the absolute level of wealth, but the relative level that is crucial. For example, take the case of Ahmed, who earns $1,000 a year. Research findings suggest that Ahmed will enjoy better health and live longer in a society where the richest people earn ten to fifteen times more than him than in a society where the richest group earns a thousand times more than him. One reason for this is that people assess their own situation and worth relative to others, and in contemporary societies such worth is to a large extent assessed using material criteria. A combined consequence of this materialist value system and increasing wealth disparities is that those with least wealth learn to see themselves (consciously or unconsciously) as least valuable and at the bottom of the status hierarchy.

Macro-Micro Change Disparities

During my interviews with people in different parts of the world about their experiences with globalization, a constant theme has been the feeling people have of a sense of being overwhelmed by wave after wave of changes that seem to begin in distant places and are beyond both their personal control and the control of local authorities. Globalization is motored by economic, technological, and political changes at the macro level. Such changes are well beyond the control of individual people and local authorities, and have a very high maximum speed. For example, political power can change hands overnight, through elections or political coups or other means. Similarly, economic policies can change quickly, when governments change or when politicians change their minds. Technological changes can also come about very quickly, and the pace of technological innovation is accelerating. For example, consider the revolutionary changes in electronic communications over the last few decades, including the World Wide Web, e-mail, Facebook, blogs, Twitter, and so on. These rapid macro-level changes are pushing along transformations at the micro level of intrapersonal and interpersonal processes.

This top-down push for change, motored particularly by technological and economic factors but in some cases also by political decisions, is often running into resistance because of the typically slower pace of change at the micro level of human cognitive styles and social relations. For example, consider how economic and political elites are using every means available, including technology, to try to bring about changes in the twenty-seven-member EU, so as to create a sense of "European identity" and loyalty to the EU. But changes in such micro-level processes are proving to be difficult and slow to bring about. The so-called *Eurobarometer* surveys show that a feeling of European identity has been slow to develop, and distrust in the European government system has in some ways increased.

The disparity between macro- and micro-level changes is less for young people and less for the most technologically and educationally advanced countries. For most older people living in (particularly the rural parts of) low-income societies in Africa and Asia, it has proved impossible to adapt to twenty-first century technological and economic changes.

Global Radical Networks

The increased interconnectedness of the world has brought new opportunities for global wrongdoings of all kinds—the international trafficking of human sex slaves, drug trafficking, weapons sales, pirating, religious and political fanatical networks of various types, economic terrorists, and religious terrorists. Globalization has expanded the market for all of these "activists." For example, globalization has been associated with human sex trafficking, surely the worst kind of slavery. Probably between one and two million children and women are forced into the sex industry each year. The research on sex trafficking clearly shows it to be another destructive aspect of the global economy.[15]

The increased interconnectedness of the world has been exploited by criminals with destructive intent. Of course there have always existed individuals with the potential to become destructive criminals, but their power was limited when they were isolated. At most, they could carry out assassinations, or publish their ideologies to influence others. In some cases they attracted enough local followers to try to launch a broader collective movement, but before the twentieth century they had to rely on primitive and expensive communications and transportation systems. They were typically unable to go beyond setting up local networks.

Globalization and advances in electronic communications and transportation has enabled crackpots and destructive extremists of all kinds to contact one another and try to cooperate. A dangerous fanatic who previously would have remained an "isolated problem" can now

contact, exchange information with, and gain support from other similarly minded fanatics and participate in coordinated operations with
them. Also, conspiracy theories of all kinds can now spread far more
easily, including the belief that the moon landings never happened, that
President Obama's birth certificate is fake, and that the 9/11 attacks
were planned by the government, "The emergence of the Internet as a
communications medium . . . makes it possible for once-scattered
believers to find one another."[16] An impact of such conspiracy theories,
which continue to be available widely on the Internet, is greater distrust of
governments.

Virtual Collective Movements

*Individually accessible, ordinary networked communications such as per-
sonal computers, DVDs, videotapes, and cell phones are . . . affecting the
shape and outcome of domestic and international conflict . . . From the
global spread of Islamist-inspired terrorist attacks, to the rapid evolution
of insurgent tactics in Iraq, to the riots in France, and well beyond, the
global, non-territorial nature of the information age is having a transfor-
mative effect on the broad evolution of conflict . . .*

Audrey Cronin[17]

Global electronic communications systems have enabled people to participate in new types of collective movements, such as *eswarm*. These
new collective movements are less dependent on traditional leadership
and can evolve "from the bottom up," for example, the massive demonstrations that took place in major cities of the United States against the
proposed immigration bill in 2007.

Virtual collective movements bypass the traditional state boundaries
and in important ways are "territorial-less." The global nature of contemporary communications has been used effectively by international
corporations to launch their products in a synchronized manner around
the world. For example, books in the *Harry Potter* series and films in the
Pirates of the Caribbean series have been launched simultaneously in over
a hundred countries, reaching enormous international populations. But
the same communications methods have also been used by radical
groups intent on disrupting security and changing the world order. Cell
phones and e-mail have boosted sales of consumer goods, as well as
radical ideologies espousing an end to American capitalism.

Widening Wealth Gap

Another tension concerns the widening gap between the richest and the
poorest groups in the era of fractured globalization: while almost three

billion people live on less than $2 a day, an average billionaire could hire two million of these poor workers.[18] Thus, in some respects we have not progressed beyond the era of the Pharos, when a few individuals could harness the labor of millions (the issue of the new global economy and security is discussed in greater depth in Chapter 6).

Of course there have always been enormous gaps between the richest and the poorest groups in society, between the kings and aristocrats and the ordinary working people in pre-modern Europe for example. But globalization has not only continued the unequal relationships between the richest and the poorest, but also through the global media and communications networks presented poor people with clear images of the life lived by the rich. Moreover, the ideology of meritocracy has been propagated, so that the illusion is created that the progress made by individuals in the status hierarchy is a result of their own effort and talent. The "American Dream" is being advertised as the global dream, and poor people are being educated to see their poverty as an outcome of their own behavior.

CONCLUDING COMMENT

> *That's the feeling inside each Emirati. When we felt we had it all, we also felt like we will lose it all.*
> Political science professor at United Arab Emirates University[19]

> *Emirates have fretted for years over the loss of their culture, as social norms became more a product of the newcomers than of nationals. Now, some are pinning their desires for a national salvation on the global economic downturn, which they hope will reduce the numbers of foreigners pouring into their country and give them a chance to reassert their customs and way of life.*
> M. Slackman[20]

Globalization is being driven by economic and technological forces, against which even the most powerful single states have very little power to resist. The largest countries are better able to absorb the shock waves of globalization, and they feel less threatened by globalization relative to small states: the United States exports particularly cultural products and know-how, while China exports mainly manufacturing goods. However, even the United States and China feel threatened by their dependence on globalization trends and their inability to defend their societies from the impact of global economic cycles. Small states often feel overwhelmed by globalization forces, with the onslaught of people, products, services, and cultural phenomena generally that pours over their borders. The only opportunity some states have to regroup and attempt to defend their collective identities is when the volume of people and things coming over their borders declines because of a global recession, as in the case of the Unites Arab Emirates (above). But even the largest states are not completely immune from the shock waves created by fractured globalization, as is clear from the American experience with 9/11.

6

Resource Crunch: The "Race to the Bottom" Global Economy

What are the factors that threaten security? One way to categorize answers to this question is to group theories on the basis of assumptions about human behavior. A first set of theories argues that security is threatened by characteristics internal to human beings, such as our irrational aggressive tendencies,[1] or our predisposition to want to pass on our genes and fight against those who carry competing genes,[2] or certain inbuilt cognitive mechanisms that cause us to differentiate between groups and discriminate against outgroups.[3] This group of researchers sees internal psychological factors, including feelings of deprivation and injustice,[4] as being the primary driving force behind conflict and threats to security more broadly. A second group of scholars focus on the role of material conditions, and environmental resources in particular. They argue that in one way or another material conditions shape psychological experiences, for example, whether a person feels deprived or not can be influenced by the actual material conditions, and competition for and access to resources. In this chapter, my focus is on this second perspective, dealing with material conditions external to the person.

I first examine the view that competition for material resources fuels conflict and threatens security. I find that this view has a lot of merit. Second, I argue that globalization is leading to two changes that further fuel competition for resources: (1) globalization has resulted in greater interconnectedness and more extreme cycles of economic boom-and-bust, a cycle that will continue over a "transitionary" period as we move toward the fruition of globalization, and (2) environmental deprivation and global warming, together with a ballooning global population, are resulting in greater scarcity in resources. Thus, more people are chasing fewer resources, with the result that there is greater pressure to beat the competition and gain access to depleting resources.

MATERIAL RESOURCES AND SECURITY

In this section I review three sets of arguments. First, the argument that competition for material resources inevitably results in security threats in the form of intergroup conflicts, at least during a period of transition, as globalization "matures." Second, I discuss the position of theorists who argue that we are inevitably moving toward an end to group-based inequalities (e.g., Karl Marx, 1818–1883), and opposing theories who argue that group-based inequalities will continue (e.g., Vilfredo Pareto, 1884–1923). Third, I explore theories that focus on ideologies that stabilize society, despite even enormous group-based inequalities.

Competition for Material Resources Causes Conflict

Threats to security arise when people compete for limited material resources, such as non-renewable natural resources, and often get into violent conflicts: this is the simple message of one set of theories, sometimes referred to as *realistic* or *materialist* conflict theories.[5] For example, why are there continued security threats in the Middle East? The answer from the realist camp is that the fight is particularly over resources such as land and water, and this is intensified by a rapidly increasing population, with high birth rates among Arabs being balanced by the importation of additional people (through immigration) on the Jewish side. Put simply, more and more people are fighting over a finite amount of resources. Not surprisingly, from this perspective, at the center of the "security problem" are the issues of settlements and territory generally, as well as water supplies (in areas such as the Golan Heights). More broadly, there are wars in the Middle East because there is oil in the region, a resource all the world wants.

The view that security threats arise out of competition for material resources is backed by impressive practical examples, such as the Middle East situation, and also empirical research evidence. For example, in his classic field studies with boys at a summer camp, Muzafer Sherif (1906–1988) conducted an elegant study with four main stages.[6] In stage one, eleven- to twelve-year-old White Protestant middle-class boys arrived at the summer camp and got to know one another. During stage two, the boys were placed into two groups, making sure that best friends were separated and placed into different groups. During stage three, the two groups of boys competed against one another for prizes, in tug-of-war and other games. Very quickly, the attitudes of the group members became biased against the outgroup and in favor of the ingroup. Group members came to dislike the outgroup, calling them names, raiding their camps, and generally being hostile toward them. Group members showed strong support for aggressive leadership.

Having brought the two groups into conflict, where each group saw the other as a threat, Sherif once more created harmony between the groups through *superordinate goals*, these being goals that each group desires to achieve, but is not able to do so without the cooperation of the other group (discussed in Chapter 4). For example, a truck bringing food into the camp "broke down" (through Sherif's intervention) and the members of both groups had to cooperate in order to bring the food into the camp. From the "realistic conflict" point of view, the situation had changed from one in which the groups were competing for material resources, to one in which they were cooperating to obtain material resources. This change resulted in the expected change in intergroup relations: the members of the two groups developed positive attitudes toward one another and had friendly relations.

The realist view clearly leads to the prediction that as the population of the world increases, there will be increased security threats because more people will be competing for certain essential resources that are finite and non-renewable.[7] For example, in the Indian sub-continent, where the population has reached around two billion people, the rapidly increasing population has been coupled with increased use of groundwater in irrigation, so that an expert report states: "In many of the most pump-intensive areas of India and Pakistan, water tables are falling at rates of 2–3 meters per year . . . It is no exaggeration to say that the food security of India, Pakistan, China, and many other countries in 2025 will largely depend on how they manage the groundwater problem."[8]

Even within the United States there are already severe water shortages in a number of states where populations continue to rapidly expand, including California and Florida, and there is intense competition between states for access to fresh water in some parts of the country.[9] Competition for fresh water and other natural resources is also increasing at the international level.[10] Perhaps the most intense competition, at least in the short term, is for fossil fuels, with oil as the most important example. From the realistic conflict perspective, the main reason why there is such intense competition between world powers in the Near and Middle East region is because of the large oil reserves there.[11]

The Fate of Group-Based Inequalities

In many utopias described by "progressive" authors, group-based inequalities are either diminished or they have disappeared. There is a general tendency for "progressive" political thinkers to strive to move society toward smaller group-based inequalities. However, another group of thinkers, who tend to see themselves as "realists," argue that group-based inequalities are natural, inevitable, and always with us. In an important sense, these two groups see different sources to security threats, the first group seeing security threatened when there are larger gaps between the resources available to different groups, the second group seeing security threatened when attempts are made to end (what they see to be natural and beneficial) group-based differences in resource availability.

Among the idealists who argued that there would be an inevitable end to group-based inequalities, the most influential is no doubt Karl Marx. Marx was not the first to describe imaginary societies where private property did not exist, and all land was communally owned. Sir Thomas More (1478–1535) has described such a society in his novel *Utopia*, published in 1516.[12] However, Marx not only described a version of utopia, he presented an elaborate model, claimed to be "scientific," according to which there is an inevitable historical march toward this utopia.[13] The continued influence of the Marxist utopia is international and considerable, so we must pay it attention.

Marx saw human societies starting with little or no group-based inequalities in material resources, moving to extreme group-based inequalities, and then eventually evolving to end group-based inequalities. Group-based inequalities in access to resources did not exist when humans lived in simple hunting and gathering groups that accumulated no surpluses in resources. As humans developed farming, raised domesticated animals, and lived in larger and larger settlements, they produced greater surpluses that served as a means by which some groups accumulated more material resources than others. The concentration of more and more wealth in the hands of an elite group culminated in capitalism, where a small number of major capitalists "own" the labor of the vast majority of people. According to Marx, the security of society in capitalism means protection of property first and foremost, because the major capitalists control the government apparatus (including the various military, police, and secret services) and use it to protect their own interests. But this class-based societal structure will come to an end, according to Marx, when the lower classes revolt, establish a dictatorship that serves their own interests, and the dictatorship of the proletariat gradually socializes people to work for the benefit of all society and not just themselves personally. In other words, people learn to be happy without group-based inequalities. Security is achieved, because everyone owns everything, the interests of everyone are equal and the same, which means there is nothing to fight over.

The Marxist utopia has inspired numerous revolutions, been used as an excuse for even more dictatorships, and given rise to countless disappointments. In practice, it has so far not been possible to organize a large industrialized society in such a way so that group-based inequalities are negligible. Right-wing theorists argue this is because it is against human nature to end group-based inequalities in material resources, because by doing so we take away the motivation for individuals to work hard and get ahead. If there is not a rich group that poor people can strive to work hard and join, why should anyone work hard?

The view that group-based inequalities are universal and apparently natural is endorsed by both classic theories, such as elite theory,[14] and modern theories, such as social dominance theory.[15] These are similar, in that they regard the source of inequalities as inherent to individuals. There is something about our psychological makeup, such as the tendency for the talented elite to want to monopolize resources (elite theory) or the tendency for individuals in varying degrees to endorse group-based inequalities (social dominance theory), that inevitably results in social stratification. According to Pareto, attempts to prevent this tendency will cause the talented elite to create security threats, by agitating for change and eventually mobilizing the non-elite to overturn the political order.

How Do Group-Based Inequalities Continue?

Given that, despite all efforts to create the Marxist utopia of a classless society and other similar utopias, group-based inequalities continue to exist. How do they survive? How is it that people who have relatively little resources put up with poverty? How is it that minorities who are discriminated against put up with their situation? Why does Jack, who works fifty hours every week and earns a poor wage as a chauffeur, put up with his life conditions when the boss he drives around does little work but enjoys an income of millions of dollars? The question of how security and stability is maintained despite huge group based inequalities has been answered in a variety of ways by competing theorists.

One set of explanations can be summed up in this way: the people are fooled into believing that even huge inequalities are fair by some kind of ideology that they buy into. In classic Marxist terms, the people suffer *false consciousness*; they fail to recognize their own class membership and the fact that the interests of their class are different from and conflict with the interests of other social classes. In the language of *System Justification Theory*,[16] a modern American theory influenced by

Marx, people put up with injustices because they learn to think through a belief system that justifies the existing social and political system. Religion often plays a central role in this system justification, and for this reason Marx saw religion as the opium of the people, lulling them into acceptance of life conditions "as is" (for further discussion on the role of religion in security, see Chapter 7 in this book).

But another group of theorists provide a very different view: in capitalist societies people put up with even huge inequalities because they come to believe that they, or at least their children, could climb to the top, or at least higher than they presently are in the status hierarchy. Thus, it is because society is seen as open and "anyone can make it if they have the talent and motivation" that people do not threaten security. The American Dream story, with Barak Obama being a recent example in this story, is part of this explanation.

Why is the American Dream so powerful? Why is it that people from all over the world embrace this story, even before they arrive in America? One answer, from the right wing, is that the American Dream fits well with human nature: people are motivated to work hard when they directly and individually benefit from their own endeavors. Penniless immigrants will work hard as long as by doing so they can individually climb up the social system; this is "natural" self-interest, which will benefit all society because individual effort will lead to wealth for all. This is the "greed is good" philosophy. I collaborated to conduct experiments in which we placed participants in "low status groups" and gave them unfair treatment, but found that they preferred to try to move up to the "high status group" individually rather than take collective action to change the system.[17] As long as they had the option to try to make it on their own, participants preferred the individualistic route.

Is the preference for individual mobility inbuilt and part of human nature? Left-wing critics would contend not. They view this individualistic tendency as part of modern capitalist culture, and a means by which capitalism survives. The more capitalistic a society, the more individualism has to be "taught" to people to ensure social stability. For this reason, the United States is shown by cross-national studies to be the most individualistic major society in the world.

A second point made by left-wing critics is that the American Dream is just that, a dream. In reality, social mobility is not significantly higher in the United States than it is in class-based England or the rest of Europe.[18] Critics point out that it is the "mirage of mobility" that dupes working class Americans to buy into the American system, even though this system gives many people an unfair deal: no health care and no social safety net when they lose their jobs or fall ill.

INSECURITY AND ECONOMIC DEPRIVATION

For many people in the world, particularly middle-income and lower-income people, economic security is a daily challenge. Will I have a job tomorrow? Will I have enough to eat? Will I be able to afford adequate shelter for myself and my family? Will I be able to pay medical bills when my children fall ill? Will I be able to pay for school for my children? How will I be able to live when I am too old to work? What will happen to me in my old age? Doubts and questions concerning economic security continually plague working people in their daily lives, far more immediately and urgently than military security and other factors identified as important by realists.

Of course, lower-income workers can be influenced to be concerned with military security, and to both fear external enemies and be ready to defend the nation against them. Recruits to the military tend to be from the lower rather than higher-income groups, and the old communist slogan that "a bayonet is a weapon with a worker at each end" has some truth to it. In times of war and national crisis, lower-income nationalists are particularly fervent and ready to lay down their lives for national interests. But this does not negate the idea that lower-income groups are on a daily basis concerned with, and give priority to, economic security.

Economic insecurity has particularly increased among the poorest people in the poorest countries in the world. The economic decline of the early twenty-first century started in the richest countries, but has also impacted the poorest: "A financial crisis that began in New York and London and spread to manufacturing in rich, then industrializing countries, has now hit the "bottom billion": the poorest people in sixty-odd countries who have seen only halting gains from globalization, but will feel its reverse, perhaps precipitously."[19]

A "race to the bottom" is taking place among the very poorest people in the world, those who have not succeeded to become part of the global consumer revolution. About 50 percent of people in the world still live on less than $2 a day; the poorest 20 percent do not even have $2 a day and can barely find enough food to stay alive. The availability of this very poor labor resource and the expansion of international transportation and communication have resulted in a twenty-first century slave trade, involving the sale of millions of (typically very young) people for exploitation (as discussed in Chapter 5).

Improvements in technologies and other factors are enabling massive increases in the production of wealth around the world, but this wealth is increasingly being monopolized by a small elite. Some of the new computer-based multi-billion dollar corporations require only a few hundred employees to fully function (as opposed to the several hundred thousand employees hired by traditional companies with similar-sized capital assets). The wealth concentration associated with the new technologies is accentuating the difference between the richest and the poorest groups in many parts of the world. This trend is as true in the United States as it is in China. At the same time, the wealth difference between the poorest 20 percent of the world's population and the richest 20 percent is also increasing. This rift is coming about during a time of rising expectations among the poor around the world, as they become more influenced by global consumer advertising.

The Rise of "Nonstandard Work"

The real change today is the greater job insecurity experienced by unionized blue-collar and white-collar middle managers, and the greater frequency with which these privileged segments of the labor force experience the features of the nonstandard work arrangements (low wages, lack of benefits, part-time employment, agency and contract labor).

Dorothy Cobble[20]

The working conditions and standard of living of middle- and lower-class working people improved tremendously over the course of the nineteenth and twentieth centuries, in large part because the norm became standard work involving steadily increasing wages, health benefits, pensions, and insurance, full-time employment, and long-term job guarantees. The rising power of labor unions and professional associations assured that the rights and interests of employees would receive strong support. After all, labor unions and professional associations could afford to pay lawyers and contribute to the political campaigns of the major parties, and so their voices would be heard.

In the United States after the Second World War, the earnings of employees went up in lockstep with increases in productivity year after year. As technological and work organization innovations were introduced and production per person-hour went up, so did employee income and benefits. But this trend changed in the 1970s, and after that employee income fell behind. The difference between the very top money earners and the rest of society dramatically increased, so that those in charge came to earn tens, hundreds, and thousands of times more than the vast majority of the employees. Even when business executives made poor management decisions that resulted in huge losses, and even bankruptcies, for their companies, the tendency has been for them to still receive multi-million dollar bonuses—and for mid-level and lower-level employees to experience pay freezes and pay cuts.

In addition to decoupling middle-class and working-class income from productivity and increasing differences between income levels across social classes, there emerged a new trend of increasing nonstandard work, meaning jobs that are not full-time, lack benefits (health, insurance, pensions, and so on), and have no future guarantees.[21] Gradually, the standard full-time, guaranteed job with benefits, that people had come to see as the "norm" is becoming more and more difficult to land; this is "nice work if you can get it"[22] but getting it is not easy for the young people entering the labor market in the twenty-first century.

The growth of nonstandard work is associated with a loss of power for the employees. About one in three working Americans now has a nonstandard job, and women and minorities are over-represented in this group. Nonstandard work has tended to grow particularly in employment sectors where there are no strong labor unions or professional associations. This is even the case for the most highly educated work groups. For example, in American colleges and universities over half of all courses are now taught by adjunct professors. These are typically people with doctoral degrees, many years of post-doctoral experience, but with no job security, no benefits, and no guaranteed future employment. Adjunct professors are hired to teach on a semester-by-semester basis, for low pay.

The "Super Fast" Economy and Insecurity

"Trillions of dollars have vanished" roared the newspaper headline, announcing yet again to the depressed public that the world has plunged into an economic abyss in 2009. Another newspaper headline roared "No bottom in sight to market decline."

> "What I want to know is, why don't they arrest the thieves who stole the money?"
>
> I had been staring vacantly at the headlines, and it took me a moment to realize that the question was addressed to me.
>
> ". . . the money?" I asked.
>
> "Yes, the trillions of dollars . . . they should arrest the thieves who stole it," repeated the speaker, a charming, colorfully dressed lady who looked to be in her seventies or even eighties. "How difficult can it be? It can't be easy for the thieves to hide all that money!"
>
> "Oh, but nobody has stolen the money . . .."
>
> "No?"
>
> "No, the money has just vanished because people lost confidence."

"Lost confidence?"

"Yes, they don't feel secure."

"What a silly idea. That doesn't sound right to me."

The charming lady walked away shaking her head, no doubt unhappy to have sought reassurance from a man who imagines that trillions of dollars can just disappear because people "felt insecure."

****

It felt like there was no ground beneath your feet.[23]

Swiss bank representative on the "financial meltdown" of 2008

The global financial crisis starting in 2008 brought to the forefront a new feature of twenty-first century insecurity: Not just the total interdependence of economies around the world, but the furious speed with which economic problems in one part of the world can create tidal waves and even tsunamis in other parts of the world. The so-called "subprime" mortgage debacle had created problems in the United States economy, and by the first half of September 2008 stock markets around the world had become stagnant. When Lehman Brothers, headquartered in New York, filed for bankruptcy protection on September 15, it speeded up a global rush by investors to seek safer havens for their capital. Very quickly, the stocks of major international companies such as Goldman Sachs and Morgan Stanley plunged and stock markets around the world almost instantly lost trillions of dollars. Even in Russia, a relatively "closed" economy, the stock market had to be closed down temporarily several times in late September 2008, because there seemed no end to the steep decline in stock values on the Moscow stock exchange. Central banks all around the world, including in Washington, DC; London; Hong Kong; Tokyo; and New Delhi, had to pump billions of dollars into the market to try to prevent a complete standstill to economic activity. In just three days, central governments had to bail out five major European banks. A $700 billion "rescue package" was approved by the United States federal government on October 3. As an editorial headline in *The Economist* put it, this had quickly become a "World on the Edge."[24]

Globalization has dramatically increased the pace of change. Almost everyone, including the financial experts, was caught out by the speed and scope of the financial crisis starting in 2008, and certainly the most serious since the Great Depression. Within a matter of weeks, even countries that seemed to have strong economies and were supposed to be immune, suddenly found themselves ensnared by the reach of these super-fast globalization trends. For example, in mid-October 2008,

Poland had seemed a safe haven from the economic storm, but only a week later the storm hit Poland, so it was reported from Warsaw on October 27 that, "Poles were jolted last week by the sudden discovery that they were not immune to the financial crisis contagion rippling across the globe. The plunging stock market here and the drastic weakening of the Polish currency proved, as in so many corners of the fast-growing developing world, how wrong they were."[25]

Of course there had been declines in world economic activity in previous eras, the most notable example being the Great Depression of the 1930s, preceded by an economic slowdown in the late 1920s and by the New York stock market crash of 1929. But the financial "meltdown" of 2008 revealed a new vulnerability in both national economies and the global economy. Vast improvements in communications and transportation systems, as well as the internationalization of trade and business, have created a far higher level of interdependency and rapid change among national economies. Of course, there are still high trade barriers that act like walls around national boundaries, including through government subsidies that lower the price of local products and inhibit free trade. But international corporations with affiliates in many different countries and economic regions can work around most trade barriers. Also, there has been an expansion of free-trade zones, such as the EU and the North American Free Trade Agreement (NAFTA). All these changes have not only strengthened economic interdependence, but also vastly *increased the speed* with which economic changes in major countries have an impact on the global economy.

CONCLUDING COMMENT

> *We're suffering from the paradox of thrift: saving is a virtue, but when everyone tries to sharply increase saving at the same time, the effect is a depressed economy. We're suffering from the paradox of deleveraging: reducing debt and cleaning up balance sheets is good, but when everyone tries to sell off assets and pay down debt at the same time, the result is a financial crisis.*
>
> *And soon we may be facing the paradox of wages: workers at any one company can help save their jobs by accepting lower wages, but when employers across the economy cut wages at the same time, the result is higher unemployment.*
>
> Paul Krugman[26]

Rapid globalization is throwing up different paradoxes fast and furiously. Perhaps the greatest unsolved paradox of all involves the environment: as national economies around the world grow, people enjoy a higher standard of living and populations increase. But as greater numbers of human beings consume more and more, environmental quality declines and our future security on planet earth is threatened.

Scientific evidence suggests that environmental degradation as a result of human activities is increasing and even accelerating. The collapsing environment is forcing increasing numbers of people to change their lifestyle, from where they live to how they earn their daily bread. Some lifestyle changes are proving to be extremely painful (e.g., fishing and herding communities who have to abandon fishing and herding because of depleted sea and land resources). As groups adjust and search to find new resources and vacant spaces, they clash with competing groups and experience greater insecurity.

Religious Insecurity

A profound puzzle confronts students of religion and society. On the one hand, theories of modernization and secularization predict that religion would lose relevance in the modern world, with science replacing religion as a basis for belief and action in everyday private and public life.[1] Developments in some parts of the world, particularly Western Europe, provide some support for this view, as religiosity and church attendance declines.[2] For example, in England and Canada, two countries where I have lived for extended periods, I witnessed a number of old houses of worship in London and Montreal being transformed to residential apartments, because local residents had simply stopped attending church services. On the other hand, religion seems to have gained considerable strength in many other parts of the world, as reflected by the rise of various types of fundamentalist religious movements, including Islamic fundamentalism in both Muslim (e.g., Iran) and non-Muslim (e.g., France) countries, Hindu fundamentalism in the Indian sub-continent, as well as the surprising surge of Protestant evangelicalism in Africa and Latin America, and Christian fundamentalism in the United States.[3] In the words of one prominent researcher, the world continues to be as "furiously religious as it ever was, and in some places more so."[4]

How do we explain this paradox? On the one hand, we have passed the 150th anniversary of Charles Darwin's revolutionary work *On the Origin of Species* (first published 1859) and science is supposed to have now replaced outmoded religion, but on the other hand there is a surge in religious movements in many parts of the world. It is equally puzzling that although religions are associated with peace, charity, and love toward others in the world, the rise of religious movements has been associated with increased intergroup conflict and even terrorism.[5] Whereas major religions encourage the faithful to love and care for others, empirical evidence shows that religiosity is associated with prejudice and closed-mindedness.[6] Religious people, for example, tend to be prejudiced against less religious individuals.[7]

The new "religious pluralism"[8] is associated with individuals having a greater choice of religious offerings, as religious communities compete in the marketplace and try to attract more followers. An idealistic view of religious pluralism might begin by viewing globalization as creating one enormous, open, religious marketplace. Just as free trade and the taking down of trade barriers would allow goods and services to compete openly in the global market, religious communities would find themselves competing openly with one another to gain followers (consumers). In such a free-trade global environment, religious communities that could best meet the needs of consumers would thrive and would gain many new converts, but religious communities that could not adequately meet the needs of consumers would lose followers. By gaining and losing followers, religious communities would gain and lose resources more broadly, including houses of worship, schools, universities, publishing houses, media outlets (such as television and radio stations), and other such assets. The outcome would be beneficial for consumers, because the religious communities that best met market demands would thrive, and other religious communities would lose market share. However, the "new religious pluralism" is associated with intolerance, closed rather than open societies, and increased prejudice against other religions.[9]

Perhaps most puzzling with respect to the main theme of this book is that religion is associated with greater security and stability, both at personal and societal levels. People who express greater religious faith have been found to also express greater life satisfaction and happiness,[10] as well as better health—so much so, that there are now structured "religious and spiritual therapies" regularly used alongside traditional medical therapies.[11] This has been facilitated through the transfer of religious and spiritual therapeutic procedures by non-Western immigrants moving to Western societies.[12] Religion comforts people and gives them a firm basis for belief and hope. This "uplifting" role of religion, and its relationship with psychology, has resulted in an upsurge of interest in religion on the part of research psychologists.[13]

At the societal level, religious organizations provide both physical and spiritual comfort to the disadvantaged, and help to make people more content and society more stable. Religion can serve as a mechanism for helping people feel satisfied with what they have, with social and political arrangements as they exist. For thousands of years, political rulers have known that their hand is considerably strengthened when they also enjoy the support of religious authorities. Rulers such as Henry VIII (1491–1547) of England streamlined this process by making themselves the head of both state and church, using the interdependent influence of both to secure their power.

However, religion is also associated with insecurity and instability. Indeed, in the recent decades the most powerful global images associated with religion concern insecurity rather than security, instability rather than stability, extremism rather than moderation. These images range from the 9/11 terrorist attacks and numerous other religiously inspired terrorist attacks in London, Madrid, Mumbai, and other internationally important centers, to Christian fanatics harassing and murdering pro-abortion medical doctors in the United States, to violent Jewish settlers fighting with Israeli security forces in defense of their illegal settlements, to Hindu and Muslim fanatics burning mosques and temples and killing one another in India, to Islamic fundamentalists taking over the anti-Shah revolution and grabbing power in Iran. In so many different domains, religious fanatics have justified violent attacks against others in the name of God.

How do we explain these seemingly contradictory trends? How is it that religion seems to be associated with both security and insecurity, stability and instability, open societies and authoritarian systems, love toward others and prejudice against them? To arrive at solutions, I return to the main thesis of this book: globalization is resulting in greater interdependencies, super-rapid and interconnected changes, and sudden intergroup contact, which in the immediate future results in increased threats to security. I begin by interpreting religion as a collectively shared belief system, moved forward and propagated across societies and across time through dynamic "sacred carriers." Of course, religion is continually changing, as are human constructions of the divine.[14] Despite the continual changes, the resiliency of religion continues as a core set of practices and beliefs in human societies.

EXPLAINING THE RESILIENCE OF RELIGION

> . . . the unique features of religion as a system of meaning may underlie its resiliency in the face of increasing modernization and globalization . . . religion will likely continue to exert profound effects during the new millennium.
>
> Silberman[15]

Human beings are motivated to make their lives meaningful, and construct and ascribe meaning to themselves, their actions, and their surroundings in all situations. The most pervasive strategy people use to make their lives meaningful is through the construction of narratives: we are natural storytellers, about ourselves and others, and the world we live in. For example, consider what takes place when we meet with family and friends: we catch up by telling stories about what has happened to us since our last meetings. The stories we tell could be about how a local politician was caught red-handed telling lies about the town budget, how I left a package in a taxi on my way home, but to my surprise the package was returned to me by the taxi driver the next morning, how a mutual friend has moved back to our neighborhood from California, and the like. Numerous authors have explored the types and structures of the narratives we create,[16] and although there are differences of opinion on some issues (such as the main types of narratives), there is general agreement that all stories are sequential, they have plots, and they involve problems and resolutions. Stories also reflect and carry forward moral values.

The motivation to ascribe meaning is particularly strong when we are confronted with phenomena that are unknown or beyond direct experience, such as life after death or how the world began. In this foundational sense, science and religion have the same origin, as my colleague Jack Haught has pointed out, ". . . science and religion . . . share a common origin in the remote and mysterious fountainhead of a simple human desire to know. Both science and religion ultimately flow out of the same 'radical' eros for truth that lies at the heart of our existence."[17]

Both science and religion involve, at the highest level of abstraction, the construction of stories that help us make sense of the world. Of course, the data for stories used in science and religion are very different (at least in the twenty-first century), but both rely on story construction. For example, consider how both scientific and religious texts present stories about the mysteries of space and time. In his discussion of *Nothing*,[18] the physicist Frank Close argues that in some ways similar processes are involved in the emergence of "nothingness" and the emergence of consciousness, starting with the Big Bang some 14 billion year ago. Of course, major religions tell the story differently, with God rather than the Big Bang as the starting point.

Scientific story telling has come to influence everyday storytelling, particularly among people who have been through modern educational institutions. For example, health education classes are now mandatory in the modern education system of many societies, and in these classes young people learn the scientific story of how babies are made. But in some traditional cultures, the story of how babies are made is told in a very different way. For example, the traditional Tiwi of northern Australia told the story of human conception in a way very different from modern Western "health classes,"

Anthropologists have long been aware that the Australian aborigines generally . . . ignored the role of the male in human conception and firmly believed that a woman becomes pregnant because a spirit has entered into her body. The Tiwi were no exception, but went a step further . . . in dealing with the dangerous situation created by the unpredictability of the spirits. Because any female was liable to be impregnated by a spirit at any time, the sensible step was to insist that every female have a husband *all the time* so that if she did become pregnant, the child would always have a father.[19]

Among the Dobu islanders of the Western Pacific, the belief is that the male has a role in human conception, but that "Semen is . . . voided coco-nut milk which has passed through the body of the male, and is ejected at the point of orgasm. This voided coco-nut milk semen is believed to fertilize the woman, causing the blood within her, which when unfertilized comes away in monthly menstrual flow, to coagulate and form the foetus. A man drinking coco-nut milk to make himself potent is liable to have obscene jests made at the expense of his action."[20]

The Tiwi of northern Australia, the Dobu islanders of the Western Pacific, and other traditional groups with distinct cultures have numerous beliefs about the beginning of life, death, the after-life, and so on, that are very different from Western beliefs. But they convey these beliefs in a way that is familiar to people in modern societies: they narrate stories. As in other societies with strong oral traditions, the young in Tiwi and Dobu societies are instructed through stories told to them from the first years of their lives. Religious and scientific stories both play a role in the socialization of children in modern societies.

Although science and religion both tell stories, the criteria we use to evaluate scientific and religious stories are now very different. Scientific stories are evaluated according to criteria that include reliability, validity, and falsifiability. But these criteria are not applied by the faithful to religious stories, because the only real need is faith. A religious story can contradict basic rules of rationality, yet still be believed by the faithful. For example, the social anthropologist Napoleon Chagnon points out that, "Most creation stories begin with two individuals who people the earth with humans . . ."[21] According to the Christian Bible, "Eve was created from a portion of Adam's body, his rib, and therefore, they somewhat incestuously go about creating the rest of us."[22] A compelling story moves us, the way a piece of art moves us,[23] irrespective of its status on the criterion of rationality. For example, the story of Adam and Eve continues to be told and re-told in modern "scientific" societies. Part of the power of this story is that it is compelling for children. For example, this is how the story is told in a typical collection of stories for children entitled *Stories from the Bible*,

The first people God made were a man called Adam and a woman called Eve. This story is about what happened to them. God made Adam from the dust of the earth. He breathed life into Adam, so that Adam became the first person on earth . . . God . . . decided to make a woman, to be Adam's wife. First He put Adam into a deep sleep, and he took one of Adam's ribs and made Eve from it, so that in an odd way they were one person.[24]

As Chagnon points out (above), the apparent contradictions in stories such as Adam and Eve do not prevent them from having a powerful impact on an audience of believers. Of course, religious stories are not unique in being compelling despite their contradictions. Fairy stories also have longevity and are typically riddled with features that are in some ways contradictory. The brothers Jacob Grimm (1785–1863) and Wilhelm Grimm (1786–1859) did pioneering work collecting and publishing fairy tales,[25] including some that have now become Walt Disney classics: *Cinderella, Sleeping Beauty*, and *Snow White*. Films based on these stories have been watched countless times by generations of children around the world.

Positioning and Storytelling

I have described human beings as being motivated to construct meaning, to make our lives "meaningful." Our most effective strategy for ascribing meaning is through storytelling, an activity common to all cultures. Storytelling is a human universal with a central role in all our lives, helping us to understand both our inner experiences and the outer world. Cultures are carried forward by stories that reflect both the shared and the unique features of each culture. Certain stories are collectively shared within each culture, collaboratively upheld, and passed on from generation to generation. Stories incorporate and pass on the beliefs of each culture, such as the above-discussed examples of the Tiwi belief that women become pregnant when spirits enter their bodies and the Dobu belief that semen is voided coco-nut milk.

The young in all groups are socialized through stories that entail the values and beliefs of their particular cultures. For thousands of years, religious stories have served this important purpose. Fairy tales have also served the purpose of passing on cultural values from generation to generation. A useful way to understand all these stories is through positioning theory,[26] which uses the metaphor of a triangle, consisting of (1) storylines, (2) positions, and (3) acts. The positioning triangle serves as a framework for defining the meaning of events. The question "what happened?" is answered by storylines. For example, an argument between a woman and a man during an emergency could be described as the end of an affair, or actually the start of a new "when opposites attract" romance. "Positions" specify the range of acceptable actions a character may perform. For example, the man involved in the argument might be described as having a duty to help the woman in a time of crisis. "Acts" refer to the speech acts that a narrator performs in telling a story. For example, "She really should have appreciated a lot earlier how much he sacrificed for her" performs the act of criticizing.

Religious stories serve a particularly powerful role in positioning individuals regarding their rights and duties, vis-à-vis other people as well as God. Rights and duties are reflected directly in the Ten Commandments and similar edicts found in all the major religions, as well as indirectly in stories of the Bible, the Koran, the Torah, and other holy books. According to *natural law theory*, rights, duties, and the law generally originate from a divine, natural source. Human beings have a duty to discover law and abide by it. In contrast, the *positive law* tradition argues that rights, duties, and laws in general are human constructions. We evolved to have a sense of fairness and to use certain rights and duties to regulate our behaviors and social relations, and the roots of our "justice behavior" can be found in lower animals and "wild justice"[27] (this topic is discussed in greater depth in Chapter 9).

SACRED CARRIERS AND IDENTITY

So far I have argued that religion can be interpreted as a means by which we ascribe meaning to our inner experiences, outer worlds, and life generally, and that stories are important ways in which religions are moved forward, passed on, and expanded across generations. An essential part of religions are the rights and duties that position people in relation to one another and in relation to God. But in order to more fully explain the power and central role of religion in human security, we need to explore two other issues: first, the role of religion in human identity; and second, the role of sacred carriers in passing on and propagating religions.

Religion and Identity

Religious meaning systems define the contours of the broadest possible range of relationships—to self; to others near and distant, friendly and unfriendly; to the non-human world; to the universe; and to God, or that which one considers ultimately real and true. No other repositories of cultural meaning have historically offered so much in response to the human need to develop a secure identity. Consequently, religion often is at the core of individual and group identity.

Jeffrey Seul[28]

There are two aspects of the role of religion in individual and group identity that I particularly highlight. The first is the role of religion in helping individuals to achieve a positive and distinct identity, postulated by social identity theory to be essential universal human needs. The second is the role of religion as an "anchor," a source of stability in times of instability and change. This second role has become more important as globalization has progressed with increasing speed.

Religion and the Positioning of Identity as Positive and Distinct

Religion serves to categorize the world into "us" and "them," those of "our faith" and "others." Again and again, religions remind in-group members that they are different from those who belong to other faiths, or to no faith at all. This serves to position the in-group as distinct and to highlight avowed intergroup differences. Thus, the followers of Christianity, Islam, Judaism, and so on, learn to see differences between themselves and others. These differences are often more symbolic than real, but they nevertheless influence behavior in important ways. As globalization creates real similarities between groups, the need for distinct identities leads to the manufacturing of symbolic differences. This process is visible in both religious and secular domains,

> The members of different groups, who actually live lives that are very similar to one another, are now constructing intergroup differences, rediscovering or manufacturing "traditions," and adopting cultural carriers that symbolize their "differences" . . . Examples of this include the numerous African cultural practices and products, such as those associated with the annual Kwanzaa celebrations held December 26 through January 1, which continue to be rediscovered and adopted as carriers by African Americans.[29]

Research suggests that the exaggeration of symbolic and real differences between groups, and the minimization of differences within groups, generally takes places as a result of social categorization,[30] but religion pushes these tendencies to extremes. Consequently, for example, Christians tend to see the differences between themselves and Jews and Muslims as greater than they really are, and to see the differences within the Christian community as smaller than they really are. Such differentiations are often reinforced by religious rules limiting or forbidding intergroup contact. For example, out-group practices, such as eating habits, are often depicted as "unclean" and "unGodly" by the in-group faithful.

But religions also position the in-group more positively in a variety of ways compared to out-groups (people belonging to other faiths). This ranges from seeing the in-group as "chosen by God" (versus the out-group "condemned by God") and "destined to enter heaven" (versus the out-groups "condemned to hell"), to more subtle positioning of the in-group as superior and duty-bound to "save" the "poor unbelievers." For example, from the fifteenth century and throughout the era of Western colonization of Africa and Asia, missionaries were often the vanguard of Western incursions into "new, undiscovered" territories. It was the task of the missionaries to convert "savage" local peoples to Christianity, and to teach them to wear "decent" (Western) clothes and adopt Western lifestyles. Following the conversion of locals to Christianity, Western companies could import Western textiles and other products in "exchange for" the raw materials (e.g., rubber, oil, timber) they exported from the Asian and African regions they had colonized. Thus, religious "trade" preceded economic trade, and this was justified according to the belief that Christianity was a superior religion that would "save the natives."

The belief that "our religion is correct and the followers of all other religions are misguided" is not unique to Christians. Fundamentalists of all religions, including Islam and Judaism, all strongly believe in the superiority of their own faith and are prejudiced against out-group members. The belief in in-group superiority sometimes leads to discrimination and violent attacks against those categorized as out-group members, irrespective of how those people actually categorize themselves. For example, as I revise this chapter, in Iran there continue to be violent attacks by fundamentalist supporters of Mahmoud Ahmadinejad against unarmed people protesting the fraudulent elections of June 12, 2009. The peaceful protesters have been labeled by Mr. Ahmadinejad and his followers as "terrorists" and "un-Islamic," working for "the enemy," and consequently legitimate targets of death squads and gang rapes. The clear evidence of atrocities taking place in the name of religion in Iran, electronically flashed around the world, has provided another sickening reminder to the world of how religion can be used to mobilize a group to commit atrocities against those categorized as "ungodly."

Religion as a Source of Stability

In addition to serving to support a distinct and positive identity for the faithful, religion also acts as an important source of stability at both the individual and societal levels. Threats to security arise in many different ways, but one thing they have in common is change—change that is associated with uncertainty, risk, and the unknown. Of course, the greatest example of this is change from life to death, and the uncertainty of what comes with death. Religions offer the ultimate inoculation against anxiety arising out of our knowledge that we will one day die. The major religions promise us that death is not an end, only a beginning, and that in the next world we (the faithful) will live on in eternal bliss.

But other kinds of changes are also posing threats. For example, globalization and revolutions in communications, electronics, among other domains, are bringing about increasingly rapid changes, re-shaping the contexts in which we work and live. Associated with these globalization changes are enormous movements of people, both across and within national borders. In most cases, these movements are brought about by economic shifts, violent conflicts, environmental disasters, and other events completely out of the control of individuals. In this context, individuals can feel overwhelmed, anxious, and helpless. Faith in religion can serve to create calm and help individuals better cope with external changes. Not surprisingly, particularly since the 1990s, there have been more formal attempts to incorporate spirituality in psychological therapy,[31] particularly for minority groups, such as African Americans,[32] who are experiencing the greatest pressure as a result of rapid globalization changes and economic shifts.

Religion is also a strong source of societal stability. A conservative interpretation of religious scripture leads to endorsement of the power hierarchy as "natural" and "God given," something that should not be altered by "human hands." For thousands of years, hereditary monarchs ruled in various countries under the justification provided by "the divine right of kinds," a justification that is still used in some countries under different guises. For example, in a number of Islamic societies (such as Iran and Saudi Arabia), the leadership uses religious justification for the continuation of corrupt political systems based on extreme economic inequality. The poor are promised their rewards "in the next world," while the rulers and their families siphon off the wealth of the nation. In the United States, religion is used by varieties of fundamentalists and television evangelists to amass fortunes and garner support for policies that perpetuate group-based inequalities.

Sacred Carriers

Carriers play a crucial role in enabling the continuation and diffusion of cultures, by serving as vehicles for passing on the essential features of cultures across generations over time and across groups in different geographical locations.[33] Carriers often come in the form of symbolic objects, such as a national flag. For example, the United States national flag, "Old Glory," is "just a piece of cloth," but it has become a piece of cloth that some people are willing to die and kill for. The symbolic importance of the American national flag is well understood by those who wish to attack the United States, when they publically burn and trample on the "Stars and Stripes."

Some carriers take on sacred meaning and come to represent values that reflect beliefs in divinity, God, creation, and religion more broadly. An example of such a sacred carrier is the Christian cross, which is displayed in countless ways, on buildings, clothing, furniture, and so on. A sacred carrier that has more recently taken on significant value in the Western context is the Islamic veil worn by some Muslim women, sometimes by choice. The Islamic veil is "just a piece of cloth," but it is a piece of cloth that some people are willing to die and to kill for.

Unfortunately (for women in particular), the Islamic veil has come to represent the values of traditional Islam. In both a symbolic and practical sense, the veil is now taken to be "the line in the sand." Muslim fundamentalists and traditionalists have taken a stand on one side of this line and are determined not to allow Western values and lifestyles to cross over. On the other hand, those who want to reform Islam and to transform Islamic communities to become more secular have attempted to liberate women from the veil as part of a larger program intended to arrive at more egalitarian gender relations in Islamic communities. Both sides view the veil as representing essential values, which they seek to uphold or to oppose.

Through globalization, sacred values that might have remained limited in their influence at the local level have in some cases become globally important. The Islamic veil is an example of this trend. The large-scale migration of Muslims to live in non-Islamic societies, as in the case of about 20 million Muslims in the EU, has meant that the role of the Islamic veil as a sacred carrier is now influential in London, Paris, and Munich, as well as Istanbul, Tehran, and Karachi.

Because the veil has become a sacred carrier, in some parts of the world violence is being used against women to enforce the wearing of the veil. Instead of allowing women to freely choose to wear or not to wear the veil when they reach adulthood, in some non-Western countries and in some families within Western countries, women are forced to wear the veil from childhood. This is part of the broader campaign of terror against Muslim women in the name of religion.

SUDDEN CONTACT, THREATENED IDENTITIES, AND RELIGION

Globalization has brought about increased movements of people and ideas, including religious ideas, around the world. What is new is the speed and extent of these movements. This has resulted in greater religious pluralism, and increased rivalries between religions, especially in regions experiencing particularly rapid changes, such as between Protestants and Catholics in Latin America.[34]

Most importantly, globalization has brought about sudden contact (as discussed in Chapter 5) between people of different faiths, and between people who are secular and those who are more traditional or fundamentalist adherents to faith. This is the situation in Western Europe, where approximately 20 million Muslim immigrants and refugees now live. The arrival of millions of South Asians in the United Kingdom, North Africans in France, Turks in Germany, and the members of numerous other Muslim societies in other EU countries has created anxiety and a sense of insecurity among many locals. This is in part because of the background of the Muslims arriving in Europe. According to the *distance traveled hypothesis*, "the greater the distance that immigrants have to travel to reach the adopted country, the more material and intellectual resources they need."[35] Muslims coming from the Near and Middle East, North Africa, and South Asia have less distance to travel, and need less resources, to reach Europe than to reach North America. Consequently, Muslims arriving in Europe are generally less well equipped to integrate into mainstream European society, compared to Muslims arriving in the United States. American Muslims are in general better educated, better equipped (both materially and educationally), and better integrated than European Muslims (there are a few exceptions, such as Somali Muslims in the United States).

On the other hand, the avalanche of Western cultural products pouring into Muslim societies is resulting in threatened collective identities particularly among traditional and fundamentalist Muslims who fear their own demise and possible extinction. This fear of extinction (discussed in greater depth in Chapter 8) has resulted in a mobilization of religious traditionalists and fundamentalists, intent on defending themselves against what they perceive to be direct enemy attacks. In this way, religious people who are outside the mainstream Western Christian tradition have come to feel threatened, and have adopted a variety of tactics, including collective violence and terrorism, to try to defend themselves and their faith.

But it is not only Muslim traditionalists and fundamentalists who feel threatened by the accelerating march of globalization. In many respects globalization is also threatening Christian traditionalists and fundamentalists, by spreading Western secular culture and varieties of *laissez-fair* moral relativism. The increasing mobilization of women and gays, and their greater influence in public discourse around the world, has also angered many traditional and fundamentalist Christians.

CONCLUDING COMMENT

Religion has historically served to make people (at least those who believe) feel more satisfied with their lot in this world, because of the rewards they expect to receive in the next world. Religion has also helped rulers to legitimize group-based inequalities, corruption, and injustices. However, on occasions religion has also served to mobilize people against injustices, so that sometimes religion has become associated with insecurity and instability rather than security and stability. Thus, although the general historical trend of religion supporting unjust systems in many parts of the world is clear, there are also exceptions where religion has in some instances served the cause of justice rather than injustice.

Globalization has resulted in dangerous and growing feelings of insecurity among religious traditionalists and fundamentalists. This is in part because accelerating cultural changes and economic shifts around the world have created greater feelings of psychological anxiety and helplessness, and religion has been made readily available to help people—particularly because the elite have made it readily available as an instrument of their continued rule. It is no accident that religious resurgence has accompanied accelerating globalization: religion is serving to relieve anxieties and lower depression as people go through the traumas associated with rapid and unpredictable globalization changes. Nowhere is this truer than in the Near and Middle East, where religion continues to be used to try to cloak corrupt and violent dictatorships, such as in Iran, Saudi Arabia, Egypt, and so on. The forces of globalization, from electronic communications systems to interconnected economies, are pushing these societies over the cliff, but so far nobody can see how far these societies have to be pushed to reach their end.

8

Terrorism and Torture: Reactions to Collective Insecurity

Torture is terrorism carried out by the state. This interpretation is generally overlooked because the two activities are typically carried out by different agents: torture is most often carried out by the state,[1] whereas what is popularly referred to as terrorism, as in "suicide terrorism" for example, is most often carried out by non-state actors against the state.[2] However, both torture and terrorism are tactics used in power struggles between competing groups, and they pose common challenges for those concerned to minimize risks associated with global insecurity.[3] It is a grave mistake to try to understand these tactics through reliance exclusively or mainly on rational, materialist models, because such models only provide surface meanings of torture and terrorism. The deeper motives behind torture and terrorism can only be fathomed out through an *irrationalist* perspective: terrorism and torture are both irrational reactions to deeply felt insecurity on the part of typically non-governmental (in the case of terrorism) and governmental (in the case of torture) groups.

According to the rationalist-materialist view, human beings are self-centered and motivated to achieve maximum satisfaction through the accumulation of resources. Human beings are assumed to enter into rational calculations of the most efficient means to achieve this goal, implying that they are aware of what they are doing and why, and will adopt the least costly and most profitable paths to achieve particular goals. Thus, for example, torture is assumed to be used when it is the most efficient and cost-effective way of gathering information, and terrorism is assumed to be used when it is the most efficient and cost-effective way to fight an enemy force. According to this rationalist-materialist perspective, "what you see is what you get," and the transparent or "surface" reasons for torture and terrorism are the correct ones. For example, when government authorities announce that they have been forced to adopt "enhanced interrogation techniques" (government-speak for torture), because they had to extract life-saving information from a captured terrorist, this surface explanation is correct according to the rationalist-materialist argument.

An alternative irrationalist perspective assumes that human beings are often not aware of the real motives behind their actions and thoughts: they often do not know what they are doing and why. This is often overlooked because they are so good at rationalizing their own actions. For example, one country invades another country and justifies the war as a means of spreading peace and democracy. Even though the war results in the displacement of millions of people and the death and injury of millions more, the war is rationalized as having saved lives. The irrationalist perspective dismisses such rationalizations. Similarly, the irrationalist perspective dismisses surface rationalizations for torture and terrorism, claiming that there are deeper motives behind such actions—beyond information gathering in the case of torture, for example, and beyond freedom fighter in the case of terrorism.

The Surface Meanings

What are the motives behind torture and terrorism? Let us begin by setting out in greater detail the answers provided by models that are rational and materialist. Arguments in defense of torture best reveal the rational and materialist understanding of why torture takes place. At the heart of these arguments is the assumption that the real motivation for torture is information gathering. This information is needed, it is assumed, to improve decision making, strengthen defenses, and become better equipped to compete against enemies. The logic is as follows: in carrying out their duties to protect citizens, government authorities gather information about potential and actual threats to the security of society. The authorities use information to prevent harm coming to citizens and the state. However, in certain situations the authorities are aware of an imminent danger, without having enough information to thwart the danger. They become aware that the only way to get this information is to force a captured member of the enemy to reveal what he or she knows.

Central to this story line is the so-called "ticking-bomb" scenario, involving terrorists.[4] Consider the following situation:

> *Two known terrorists are captured in the capital city. After cross-examination, the younger, less-experienced man reveals that the two of them are part of a*

terrorist cell and have over the last three months assembled a large bomb. The older man, the leader of the terrorist cell, has strategically placed the bomb in a crowded location in the city. The bomb is programmed to detonate in the next twenty-four hours, and only the man who placed it knows its exact location. The authorities use "soft" tactics to cross-examine the terrorist leader for an hour, but he refuses to tell them the location of the "ticking bomb." The authorities are faced with the dilemma of either resorting to torture to try to get the terrorist leader to reveal the location of the bomb, or risk hundreds of innocent people being killed when the bomb explodes.

This type of "ticking bomb" scenario is routinely invoked by those who defend the use of torture. Irrespective of whether the argument is that torture should be used only in extraordinary circumstances and should require special legal permits,[5] or whether torture is depicted as just another tactic to be routinely used in the "war on terror,"[6] the underlying assumption is that torture is carried out to gather information that is vital to the national interest. An enormous effort was made by the George W. Bush administration to convince Americans of the necessity of torture as a weapon in the "war on terror," without actually using the word *torture*.[7]

After the story of Abu Ghraib prison broke in 2004, and photographs of some of what had taken place inside the prison were flashed electronically around the world, the media in Europe (including even the right-wing newspapers) described the events using the word *torture*. Indeed, throughout the world most people turned against the U.S.-led invasion of Iraq in part because of what they interpreted to be torture of Iraqi prisoners by American guards. Only in the United States has the mainstream press continued to avoid using that word, and instead used government-endorsed terms such as "enhanced interrogation techniques." Of course, in this and some other cases[8] the American press continues to fail in its duty to serve as an independent guardian of truth and justice.

Although limpid in its criticisms of American government foreign policy, the American press has at least come to question the validity of the rationalist-materialist view of torture, which argues that torture is necessary because it is needed for information gathering. Importantly, the implication is that when information can be gathered through other means, or when there is not an urgent need for additional information, then torture would not be carried out. After all, why would authorities expend energy torturing people if there was no tangible benefit, something substantive to make the expenditure of resources worthwhile?

This question is particularly relevant at the dawn of the twenty-first century, when the only superpower in the world, the United States, at least for a while adopted a policy of using torture. Techniques such as "water boarding," that were clearly identified by United States authorities as torture during earlier wars (for example, during the Vietnam war, in the case of water-boarding) were used by American forces with the approval of government authorities at the highest levels in the immediate post 9/11 era.[9] Of course, the United States followed the path taken by previous empires, and is experiencing contradictions that in some ways were faced by empires as far back as Achaemenian Persia who also used torture for "rational" reasons.[10]

Terrorism has also been justified as "rational," by a variety of groups who have used some common rationalizations. From the terrorists' point of view, the reasons for adopting terrorism as a tactic include:[11]

- The high value of the goal, which is so great that any and every means is justified. Just as supporters of torture argue that "the ends justify the means,"[12] supporters of terrorism argue that their "holy" goal justifies the means available to them (i.e., terrorism).
- Terrorism is the only weapon available to the "righteous" in their fight against the evil enemy.
- Acts of terror deal a blow against the enemy and inspire the ingroup (whether it be a national group, a religious group, a language group, an ethnic group, an ideological group such as "radical greens," or some other collective) to rise up and revolt against the enemy.
- The individual terrorist is making the ultimate personal sacrifice for the sake of the "great collective goal." The motivation for terrorism is not personal ends, but collective ends.
- The target of terrorist attacks is selected because of its "evil nature," and to support good in the world.

The most well-known example of terrorism as a tactic is the suicide terrorist, and this endorses the idea that the decision to carry out terrorism is made by a lone individual, making decisions independently and rationally. However, as I point out later in this chapter, the processes that lead to terrorism are collective first and foremost, and the rationalization of terrorism is supported by collective constructions.

From the terrorists' point of view, then, there are a number of seemingly rational reasons for adopting terrorism as a tactic—just as rational reasons have been put forward for why torture is necessary. But I want to offer an alternative irrationalist view of both terrorism and torture. I argue that when we pull back the curtain and look behind the cover stories, there are deeper, irrational reasons for why torture and terror-ism take place.

AN IRRATIONALIST VIEW OF TORTURE

All the interrogators and torturers call themselves doctors, or sometimes engineers. They, too, are professional technicians . . . The next day I am given my first dose of torture . . . I am given seventy-five blows on the soles of my feet with a plaited wire whip; one of my fingers is broken; I am threatened with the rape of my wife and daughter; then a pistol is held to my head at the temple by another torturer, Dr. Azumi, and, in fact, I hear it fire. I faint.

Description by the scholar Reza Baraheni of his experiences as a political prisoner in Iran.[13]

The rational account of torture contends that torture is necessary to gather vitally important information needed to protect the national interest and to save innocent lives. We saw that the "ticking bomb" scenario is often invoked as a justification for torture. The "ticking bomb" will go off, unless the captured terrorist can be forced to tell the authorities of its location. The authorities try to persuade the captured terrorist using "soft" techniques, but he will not talk and they sense that time is running out. The lives of innocent people are at stake. The only possible solution is to torture the terrorist so that he will divulge the location.

An important feature of the rational-materialist approach is the pro-fessionalization of the act of torture. This is achieved in part to create a distance between the "professional" and the "client." Consider, for example, how through training in medical teaching hospitals a profes-sional distance is created between the medical doctor and the patient. There is a tendency for medical students to personalize the experiences of patients, and even to imagine that they are suffering from the ill-nesses they are studying. However, as medical students take on the pro-fessional role of 'medical doctor,' they learn to keep a distance between themselves and their patients and their illnesses. The end result is that they become professionals who can be friendly with their clients with-out becoming friends.

It is vitally important that the medical student learns to keep a distance between herself or himself and the patient. In the first few years, a lot of medical students personalize everything, they even imagine they have the illnesses they are studying. But by the time they have become specialists, they learn to keep a distance between themselves and the patients and their illnesses. They learn to be friendly without being friends with the patient. That distance is essential if they are going to succeed in the medical profession.

The professionalization of torture by the state also means that the torturer maintains a gap with the "client" (torture victim). Often, this is done by the torturers adopting titles (as described by Baraheni, above), such as "doctor" or "investigator," or even "engineer" and "researcher," and insisting that the "clients" refer to them using these "formal titles." Another strategy, commonly used in the United States after the 2003 invasion of Iraq, has been the adoption of technical language, such as "enhanced interrogation techniques" or "aggressive interrogation procedures," which are intended to create the illusion of "science" being the basis of such "expert techniques" or "specialized procedures." These legitimization efforts have been aided by the participation of some professionals, including members of the American Psychological Association, in acts of torture.[14] The general thrust of this strategy has been to give the illusion that "harsh persuasive methods" or "enhanced interrogation techniques," and the like, are (1) not torture (even though procedures typically used, such as water-boarding, clearly meet international and also traditional U.S. standards for torture) and (2) are implemented by specialized experts, who should be left alone to do their jobs, which are too complicated for the general public to understand.

In short, information is needed from the terrorist, and the "experts" should be left alone to deal with the task of gathering the information. But there are a number of major flaws in this argument. An important implication of the "ticking bomb" argument is that torture is only carried out for the purposes of information gathering, and torture tactics are directed at making the prisoner talk. However, various different bodies of evidence contradict this view. Below are some of the deeper reasons for torture.

Displacement of Aggression

What have been the experiences of the American public and the American government since the terrorist attacks of 9/11? Among the complex array of experiences, one of the most prominent themes is undoubtedly the experience of deep frustration—frustration at failing to capture Osama bin Laden; frustration because of having to borrow trillions of dollars to spend on fighting what seems like an endless war (*The Forever War*,[15] as one author describes it) in Iraq, Afghanistan, Pakistan, and other distant countries; frustration out of having to waste so much time in airport security lines, and so on. The entire "war on terror" has been a hugely frustrating experience for the American public and government, made worse by the economic downturn that accelerated in 2008.

Freud wrote with penetrating insight about the role of frustration in group and intergroup dynamics.[16] All human relationships, Freud argues, involve both positive and negative sentiments. Even within a group where members express love for one another, such as in a family or a nation, there are also negative sentiments. A vitally important role of the group leader is to help channel negative sentiments onto outside targets, and not allow negative sentiments to find targets inside the group. Thus, for example, when a group experiences frustrations, the group leader can channel negative feelings onto a target outside the group. Typically, these external targets are marked by being dissimilar to the ingroup; for example, in terms of ethnic or religious membership.

The first group of experimental researchers who systematically explored the consequences of frustration assumed that there is a direct causal link between frustration and aggression.[17] For example, the individual who feels frustrated because he is mistreated by his boss at work, or the group members who feel frustrated because of a sharp decline in economic conditions, are going to behave aggressively, probably against a weak target who is unable to hit back. Subsequent research has shown that although frustration can lead to aggression, this is only one of a number of possible outcomes.[18] For example, it is possible that frustration becomes channeled into creative activities.

Although frustration does not necessarily result in aggression, a succession of frustrating experiences makes it more likely that a cascade effect leads to displacement of aggression. This is a possible explanation of, first, support for torture among over half of the American population (according to Pew Research Polls) and, second, the endorsement of torture by the highest level government officials, at least during the period of the George W. Bush administration. From an irrationalist perspective, the argument is that the "war on terror" has been a highly frustrating experience for the American public and government, and as a result there has been a greater tendency to endorse torture against suspected terrorists. Of course, this displacement of aggression has not been consciously decided, and is not openly admitted.

Retributive Justice: The Revenge Motive

In my own case (and I would consider it typical of the general attitude of an officer at the time) torture was regarded as a means to an end. The objective was to obtain a confession from the detainee, purely and simply. The authorities constantly enjoined on us the need to obtain confessions in order to save the lives of military personnel who might be in danger of attack by revolutionary groups . . . However, subsequently the idea began to lose its force and changed into the application of torture for its own sake, as part of a routine, and also as an act of vengeance against the detainee.

Statement to Amnesty International, by an Officer in the
Uruguayan Army who carried out acts of torture.[19]

My argument on this point is that torture is also motivated by an urge to avenge, to harm a perceived wrongdoer in return for alleged misdeeds. Captured terrorists are viewed as responsible for harming the United States in various ways, for killing and injuring American citizens and damaging American economic interests. Empirical research evidence suggests that such wrongdoers become the targets of retributive justice and the urge to get revenge, an urge that has little to do with prevention and reform of captured wrongdoers.[20] Just as there is some support for the death penalty as a way for revenging wrongdoings ("an eye for an eye"), there is also some support for waging war in the Middle East as a way of avenging things perceived to have been done against the United States.[21]

What about the argument that torture is really carried out to get information? Experimental research suggests that the actual possibility of obtaining information is not the key factor influencing how likely it is that torture will be used against a detainee. For example, in a study carried out with American participants, a vignette was presented about an individual captured by Coalition forces in Afghanistan.[22] The participants were told that there was a 0 percent, 5 percent, 60 percent, or 95 percent chance that the captured individual had information that could prevent further terrorist attacks. The results suggest that it was the desire to punish the detainee, rather than the efficacy of punishment for getting information, that guided how participants assessed and reacted to the situation.

The bottom line is that when people are in a position to punish others, they are guided by how much they believe the target deserves to be punished. The main motivation for punishment is getting even, rather than getting information.[23]

Just World Motive

Why do surveys show that over a half of the American population support harsh interrogation techniques, otherwise known as torture? Why is it that (according to experimental evidence) people are motivated to get revenge against wrongdoers? An underlying explanation is provided by "just-world theory," which proposes that people have a need to see the world as just.[24] The main reason for the justice motive is self-protection: if I believe that bad things happen to bad people for a just reason, then (1) I am safe (because I am a good person), and (2) there is no need for me to intervene.

The justice motive can help to explain a number of otherwise puzzling trends since the 2003 U.S.-led invasion of Iraq, and the post 2008 build-up of U.S.-led military activity in Afghanistan and Pakistan. First, there was a general apathy of the American public toward the plight of Iraqi, Afghani, and Pakistani civilians. The invasion of Iraq has had devastating consequences: probably around 500,000 Iraqi deaths, many more seriously injured, and millions of refugees. In addition, it is a great tragedy that Iraqi women have experienced a long leap backward, particularly in Basra and other parts of the south where a regressive interpretation of Islamic law has been implemented through the authorities *put into place by the U.S.-led intervention*. It is ironic that American women, who have fought so hard for gender equality at home, have stood aside and watched as women in southern Iraq have become far less free since the U.S.-led invasion of Iraq. The implementation of stricter interpretations of Islamic law in southern Iraq has put Iraqi women back a century, and yet "liberated" American women have not raised their voices to object. Second, the American population has continued to remain largely apathetic toward the issue of torture, despite knowing about U.S. government supported torture programs through the Abu Ghraib and other scandals.

In addition to revenge, an important factor explaining these reactions is the justice motive: the need to see the world as just, and believe that people get what they deserve. If detainees are tortured, then they must have done something wrong; and as for the hundreds of thousands of Iraqis who have been killed, and millions of others displaced and seriously injured, it must be because they deserved it, too!

Shame and Humiliation

Then a woman in civilian clothes entered the room and [the male interrogator said], "Well, we'll leave you with her, maybe this will change your mind." I kept my head down, I did not know what was going on, I was trying not to talk to her, but she started to undress. And while she was talking to me in English, this lasted for a long time. I was still looking down, I was not looking at her, I did not know if she was completely naked or still in her underwear. But she started to touch me and then after a while, after about an hour, a guard came in and said, "Okay, it's not working, that's enough." And I could hear the laughter of the people who were watching this from behind the mirror . . . this was just a very humiliating experience.

> A male prisoner at Guantánamo Bay, Cuba, describing
> his treatment, after he repeatedly denied being a
> member of Al Qaida.[25]

In May 2009, President Obama announced that additional photographs showing the torture of detainees from Iraq and other Muslim nations by American troops would not be released, because such images might inflame anti-American sentiments and put the lives of American troops in greater danger. Some news about the additional torture photographs did leak out, revealing the typical patterns of Muslim prisoners being abused: rape, sexual assaults of various grotesque kinds, and the abuse of detainee bodies in many ways. Again and again, torturers in different countries and different situations sexually assault detainees. Photographs from Abu Ghraib prison show naked, blindfolded Iraqi detainees heaped on top of one another, forced into humiliating positions and sexual relations. Why is this? Is this really about obtaining information needed to prevent the next terrorist attack?

Obviously the "ticking bomb" scenario is completely inadequate for explaining sexual assaults against detainees. The deeper motive for such sexual assaults is to humiliate detainees, to make them feel ashamed (of course, we cannot rule out the motive of gaining sadistic pleasure on the part of torturers). To achieve this goal, torturers try to find culturally appropriate methods. For example, U.S. torturers "working on" male Muslim detainees came to the conclusion that sexual attacks by American females would be particularly effective, and so they experimented with this tactic (for example, as reported by the male prisoner held at Guantánamo Bay, Cuba, above). The shame and humiliation that torturers attempt to instill is intended to be painful, but it is also intended to hammer home the point that the detainees have no control at all, not even over their own bodies.

Instilling Collective Helplessness

Torture has been interpreted at the individual level, and this is a profound mistake. The ultimate goal of torture by the state (or representatives of the state) is not just to use shame, humiliation, and fear to instill a sense of helplessness in the individual being tortured, but in an entire population. The primary target of torture is not the individual, but society as a whole.

This is why the state on the one hand is (supposedly) reluctant to reveal the details of torture programs, and officially insists that there are no such programs, but unofficially leaks information about torture programs and refuses to shut down the apparatus of torture. The message being sent by the state is: look at these photographs of raped, mutilated bodies! If you step out of line, the same thing will happen to you. If you turn against us, you too will disappear, you too will end up in a black hole, and you could be there for the rest of your life, with no possibility of release and no possibility of a day in court. This same message is sent out by societies that in other ways are very different, such as Iran, Russia, and the United States.

The ultimate goal of torture is to bring about a feeling of helplessness in a society. In this sense, the torture carried out by the government in Iran in the name of Islam is no different from the torture carried out by the U.S. military in Iraq in the name of democracy and freedom, or by Russia in Chechnia in the name of "the people." Similarly, the information leaked about torture in all three cases is intended to serve the same purpose, that of instilling fear and a sense of helplessness in a population. Obviously the senior officials in the George W. Bush administration who "unofficially" directed lower officials to use torture in Iraq and the senior officials in the Iranian and Russian governments who enable torture against political prisoners in Iran and in Chechnia are not interested in individual detainees. Their deeper goal is collective: to control the Iraqi, Iranian, and Chechnian populations, and to achieve control over these populations.

The target of torture is not only, or even mainly, the detainees being tortured. Rather, the target of torture is the much larger population outside prison, a population that might be intimidated by the threat of torture. The photographs and rumors about torture are not spread to scare those already inside prisons, those inside prisons already know about torture first-hand, but the much larger population still outside prisons. The inmates of Abu Ghraib did not need photographs to tell them about torture, they experienced torture every day; the photographs and stories about torture distributed in Iraqi society were for the control of that society.

Influencing In-group Supporters and Opponents

In addition to targeting out-group members, torture is intended to influence two groups of in-group members. A first group are extremists, who might be hard core supporters of the government, and who want to "see something done" against the enemy. Particularly when the enemy is elusive or too large to take on, a government may find it difficult to satisfy extremist supporters who demand action. This is often the case when a government is fighting against underground organizations that it labels "terrorist" but is not able to find and destroy (as is the case for the U.S. government in Iraq, Afghanistan, and Pakistan, and the Russian government in Chechnia). Torture becomes a tactic that a government can use to show it is taking action against the enemy, and such illegal action is generally supported by authoritarians who believe that the terrorists being tortured "get what they deserve."

The psychological research on authoritarians and other extremists who support a policy of torture against the enemy has focused on right-wing authoritarians.[26] This is understandable in a Western democratic context, where the threat to liberty has arisen for the most part from right-wing extremists, particularly in the face of external threats, such as communism in the 1950s and the Islamic extremism since the late 1990s. The rise of right-wing authoritarianism in the United States and Europe has been palpable particularly since the late 1990s. However, it is an enormous mistake to assume that there is no threat from left-wing authoritarians. Closed societies ruled by left-wing dictators (e.g., Joseph Stalin) are no better than closed societies ruled by right-wing authoritarians (e.g., Adolf Hitler).

A second group of people that torture is intended to influence is members of the opposition, not so much organized political parties who are active as part of mainstream politics, but more fringe opposition groups, isolated activists, and rebels. The threat of phone tapping, surveillance, and possible torture serves to dampen political activity at least among some political groups outside the mainstream. This in part explains the weak opposition in the United States to the clamping down of civil liberties and the implementation of torture programs during the immediate post 9/11 years.

AN IRRATIONALIST VIEW OF TERRORISM

Reporting from Sri Lanka between 1985 and 1991, I saw Buddhists slaughtered in their holy city of Anuradhapura. I sat in a Colombo hospital with a woman coughing blood as she told me how her son had died as they rode toward the city on a shopping trip. "He saw them get on the bus wearing uniforms, and then he saw their rubber sandals and he said, "Mummy, these are not soldiers' " In a second, the boy was dead and she was badly wounded. I never knew whether she survived. Multiply these stories many times over . . .

A report of terrorist violence in Sri Lanka[27]

How can we best make sense of terrorist attacks, such as the one described above by a mother in Sri Lanka?[28] At one level, such terrorist attacks are intended to cause physical damage, and to weaken and ultimately topple government authorities. The logic and justification for terrorist attacks appear to be rational and materialistic. The pronouncements of the terrorists themselves, whether they are secular groups such as in Sri Lanka or faith-based groups as in Iraq, Afghanistan, and Pakistan, express supreme confidence in their avowed reasons for carrying out terrorist attacks: "I am doing my national/religious duty; I am sacrificing myself in the holiest cause of all."

Similarly, the authorities attempting to capture or kill terrorists see their goal within a rational-materialist framework. Terrorists are attempting to kill or injure innocent people, or to harm property, and must be stopped. The analysis is in terms of the here and now. Government authorities, including security forces, have been less concerned with the larger contexts that give rise to the terrorist attacks. Such a situational perspective is avoided, because it is assumed to distract security forces from the immediate task of capturing or killing the terrorists, a task that requires focus on individuals or groups as agents—not on situations.

But I want to step back from the immediate to consider the longer term, and from the rational-materialist account to consider irrational factors. Terrorism is far better explained, I argue, in a macro context of global and cultural evolutionary changes, which both terrorists and security forces neglect. The rationalizations for why terrorism occurs tend to be irrational, in the sense that they do not show awareness of the macro factors that really result in terrorism.

The Big Picture

Knowing about evolution and human origins helps us to understand what makes us human and informs us about our possible destinies, the choice of fate largely to be determined by how we treat one another and our planetary home.

P.R. Ehrlich and A.H. Ehrlich[29]

My objective in this discussion is to interpret radicalization and terrorism within the context of long-term evolutionary processes and ongoing globalization. Thus, I am considering the macro context of extremist thoughts and actions, both in terms of time and space. This seemingly obvious approach is very much against the current trend, driven by political factors, of considering radicalization and terrorism in a "here and now" reactive manner: each terrorist threat or plot or actual attack brings a frenzy of activities from the media, the authorities, and the "expert" community. Of course, it is necessary to deal with imminent threats, but my concern in this discussion is the neglected but necessary "big picture" and the long-term view of events.

As Ehrlich and Ehrlich have pointed out, we human beings have become *The Dominant Animal* on planet earth, but through our actions we risk destroying our natural habitat. We are experiencing rapid changes, one aspect of which is dramatic declines in diversity among animals and plants, as well as among human cultures and languages. We need to appreciate the interrelated nature of declining diversity in these two "parallel" domains,[30] but also to better understand the unique human reactions to declining diversity in human cultures and languages. I argue that human groups (ethnic, religious, linguistic, and so on) have a variety of defense mechanisms of varying functionality when faced with what they perceive to be possible extinction, and among these defense mechanisms are radicalization and terrorism.

Catastrophic Evolution and Sudden Contact

Migration has been an integral part of human evolution.[31] Genetic research involving the tracking of the Y-chromosomes lineages has shown that by 10,000 years ago, human beings had emerged out of Africa and reached all of the major land masses on planet earth.[32] The intermingling of human groups over the last few thousand years has had important biological and cultural benefits, not the least of which is the beneficial outcome of cross-breeding (discussed by Darwin[33]). Thus, migration has been both "natural" and beneficial. But having reached the major land masses, large numbers of human beings have continued to migrate, and particularly in recent decades this movement has involved "contact without preparation" (discussed in more detail below) between people with different ethnic, religious, cultural, linguistic, and other such characteristics.[34]

Because of the nature of transportation and communication technology, until very recently in human history the migration of human groups took place at a relatively slow speed. The first humans arrived in North America by foot and by slow-moving rafts. Today, over a million people a year legally immigrate to the United States, arriving in their adopted land mostly using rapid air transportation. The sheer speed at which large numbers of people move from place to place in the twenty-first century can create *sudden contact*, the coming together of different groups with low preadaptiveness (after Ehrlich[35]), meaning that there is a high probability that a life form will experience rapid decline or even extinction after contact. In the North American context, this translates to the decline and extinction of immigrant cultures and languages. For example, millions of German-speaking immigrants came to America in the nineteenth century[36] and lived in settlements that were almost completely German-speaking, but by the twenty-first century these immigrants had "melted away" into the English-speaking American mainstream. The classic theme of American immigration has been one of new groups occupying segregated sectors of society and retaining their heritage life-style, but subsequent generations disappearing into the American mainstream "melting-pot"[37].

In the global context, sudden contact has been taking place between colonial, and later imperial, powers and indigenous non-Western peoples. The outcome of Western powers expanding their influence, as colonists and later as imperialists, around the globe has been a sharp decline in cultural and linguistic diversity. Of course, the decline in linguistic diversity is easier to quantify (compared to changes in "woolly" culture): over the last five centuries, the number of living languages has declined by over 55 percent to about 6,000, and by the end of the twenty-first century the number is likely to decline to about 2,000.[38] These transformations can best be understood in relation to the "fractured" manner in which globalization is taking place.

The "Good Copy Problem" and Identity Threats

In exploring the "identity crisis" being experienced by Islamic communities around the world, it is useful to examine the nature of the "good copy problem"[39] (discussed in Chapter 1). This problem arises whenever a minority group adopts a model of the ideal, a model of what they aspire to become, that is not authentic to them, but has its roots in the outgroup majority culture. All kinds of minority groups have confronted this problem in the past. For example, when women entered management and various leadership positions in the workforce, they (at least initially) adopted the male model of leadership. Of course, women could only become a "good copy" of the original male image. Being a mere "good copy" of an original raises problems of authenticity and originality.

The "good copy problem" particularly confronts many non-Western communities. This is because the ideals models being propagated around the world tend to have Western sources, and are spread through the Western-dominated media. These ideals are particularly targeting young people under the age of twenty-five, who make up about 60 percent of the population outside the Western industrialized world. Many young Muslims are being influenced by the ideals of Western societies, and being moved to try to become "good copies" of Western models. The way forward, real progress, seems to be synonymous with taking on Western characteristics. Step into a class in any leading university in Istanbul, Mumbai, or Beijing, for example, and in terms of the clothes they wear, the music they listen to, the films they watch, the books they study, and many other characteristics, the students will be similar to those in university classes in the EU or North America.

From the perspective of fundamentalist Muslims, globalization threatens to make extinct their "pure" Islamic way of life. Muslim youth are being lured to a way of life that is alien to pure Islam. The only way to avoid extinction is to fight back, using every means available. A vitally important weapon adopted by fundamentalists is symbolically powerful cultural symbols, "sacred carriers" such as the Islamic veil (as discussed in Chapter 7).

CONCLUDING COMMENT

Both torture and terrorism have been supported through rationalist-materialist arguments, such as the idea that torture is necessary for extracting vital life-saving information in the so-called "ticking bomb" scenario, and that terrorism is a logical tactic against a much more powerful opponent. But in reality torture and terrorism can be explained far more effectively through an irrationalist account. The deeper reasons for both torture and terrorism have more to do with displacement of aggression and the desire to bring collective shame and humiliations, as well as helplessness, to a group. Both torture and terrorism more often result in greater material destruction and more loss than gain.

Part III

Toward Solutions

The search for long-term security solutions must begin by setting aside entrenched dogmas and the accepted norms for how to interpret, view, and debate security. The contrast and rivalry between traditional realists and the more recently established human security camps have to some extent been fruitful, but now we must adopt an even broader perspective, to more fully incorporate human irrationality and human identity needs. Threats to collective identity are at the heart of the new global insecurity, and the most important factors impacting this process are irrational ones.

Collective identity threats are the main source of security threats in the twenty-first century. For example, the root of 9/11 and, more broadly, terrorism by Islamic fundamentalists is their fear of being sidelined and eventually made extinct. Globalization in practice has meant the spread of Western and particularly American secular values. Minority groups, such as Islamic fundamentalists, feel particularly vulnerable in the face of this onslaught of American culture.

The threat perceived by minorities might have been managed more effectively if changes in the intergroup landscape had come about far more slowly. However, as discussed in Chapter 5, globalization has brought about sudden contact on a large scale: the coming together of enormous numbers of people from different cultural, religious, linguistic, political, ethnic, and national backgrounds, without preadaptation to prepare them for such interactions. In this context, some groups, typically those with less power and resources, decline and vanish. Most often, the members of these less powerful groups adapt by becoming absorbed into more powerful groups.

Groups that are confronted with the possibility of decline and extinction typically experience collective identity threats, anxiety provoking insecurity, and adopt defense tactics. These tactics range from terrorism to peaceful collective mobilization. Whatever the tactics used by minorities in the face of potential decline and extinction, the consequence is often perceived threat and insecurity on the part of majority groups, which can result in further intergroup conflict. There is an urgent need to develop more effective policies for managing relations between groups, particularly in a global context in which diversity is the norm, and groups that differ in terms of religion, ethnicity, language, and so on, are continually interacting with one another.

But it is not enough to develop policies for managing diversity at local, national, or even regional levels. More efforts need to be made to develop and highlight a *long-term global diversity policy plan*, one that takes into consideration priorities, resources, potentialities, and so on, of the world as a whole. This requires that far more attention be given to the present and future state of humankind, and not just particular selected nations.

Should the world become a place with less or more diversity in terms of human cultures and languages? Is it better to facilitate assimilation processes, so that we come to share a common world culture and speak the same few or even one language? Surely assimilation would help to bridge gaps? Surely if all humans spoke the same language there would be fewer communication errors, misunderstandings, and conflicts? Or, is it better to support greater diversity in human cultures and languages? Is it better to strengthen and celebrate differences between groups? If we decide that diversity has benefits, how can we help to sustain minority cultures and languages? These are among the questions that need to be addressed, on the road to developing a global diversity management plan as part of a world development plan more broadly.

The development of effective policies for managing diversity and intergroup relations is the greatest long-term challenge facing students of security studies. In turning to this challenge, I critically review the two main traditional policies, assimilation and multiculturalism, and put forward a more effective alternative, omniculturalism.

9

Omniculturalism: The Third Path to Managing Diversity and Overcoming Insecurity

Human beings achieved impressive advances in medical and engineering sciences over the course of the twentieth century, but in broader terms made far less progress toward ending war and attaining peace and justice in intergroup relationships and security. In his profound analysis of genocide in the twentieth century, Weitz[1] highlights the question of how we can organize relationships between human groups and manage diversity to achieve a more peaceful and secure world. What is the best policy to adopt for managing and improving relations between people from different cultural, linguistic, racial, ethnic, and religious backgrounds? In the twenty-first century, the continuation of violent intergroup conflicts around the world, increased radicalization of certain major religious groups, and the proliferation of international terrorist movements have made the challenge all the more urgent.[2] Those interested in improving security must directly concern themselves with policies for better managing relations between groups.

My first objective is to make the case that a multidisciplinary approach is needed to find better solutions for managing diversity and improving security in the global society. Of course, the psychological foundations of policies for managing diversity necessitate that psychological science contributes directly and substantially to ongoing explorations of how best to manage intergroup relations in a world of limited and in some key respects shrinking resources; linking contributions being made by biologists,[3] sociologists,[4] political scientists,[5] among others. Policies for managing diversity have had important consequences in a number of domains of central concern to psychological science, including mental health[6] and education.[7] However, from a psychological perspective there are major shortcomings in the two main policies traditionally adopted for managing diversity: *assimilation,* the washing away of intergroup differences, and *multiculturalism,* the highlighting, strengthening, and celebration of intergroup differences. It is essential that we explore a more effective alternative strategy for managing diversity and coping with global insecurity, one that is available based on a foundation of psychological science. The basic features of this alternative strategy are presented here.

First, I critically assess the psychological foundations of the two traditional strategies for managing diversity. The more historically dominant policy, assimilation, has the ultimate goal of achieving a more homogeneous society through minimizing intergroup diversity and maximizing intergroup similarities. The ideal outcome of assimilation policy is a celebration of individuals (independent of groups) and a washing away of differences between groups. Assimilation has historically been associated with the American "melting-pot" process and meritocracy. According to the "American dream" ideology, America is the land of opportunities where any individual can become successful and reach the top, through sufficient individual effort, personal responsibility, and the requisite talent. More recently, assimilation has become associated with the assumed homogenizing impact of globalization at the international level.[8] It is assumed that the internationalization of trade, transportation, and communications will result in a global village with increased similarities between all people around the world.

The end goal of multiculturalism, the second major established policy, is the maintenance and celebration of group-based differences, typically formalized in government and sometimes private sector policies that support cultural and linguistic diversity. Multiculturalism has been associated with the collective mobilization of minorities since the 1960s, with national policies adopted by governments in Canada, Australia, and some other countries since the 1970s, and with "identity politics" more broadly.[9] Multiculturalism offers an alternative vision to the "melting pot": individuals can become more constructive citizens when their identity is securely rooted in their distinct collective heritage cultures, and their cultural group is esteemed for itself in the larger society. In critically assessing the psychological foundations of both multiculturalism and assimilation, I also point out their more serious psychological shortcomings, and argue that a third, more viable alternative needs to be developed on the basis of psychological science.

The third alternative I introduce is *omniculturalism,*[10] which involves using a foundation of psychological universals as a launching pad for valuing distinct identities. The policy of omniculturalism arises out of well-established ideas in psychological science, such as Muzafer

Sherif's[11] (1906–1988) concept of superordinate goals (discussed earlier in Chapters 4 and 6). A superordinate goal in the twenty-first century is saving the environment, because the cooperation of all countries is required to attain this goal. Empirical research suggests that when the members of different groups come to see themselves as having a common or superordinate identity, the biases that existed between the members of the original groups decrease or end.[12] But omniculturalism goes beyond the first step of developing a superordinate identity.

The end point of omniculturalism is a society whose members first recognize the importance of their common similarities and bonds, and then, secondarily, celebrate, uphold, and share the distinctiveness of different groups, local identities, and lifestyles. In omniculturalism, the celebration of human commonalities shared by all groups serves as the prerequisite for and a stepping stone toward the celebration of intergroup differences. By first socializing the young to recognize and act on basic human psychological similarities, omnicultural policy diminishes the tendency for group-based differences to become highlighted, exaggerated, and used as the primary basis for relationships. In turn, this will lessen the tendency for prejudice and discrimination.

THE TRADITIONAL POLICIES FOR MANAGING DIVERSITY

The two traditional policies for managing diversity toward achieving intergroup peace and security, assimilation and multiculturalism, are both based on major psychological assumptions. I point out that, first, at least some of the psychological assumptions underlying both policies are flawed and, second, the overarching direction of both policies is problematic and not conducive to intergroup harmony. I will begin by discussing the case of assimilation, which on the surface at least seems more in line with prevailing globalization trends.

Assimilation

"God's crucible, the great Melting Pot where all the races of Europe are melting and re-forming"[13] is how the playwright Israel Zangwill captured the vision of America in his 1909 play *The Melting-Pot*—a place where all group-based differences are washed away. In this form of assimilation, *melting-pot assimilation*,[14] all groups contribute to the emergence of a new culture.[15] A second kind of assimilation, *minority-assimilation*, involves the minority groups "melting into" the culture of the majority group. Minority-assimilation is associated with the University of Chicago's School of Sociology,[16] and the "classic" picture of immigrant integration into

American society: first-generation immigrants live in inner-city ethnic neighborhoods and continue in the habits of the heritage country, but subsequent generations work their way up the social status system, move out to the suburbs, and adopt the life style and language of mainstream America.[17]

At both national and international levels, assimilation is assumed to be made inevitable by the demands of new economic and technological forces. Market conditions demand that individuals be mobile to take advantage of the best employment and quality of life opportunities. As a consequence, geographical mobility is increasing, and participation in traditional communities and group activities is decreasing.[18] The movement of people, goods, and services around the world is part of a trend of increasing globalization and increasing intergroup contact. Although globalization is not always synonymous with westernization, since China, India, Brazil, Nigeria, and some other non-Western countries are also increasing their international influence through globalization,[19] it is seen to be synonymous with increasing homogeneity in lifestyles around the world.

There are a number of factors that have made assimilation an advantageous policy from the perspective of both national governments and newly emerging regional units, such as the EU where central and local authorities are competing for influence.[20] Assimilation involves the "washing away" of ethnic, tribal, racial, and local differences and loyalties. Under such conditions, it is more likely that loyalties to a central authority and stronger identification with relatively recent national states and regional unions will emerge. In turn, citizen loyalty will enable the central authority to govern with greater credibility and effectiveness.

Four central psychological assumptions underlie assimilation policy. Some aspects of each of these assumptions are supported by empirical research, but other central aspects of these assumptions are seriously flawed.

Consequences of Contact

Assimilation policy begins with the assumptions that contact between people from different cultural, religious, ethnic, racial, and linguistic backgrounds will result in more positive relationships (and eventually the voluntary merging of groups). Allport[21] proposed basic preconditions that must be met in order for intergroup contact to have positive outcomes, but recent meta-analytic studies suggest that contact can bring about more harmonious intergroup relations, changing majority group attitudes particularly,[22] irrespective of the specific conditions in which it takes place.[23] Well-established research evidence on the "mere exposure effect" is in line with this idea: our liking for things increases with increased exposure to them.[24]

However, ongoing research on the contact hypothesis[25] is limited because it ignores historically important exceptions, such as the case of *sudden contact* and *catastrophic evolution*, when groups with little or no history of contact are suddenly brought together, with the resulting sharp decline and sometimes extinction of one or both of them.[26] For example, between the sixteenth and nineteenth centuries, Western European powers came into sudden contact with native groups in Africa, South and North America, and Asia, the result being sharp declines, and even extinctions, of many indigenous peoples.[27] Perhaps the concept of catastrophic evolution is best illustrated by "language death": since Columbus landed in America, the number of languages in the world has declined dramatically, and minority languages continue to disappear at a steady rate in the twenty-first century. Thus, rather than leading to more positive relations between groups and the voluntary merging of groups, the historic trend clearly shows that intergroup contact has resulted in the often forced decline and even extinction of numerous minority groups around the world.

Similarity-Attraction

Assimilation is intended to lead to a society composed of members who are relatively similar to one another, and in this way society is assumed to benefit from the long-established relationship between similarity and attraction.[28] All things being equal, people tend to be more attracted to others who are more similar to themselves. The vast majority of similarity-attraction research studies have focused on interpersonal relations,[29] but there have also been a small number of intergroup studies and these have confirmed that group members are more positively inclined toward more similar outgroups.[30] Thus, similarity-attraction research seems to confirm the benefits of assimilation policy.

But insights from psychoanalysis and evidence from experimental social psychology cast serious doubts on key aspects of this picture. Freud argued that minor differences can be used to differentiate and distance others, and that it is possible to bind people together in love as long as "there are other people left over to receive the manifestations of their aggressiveness."[31] Research in the tradition of the minimal group paradigm provides robust experimental evidence to support the view that even trivial differences can serve as the basis for intergroup differentiation and bias.[32] Experimental evidence using the minimal group paradigm (discussed in Chapter 5) demonstrates that individuals can show bias in favor of the in-group and against the out-group even when the differences between the in-group and the out-group are trivial on an objective basis, group members do not know the identities of in-group and out-group members and will not interact with them in the future, and the bias that group members show will not directly reward themselves. Thus, no matter how many characteristics people come to share (e.g., language, civic knowledge) through assimilation policies, it will still be possible to identify or manufacture differences, even on a trivial criterion, to serve as a basis for intergroup differentiation and discrimination. Besides, physical markers such as skin color will continue to distinguish between people, making it impossible to achieve assimilation on all criteria relevant to group-based differentiation and discrimination.

Assumed Benefits of Homogeneity

Assimilation policy is supported by two further related arguments, the first being that societal homogeneity is associated with cohesion and peace, whereas diversity creates opportunities for intergroup rifts and conflicts. For example, research shows a surprisingly high level of intolerance between Asians, Blacks, Latinos, and Whites in at least some major U.S. urban centers.[33] Whereas societies such as Japan are cited as evidence of the benefits of homogeneity, Canada seems to provide a practical example of the dangers of diversity, with separatist movements almost managing to break up the country since the 1960s.[34] A second, related argument is that homogeneity supports democracy, whereas diversity works against democracy but supports authoritarianism.[35] For example, in societies characterized by ethnic diversity, there is a danger that voters will give political support to candidates based on ethnic allegiances, rather than political values that reflect the interests of the entire society.[36]

The above arguments—that homogeneity is necessarily supportive of cohesion and democracy, and diversity results in intergroup conflicts and hurts democracy—have been criticized, both on the grounds that they are not supported by consistent research evidence[37] and that they are contradicted by practical examples. For example, Japan and Germany in the 1930s became increasingly more homogeneous through the policies of rising fascism, and clearly neither became more democratic or cohesive. On the other hand, India and the United States enjoy ethnic, religious, and linguistic diversity, yet they continue to function for the most part as cohesive democracies.

Meritocracy

Assimilation can be argued to be the best policy for meeting the conditions for *meritocracy*, a sociopolitical system in which the advancement achieved by each individual depends on personal merit, independent of group memberships. The claim is that assimilation will enable everyone to become culturally literate,[38] so that all individuals start on a level playing field and no group is detrimentally impacted by (possible) cultural biases in selection tests, such as the Scholastic Aptitude Test (SAT), that influence the allocation of resources in society. Assimilation will mean that everyone not only speaks in the same language, but also has a minimal level of cultural competency, so that a more level playing field is achieved.

However, a critical shortcoming in the above argument is that assimilation is not intended to diminish economic disparities, so it will not bring about a level playing field in what is arguably the most important area: material resources. The advantaged group will continue to increase their relative superiority because of their greater economic assets.[39] The socioeconomic status of parents continues to be an important factor determining cognitive and physical development,[40] and increasing income disparities[41] suggest that assimilation will be severely challenged to enhance meritocracy.

In conclusion, then, there are major flaws in the psychological assumptions underlying assimilation policy. On the one hand, the assimilation goal of "washing away" intergroup differences is in practice impossible; even if minority groups are wiped out, politically defined differences, even minor ones, can be used to create new "outgroups." On the other hand, the decline of distinct collective heritage cultures and identities can leave minority groups more vulnerable, since they have to face discrimination without a self-protective sense of collective identity and pride to fall back on. Particularly since the 1960s support has grown for an alternative policy, multiculturalism.

Multiculturalism

Whereas the goal of assimilation has been to increase similarities and forge a homogenous society to meet a standard set of cultural criteria, multiculturalism came to fruition through the ethnic revival of the 1960s[42] and was intended to highlight, support, and celebrate diversity.[43] The term *multiculturalism* has sometimes been used merely to describe any society or organization comprised of people from different ethnic, racial, national, religious, or linguistic background. Another feature of the broader use of the term has been in association with cultural relativism, and the perspective that evaluations of phenomena should be made according to the criteria of the culture in which they have evolved. Associated with cultural relativism is the idea that what is considered abnormal and dysfunctional behavior in one culture can be functional in another,[44] that cultural diversity is in itself of value, and educational institutions in particular benefit from having a culturally diverse student body, faculty, and curriculum.[45]

With respect to the question of "how" a society can best become multicultural, a first strategy is *laissez-faire multiculturalism*, whereby market forces are allowed to shape developments with minimal government intervention. Such a free market approach could result in ethnic economic enclaves, sectors of the economy dominated by particular ethnic groups who develop sufficient economic clout to become in some key respects self-contained (such as ethnic enclaves in New York and Los Angeles).[46] The particular needs of the ethnic community would be met by specialized shops, television and radio stations, newspapers, cultural centers, and other services. The success and failure of such businesses, and the size and vibrancy of the ethnic economic enclave, would depend on market conditions.

An alternative model is *planned multiculturalism*, whereby governments directly intervene to support heritage cultures and languages. For example, such support would take the shape of government grants to heritage language schools, media outlets, and cultural centers. In Canada, Australia, New Zealand, and other democracies where a moderated form of planned multiculturalism has been practiced, the support provided by the government for the maintenance of minority heritage cultures and languages has in practice been influenced by the relative size of the different minority populations, so that the largest groups have tended to receive more support.

Both in its laissez faire and planned forms, multiculturalism could be argued to be particularly in line with the values of democracy. Rather than "washing away" group-based differences toward meeting an elite majority group model of the ideal, as is the goal of minority assimilation, multiculturalism policy provides space, opportunities, and support for group-based diversity to be recognized and celebrated.[47] However, multiculturalism policy also has major shortcomings, in large part because it is based on a number of questionable psychological assumptions.

Cultural Retention and Cultural Relativism

When introducing legislation in support of multiculturalism policy in the Canadian Parliament in 1971, the Canadian Prime Minister Pierre Elliot Trudeau (1919–2000) stated that "there is no official culture, nor does any ethnic group take precedence over any other."[48] Underlying this statement is the relativist assumption that all cultures and languages are of equal value and deserve equal government support. In the free market of cultures, the government would not make value judgments, but would support all groups motivated to retain their distinct heritages.

A central challenge of multiculturalism policy is the danger of sliding into cultural relativism, whereby phenomena can only be assessed within the value system of the particular culture from which they arise. From this perspective, for example, whether a particular behavior of a female or male is "correct" depends on the cultural context. If in culture C1 it is deemed correct to treat females as adults when they reach 9 years of age, and in culture C2 females are treated as adults when they reach 18 years of age, then these different criteria for when females should be treated as adults have to be assessed according to the different normative systems of cultures C1 and C2, and not according to scientifically asserted universals in the psychological and biological development of human beings (some such universals are proposed by cultural researchers[49]).

Of course, it could be claimed that the laws and constitutions of democracies would guarantee the rights of individuals, and serve as a guard against abusive group practices, such as polygamy and the forced marriage of young girls. However, not all countries are democracies, and, second, some democracies, including Canada and the EU, still do not have ratified constitutions, and "across the board" government support for diversity can raise problems for minorities (particularly women and children). For example, consider the thorny issue of the Islamic veil, and the question of whether the millions of Muslim families living in Western societies have the right to force their daughters to wear the veil in public, and whether the government has the duty to allow the wearing of the veil in public schools.[50] A relativist position on such issues can harm the rights of women in particular.

Retention of Heritage Cultures

Underlying multiculturalism policy is the assumption that immigrants are motivated to retain their heritage cultures. According to this view, immigrants move to the adopted lands to take advantage of economic and educational opportunities, as well as political freedoms, but not necessarily, or even ordinarily, to abandon their heritage cultures.

Evidence is ambiguous on the question of immigrants wanting to retain their heritage cultures.[51] For some minorities, heritage culture retention could serve to make them more visible targets for discrimination, which some researchers argue is in-built by default in traditional social relations[52] and can actually be exacerbated by diversity management policies.[53] In the context of multicultural Canada, there has for some time been evidence that the longer visible minority immigrants stay in the country, the more they feel like outsiders.[54] Thus, policies that help minorities become more visible could be serving to make them easier targets for discrimination.

The Multiculturalism Hypothesis

At the heart of the Canadian policy of multiculturalism is what became known as the *multiculturalism hypothesis,*[55] which states that national unity must be based "in one's own individual identity; out of this can grow respect for others and a willingness to share ideas, attitudes, and assumptions."[56] A straightforward interpretation of the multiculturalism hypothesis[57] is that confidence in one's own group identity will lead to, first, openness toward out-group members and, second, a willingness to share and exchange one's own cultural heritage and that of others. A number of classic[58] and contemporary[59] researchers have endorsed the optimistic viewpoint that love and loyalty for the in-group is not a precursor of hate for out-groups; rather, it is a basis for acceptance of others and differentness.

This optimistic view represented by the multiculturalism hypothesis contradicts at least three pessimistic alternatives. First, there exists a long-established[60] theoretical position proposing that ethnocentrism is universal, involving positive bias in favor of the in-group and hostility toward out-groups. Second, social identity theory,[61] the most influential intergroup theory since the 1970s, has also been interpreted to predict that the more strongly individuals identify with the in-group, the more negatively biased they will be against outgroups.[62] Third, there seem to be important historical examples of groups (e.g., the Nazis) that espouse strong confidence in their heritage cultures, but are not at all accepting toward out-groups. Of course, it may be that such groups are not really confident, but suffer inflated and unstable self-esteem.[63] Also, recent empirical evidence highlights cases showing different patterns for minorities and majorities. This disparity implies that the pessimistic view of in-group identification being associated with negative out-group bias is more true for minority group members, and the optimistic view of in-group identification being associated with greater acceptance of out-groups is more true for majority group members.[64] The implication is that the validity of the multiculturalism hypothesis can vary with the minority-majority status of the group. At most, then, the multicultural hypothesis is shown by psychological research to be valid only under very limited conditions and only for some groups.

In conclusion, the two alternative traditional policies for managing diversity are founded on questionable psychological assumptions. Assimilation policy attempts to "wash away" intergroup differences and create a culturally more homogeneous, meritocratic, democratic society, one with maximum similarity and minimal rifts. But assimilation policy neglects the research evidence demonstrating a tendency for human beings to construct *distinct* identities[65] and to manufacture major intergroup differences on the basis of even objectively trivial criteria.[66] Besides, we have to keep in mind the impossibility of eliminating all differences in physical appearance (e.g., skin color). In practice, the end goal of avoiding intergroup discrimination and peace through assimilation, homogeneity, and minimal diversity is untenable.

On the other hand, multiculturalism policy adopts the goal of supporting and celebrating diversity, and starts with the assumption that minority groups are motivated to retain their heritage cultures; however, this is often not the case, particularly for visible minorities. Moreover, the policy of support for diversity often slips into cultural relativism, with dire consequences for women and others who are deprived of equal rights in certain cultures, and who would benefit through the universal application of human rights principles. In addition, research evidence has brought into question the validity of the multicultural hypothesis, the keystone of multiculturalism policy. Pride and confidence in one's own heritage culture does not always, or even often, result in greater openness toward out-groups. Weaknesses in the two traditional policies bring into sharp focus the urgent need for a more constructive alternative in this era of rapid globalization and fast shifting patterns of intergroup contacts.

OMNICULTURALISM: THE THIRD WAY FOR MANAGING DIVERSITY

The third way I propose for managing diversity involves learning and celebrating; first, foundational scientifically-established universals and, at a second stage, distinct collective identities. The end goal is a society bonded by and founded on human commonalities, but also building on this foundation to celebrate and share distinct cultural outgrowths. Whereas the end goal of assimilation is commonality and the end point of multiculturalism is the celebration of intergroup differences, the end goal of omniculturalism is the recognition and celebration of primarily research-based human commonalities and, secondarily, group based differences.

Omniculturalism is not simply a combination of assimilation and multiculturalism. First, whereas assimilation attempts to arrive at a more homogeneous society guided by the criteria of the dominant culture (in the case of minority-assimilation) or all cultures (in the case of melting-pot assimilation), omniculturalism attempts to establish a foundation of similarity guided by psychological science. Second, whereas multiculturalism attempts to arrive at a diverse society that celebrates intergroup differences identified by group members, omniculturalism first celebrates intergroup similarities and only subsequently and secondarily celebrates intergroup differences. The intergroup similarities that are celebrated form the foundation for the identification and celebration of intergroup differences.

A policy of omniculturalism rests on the assumption that there is research evidence in support of human universals in important domains of thought and action. Psychological science has established a number of important universals, including ones in cognitive, developmental, and social domains.[67] Although psychological universals are less extensive than claimed by some traditional psychologists,[68] research evidence suggests universals in domains such as the ability to discriminate on the basis of conceptual primitives of geometry,[69] the tendency for similarity to be positively associated with attraction,[70] and for well-learned tasks to be performed better and poorly learned tasks to be performed worse in the presence of others.[71] Of direct relevance to the cognitive foundations of intergroup relations, evidence suggests certain universals in categorization processes.[72] Despite controversy, then, even when serious attention is given to culture, some psychological universals can be identified.[73] Of particular concern to us in this discussion are universals directly relevant to the management of diversity. The illustrative example I discuss below is subjective justice, selected because this issue is at the center of intergroup relations. The perception of injustice, leading to claims such as "we are not being treated fairly" and "our rights have been violated," is commonly associated with intergroup hostility and conflict.[74] My argument, supported by research evidence, is that although there are variations across cultures in subjective justice, there are also a number of important, foundational evolutionary-evolved universals.

Subjective Justice and Universals

First, there is impressive research evidence in support of the proposition that people are motivated to perceive the world as just, and experience discomfort when they come to believe that injustice is being practiced against others or themselves. One well-established line of research derives from *equity theory*,[75] which focuses on how people subjectively interpret their inputs and outcomes in a relationship to arrive at a particular sense of fairness. A second research tradition in support of the view that people are motivated to perceive the world as just derives from *just-world* theory.[76]

There has been a tendency to place emphasis on the negative implications of research stimulated by equity theory and just-world theory, such as the tendency for people to "blame the victim" in situations where others end up suffering, for example, when they are attacked, robbed, raped, or injured in other ways.[77] However, an alternative, more optimistic interpretation is to highlight the shared tendency of people to want to arrive at a just world. People feel discomfort when they perceive injustice, and even greater distress when they themselves injure or kill others.[78]

It could be claimed that the motivation to perceive the world as just is not a sufficient basis on which to build a just world in practice. Classic equity theory[79] and more recent ideologically oriented theories, such as system justification theory,[80] highlight the cognitive manipulations that can lead people to perceive the world as just, irrespective of the objective state of affairs. For example, Joe can exaggerate the contributions of his group to the peace process, and minimize the constructive contributions of a competing out-group, so as to justify the aggressive tactics of the in-group. But this criticism ignores the *direction* of the initial motivation: people *want* to see the world as just rather than unjust, and this shared "justice motive" is a powerful platform on which to build a more just social world.

Because human beings are strongly motivated to perceive the world as just, extreme measures have to be taken to influence people to treat others in ways that make the world seem unjust. For example, in the classic studies of Stanley Milgram[81] (1933–1984) and others[82] demonstrating conditions in which some persons do harm to others, the experimenters created situations in which the "harm doers" could place responsibility for their actions on authority figures or other non-dispositional factors. In this way, any injustice in the world could be attributed to external factors, not to the self.

Thus, a common starting point for all the members of society, irrespective of their group memberships, is that everyone desires to live in a just society, and to see themselves as behaving fairly rather than unfairly. This similarity can serve to unite rather than divide society when it is treated as a common starting point for socialization. In the training of young people, in particular, emphasis should be placed on this profound shared human psychological characteristic: both "we" and "they" want a just world and feel discomfort when we see injustice.

Primitive Social Relations: The Example of Turn-Taking

There are also specific *primitive social relations*, elementary behaviors that evolved as part of a repertoire of skills necessary for group survival,[83] that can serve as a common basis for organizing justice relations between groups in diverse societies. Primitive social relations evolved out of common human survival challenges, and some of them have served as a behavioral basis for justice practices in modern societies. For example, turn-taking is universally practiced by human beings, and is an integral part of communications even before verbal communications.[84] Although the rules of communications often vary across cultures, the practice of turn-taking is universal. Very early in their socialization, children imitate turn-taking, and learn to recognize when turn-taking has been violated.[85] The ability to participate in conversations with others depends on turn-taking practices; irrespective of the language being used, communications break down when turn-taking is not practiced. Even when an absolute dictator is giving orders, he has to allow others "their turn" to report they have received orders, understood orders, carried out orders, and so on.

In modern Western societies, the primitive social relation of turn-taking serves as a basis for a wide variety of complex behavioral repertoires, including in legal, social, and political spheres. Consider, for example, how turn-taking takes place (for the most part smoothly) in city traffic, even in the absence of traffic lights and police officers. Turn-taking is an important normative strategy, one of a number that allows people to maintain good order without formal law.[86] In law courts, turn-taking is formalized in procedures for calling and cross-examining witnesses, presenting evidence, and the like. In the political system, turn-taking is central not only to the procedures of political debates, but also to the sharing of political power through term limits, which results in turn-taking in the holding of political office by representatives of different political parties.

Although turn-taking is practiced in some ways by all people, turn-taking has not influenced the political and legal activities of all societies in the same manner. There are cross-cultural variations in who has the right to "a turn" to be heard, and how much value is given to the voice of each group. For example, in fundamentalist Muslim communities the testimony of a woman carries less weight than that of a man, and in major Muslim countries such as Egypt and Saudi Arabia, political leaders do not practice democratic procedures for turn taking. Despite such variations, turn-taking can be used effectively as a basis for achieving more just intergroup relations in diverse societies. For example, consider how people in fundamentalist societies can come to use turn-taking in modern traffic situations. Despite what might seem to be chaotic traffic in Tehran and other major Iranian cities, turn-taking is practiced by both women and men Iranian drivers in city traffic. The order in which cars take turns at crossroads in Tehran depends on the order in which cars arrived, and not on the gender and other group characteristics of the drivers. This illustrates how females and males can learn to take turns as equals in an Islamic country governed by fundamentalists (of course, for this to happen, women have to have the right to drive cars, a right they already enjoy in Iran but do not yet have in some other parts of the Muslim world, such as in Saudi Arabia).

Thus, the skill of turn-taking appears early in human development, is a commonly shared behavior, and can serve as a platform for moving human societies to become more fully democratic. Omnicultural policy requires more explicit focus on turn-taking, helping the members of a society to build shared political, social, and legal practices based on basic turn-taking skills.

The Motive to "Have a Voice"

People are not solely motivated to achieve voice in society out of a concern with the bottom line and what they can get out of the justice system. Rather, they are in some situations even more concerned about adding their voices and making a contribution to the decision-making process. Of course, the motivation to make a contribution to decision making can also be interpreted as self-interested concern for the bottom-line, on the basis of the claim that people are concerned with procedural justice only because the process of decision making will influence how rewards are distributed to themselves and others.[87] But empirical evidence shows that the contributions and concerns of individuals in the domain of justice go well beyond self-interest and the material bottom-line; people derive psychological benefits from contributing to group life and having a voice in the community.[88] They want to have their say not only because of a desire to get their share of material rewards, but also because making contributions and participating in a collective can itself constitute a reward.

In democratic societies, the commonly shared motivation to have a voice in the community, to contribute, and to be a part of collective life can serve as a basis for reversing what has been identified as a decline in some types of social capital[89] in the larger society. It may well be that participation in some types of group and community activities has suffered a decline in the United States and elsewhere,[90] and that this decline reflects a global trend associated with increasing individualism, geographical mobility, and specialization and fragmentation in various domains.[91] On the other hand, research on procedural justice clearly shows that people are motivated to be involved in decision-making processes, to have a voice in collective life, and also psychologically benefit from such involvement.[92] This tendency can serve as a basis for stronger rather than weaker communities.

Thus, people find it more satisfying to participate and to have a voice in decision-making processes. Even when they do not benefit materially from participation, they still can benefit from being heard and participating in the collective process. The motivation to "have a voice" can serve a vitally constructive role in the transition to more democratic forms of governance in both Western and non-Western societies. In democracies such as the United States, although voter participation has declined over the last century,[93] there is hope for greater participation in the twenty-first century; one challenge is to persuade more citizens that their voices can and should be heard through elections. In dictatorships where elections are held, such as Egypt and the Islamic Republic of Iran, a challenge is to extend turn-taking to allow the participation of candidates for political office that represent a wider range of political positions.

The Evolutionary Roots of Fairness

I have argued that certain important features of subjective justice are universal and derived from common functional challenges faced by human beings in their long evolutionary history. If this is the case, then might we find traces of such "functional justice behavior" even among lower animals? Indeed, research evidence demonstrates that certain animal behaviors can be interpreted as "fairness" in practice.[94] At a basic level, monkeys use turn-taking to reciprocate.[95] At a perhaps more complex level of behavior, monkeys became less cooperative when they witnessed other monkeys receiving better rewards for exerting less effort or no effort at all.[96] Such "fairness" can be mediated by contact with another animal, as when mice displayed behavior that could be interpreted as "empathy" when they witnessed a cagemate, but not a stranger, suffer pain.[97] Both animals and human beings acquire behaviors that reflect "rules of fairness" during game playing in their youngest years,[98] although some form of inbuilt moral grammar might also play a role.[99] Also, evidence presented by ethologists[100] suggests that aggression in both human beings and animals can be limited through inhibitory mechanisms commonly shared within species, suggesting a functional basis for limiting harm done to others.[101] In line with this functional or "experiential" approach, some legal scholars[102] have argued that human rights have evolved through human beings suffering through "human wrongs," so that, for example, the terrible "wrongs" of the Second World War resulted in a corrective, the Universal Declaration of Human Rights (adopted by the General Assembly of the United Nations in 1948). Thus, "rights" arise from "wrongs." Whatever the specific origins of subjective justice, one of its manifestations is moral systems that have certain basic similarities across cultures (such as prohibition of killing and injuring others, the lauding of truthfulness, and so on).

The first part of omnicultural policy is the establishment of a common foundation for society, based on psychological universals; the second part is the celebration and sharing of group differences, the topic I turn to next.

A Universal Need for Distinctiveness: The Second Part of Omniculturalism Policy

The second stage of omniculturalism policy is based on the assumption that human beings have a need to achieve distinctiveness, and that this need will not be satisfied during the first omniculturalism stage involving a focus on psychological universals. Groups attempt to achieve distinctiveness by, for example, constructing and maintaining special traditions and positioning themselves as different.[103] When groups are denied the right or means to "be themselves," to maintain and develop what they believe to be their "different" way of life and authentic identity, group members often feel that they have been treated unfairly, that their rights have been denied.

In many intergroup situations, perceptions of fairness are related to the issue of collective identity, what kind of a group people believe they belong to, and particularly how their group is evaluated by others. Claims that the in-group is being treated unjustly often revolve around the issue of identity. For example, inadequacy of collective identity has been proposed as being central to twenty-first century Islamic radicalization and terrorism.[104] Social identity theory[105] proposes that people are motivated to achieve a positive and distinct identity, and considerable research evidence supports this view.[106] The role of distinctiveness of group identity has been a focus of psychological research, and evidence shows that people use various strategies to position their group as not only positive but also "different."[107] Thus, there is consistent research support for the view that the highlighting and celebration of group distinctiveness can under certain conditions serve a constructive function in diverse societies.

Traditional assimilation and multiculturalism policies have taken two extreme and opposing approaches to dealing with distinctiveness of identity, neither of which is successful. On the one hand, assimilation policy attempts to achieve homogeneity and one uniform identity that covers everyone, by melting away intergroup differences. This leaves too little room for differentiation and the need for distinct identities, particularly among minority groups. On the other hand, multiculturalism highlights, celebrates, and often exaggerates differences, and in practice leads to relativism, and sometimes an "everyone is a star" approach in schools and other institutions. Thus, the exaggeration of intergroup differences without a prior, and I argue prerequisite, recognition of foundational commonalities also results in grave challenges to peaceful and constructive societal relationships. Omniculturalism begins by laying out the foundational research-based commonalities shared by the members of different groups, and on this common foundation moves on to highlight distinctive features of each group. According to omniculturalism policy, the celebration of differences takes place only *after* people have appreciated and celebrated their commonalities.

In practice, this means that in schools, omnicultural policy leads to a priority on teaching and celebrating human psychological universals. The questions of "What is a human being?" and "What do human beings have in common?" are first addressed, so that children begin their educational experiences by learning about their shared characteristics on the basis of psychological science. Of course, this picture should be communicated to children through age-appropriate pedagogical methods and language. Only after children have learned to see people through the lens of shared characteristics, does the second phase of omniculturalism begin and the celebration of group-based differences takes place. The timing of this transition from the first to the second stage of omniculturalism should be decided on the basis of cognitive development of children, as well as the degree of diversity, the nature of intergroup relations, and societal conditions more generally.

Thus, omnicultural policy is best suited to creating the optimal conditions in which the highlighting and celebration of intergroup differences can have constructive consequences and enable the sharing of distinct cultures across groups. An essential part of this optimal condition is that the members of different groups in a society share a *primary identity* based on their common characteristics, such as their motivation to participate in a just society, in which they have adequate voice, and everyone takes turns in enjoying and fulfilling both rights and duties. Throughout the early stages of the socialization process in particular, this primary identity must be given priority over the *secondary identity*, based on membership in sub-groups (e.g., ethnicity, profession, and so on) within the larger society.

CONCLUDING COMMENT

Particularly in twenty-first century North America and in Europe, governments are confronted by the enormous challenge of how to better achieve peace and overcome feelings of insecurity in societies characterized by diversity. Each year, millions of new immigrants and refugees, mostly originating from Africa and Asia, move to North America and to the EU. These newcomers add to the religious, ethnic, linguistic, and racial diversity of Western societies; an example being the approximately 20 million Muslims now living in Europe, and the roughly 50 million Latinos residing in the United States. The enormous scope of this challenge demands a critical re-thinking of traditional assimilation and multiculturalism policies, which are based on seriously flawed psychological assumptions. The policy of omniculturalism is a more constructive alternative, founded on psychological universals.

Omniculturalism policy is best suited to overcome the excesses and imbalances of assimilation and multiculturalism policies, and to meet the challenge of global insecurity. This correction can be effectively achieved through the education system, through naturalization procedures for new citizens, and in all domains where the socialization of individuals takes place toward their more active participation in the larger society. Scientific research can contribute enormously to this endeavor, by identifying important behavioral and cognitive commonalities that are particularly relevant to managing diverse societies. In this discussion I explored the illustrative case of subjective justice, but other important examples are also available. For instance, developmental science research can serve as a basis for establishing universal policy guidelines for socializing and educating children of different ages in diverse societies, independent of group membership.[108] Finally, the primary focus of omnicultural policy is subjective insecurity and procedural justice; however, a long-term goal should be the increased objective distribution of rewards through the fairer participation of individuals in justice processes.

An important part of the solution to the new global insecurity is to develop *contextualized democracy*, democratic systems based as much as possible on local cultural practices. The starting point to developing contextualized democracy is the recognition that there are vast differences between democracies in the West: American democracy differs from Canadian democracy which differs from German democracy which differs from Swiss democracy, and so on. Similarly, we should not expect Indian democracy to be identical to Pakistani or Iranian democracy (when it develops). Of course, there will be important features common to all these democracies, such as minimal level of openness and freedom, for both women and men. Despite these important similarities, the idea of contextualized democracy should guide our efforts to meet the challenge of insecurity in different parts of the world.

Notes

Chapter 1

1. My focus is particularly on the subjective experience of threats. I interpret *insecurity* as the absence of security, although I acknowledge that subjective feelings of insecurity can be divorced from objective criteria for security. For a preliminary review of different approaches to understanding human security, see M. Weissberg, *Conceptualizing Human Security. Swords and Ploughshares: A Journal of International Affairs*, XIII (2003): 3–11. The more traditional "realist" approach to security, giving priority to the sovereign state and military strength, is reflected in discussions in M. I. Midlarsky, *Handbook of War Studies* (Boston: Unwin Hyman, 1989). My emphasis on the subjective experience of security and insecurity is in line with a move away from positivism, a move that is clearly evident in the best scholarship from at least the nineteenth century. Writing about the pre-eminent nineteenth century historian Jacob Burckhardt (1818–1897), Oswyn Murray (Introduction to *The Greeks and Greek Civilization*, J. Burckhardt (New York: HarperCollins, 1998) states,

> For Burckhardt the explanation of events lies not in their causes but in the interrelations between them, of which the idea of cause is only a partial and pseudo-scientific two-dimensional reflection. Societies are not a linear series of events, but highly complex and interconnected systems, where a change in any element may provoke multiple effects elsewhere. Moreover, what people believe and how they behave are far more important than whether their beliefs are true or useful: it is not the event which matters, but the perception of that event as a "fact," which is neither true nor false, but simply believed (p. xvii).

2. Much has been written about the failure of traditional security institutions over the last half century. For example, Matthew Aid, *The Secret Sentinel*

(New York: Bloomsbury Press, 2009) and C. Abbott, P. Rogers, and J. Sloboda, *Global Responses to Global Threats: Sustainable Security for the Twenty-first Century* (Oxford: Oxford Research Group, 2006) provide a penetrating assessment of the National Security Agency, with its 10 billion dollar budget and more than 60,000 employees. However, there is little attention given to the impact that globalization has had on feelings of insecurity, and the enormous complexities and new challenges created by globalization for security agencies.

3. F. M. Moghaddam, *From the Terrorists' Point of View: What They Experience and Why They Come to Destroy* (Westport, CT: Praeger Security International, 2006).

4. "The message from Westernized Islamic elites is clear: the best that youth from Islamic societies can achieve is to become a 'good copy' of Western ideals; they can never be as good or better than the original Western models" (F. M. Moghaddam, *From the Terrorists' Point of View: What They Experience and Why They Come to Destroy*. Westport, CT: Praeger Security International, 2006, p. 38).

5. Thucydides, *The Peloponnesian War*, trans. J. H. Finley, Jr. (New York: The Modern Library, 1951), 489.

6. The realist tradition is assumed to continue to modern times particularly through the ideas of the Italian diplomat Niccolo Machiavelli (1469–1527). See N. Machiavelli, *The Prince*, ed. and trans. R. M. Adams (New York: Norton, 1977, first published 1513); the Dutch jurist Hugo Grotius (or Huig de Groot, 1583–1645); the English political philosopher Thomas Hobbes (1588–1679); the Prussian military thinker Karl Marie von Clausewitz (1780–1831); and the English historian Edward H. Carr (1892–1982).

7. R. Paris, "Human Security: Paradigm Shift or Hot Air?" *International Security* 26 (2001): 87–102, discusses these and other terms reflecting attempts to expand the concept of security.

8. United Nations Development Program. *Human Development Report* (1994). Retrieved Dec. 9, 2008, at http://hdr.undp.org/en/reports/global/hdr1994/chapters.

9. The emphasis on choices available to ordinary people, and the general shift to human development and human security, owes much to the writings of A. Sen, *Development as Freedom* (New York: Knopf, 1999). To enjoy the freedom to choose between different lifestyles, individuals must experience (among other things) freedom from insecurity.

10. United Nations Development Program, p. 22.

11. For a broad overview of contemporary perspectives in security studies, see A. Collins, ed., *Contemporary Security Studies* (Oxford, UK: Oxford University Press, 2007). The continued domination of the 'military' viewpoint in security studies is reflected in the focus on war, both in terms of the moral question of "just war" (e.g., M. Walzer, *Just and Unjust Wars*, 4th ed. (New York: Basic Books, 2006)), and the issue of tactics in the 21st century (e.g., O'Hanlon, M. E. (2005). *Defense Strategy for the Post-Saddam Era*. Washington, DC: Brookings Institute Press). An important component of this military focus is the central role of policies toward non-proliferation of nuclear weapons (e.g., S. Sagan, "The Perils

of Proliferation: Organization Theory, Deterrence Theory, and the Spread of Nuclear Weapons," *International Security* 18, (1994): 66–107), and what is perceived to be the rising military threat of China (e.g., D. Shambaugh, "Containment or Engagement? Calculating Beijing's Responses," *International Security* 19 (1996): 149–209).

12. V. Ferraro, "Globalizing Weakness: Is Global Poverty a Threat to the Interests of States?" *Environmental Change and Security Program (ECSP) Report*, no. 9 (2003): 13.

13. For a brief but insightful discussion of the cold war era, see R. J. McMahon, *The Cold War: A Very Short Introduction* (Oxford, UK: Oxford University Press, 2003).

14. There has been some broadening of the concept of security since the collapse of the Soviet Union, see D. Baldwin, "The Concept of Security," *Review of International Studies* 23 (1997): 5–26; D. Campbell, *Writing Security: United States Foreign Policy and the Politics of Identity* (Minneapolis, MN: University of Minnesota Press, 1998). For example, image and identity in the international context have gained more attention as part of a broader view of national strength.

15. In human security discussions about "food security," the focus is on "do we have enough to eat." But another approach to food security concerns agricultural bioterrorism. In the United States, "deliberate threats to agricultural plants and animals has involved organized groups opposed to the use of animals in research or opposed to genetic engineering of crops" (National Research Council, *Countering Agricultural Bioterrorism* (Washington, DC: The National Academies Press, 2003), 88).

16. D. Croxton, *Peacemaking in Early Europe: Cardinal Mazarin and the Congress of Westphalia, 1643–1648* (London: Associated University Presses, 1999), discusses the proceedings leading to the Peace of Westphalia, often wrongly referred to as the "Treaty" of Westphalia (there was more than one treaty).

17. J. Donne, *Devotions upon Emergent Occasions*, ed. A. Raspa (Montreal: McGill University Press, 1623/1975).

18. F. Delpeuch, B. Maire, E. Monnier, and M. Holdsworth, *Globesity: A Planet Out of Control?* (London: Earthspan Publications, 2009) reviews the evidence for "globesity."

19. See N. Myers and J. Kent, *The New Consumers* (Washington, DC: Island Press, 2004), for a highly informative discussion of "new consumers" around the world.

20. F. Hiatt (2007), "The Vanishing Foreign Correspondent." *The Washington Post*, Jan. 29, p. A15.

Part I

1. S. Freud (1900–1901), "The Interpretation of Dreams" (second part), in *The Standard Edition of the Complete Psychological Works of Sigmund Freud*, Vol. 5, ed. and trans. J. Strachey, 593 (London: Hogarth Press) (original work published 1953).

Chapter 2

1. J. J. Prinz, "Is Morality Innate?," in *Moral Psychology*, vol. 1., ed. E. Sinnott-Armstrong (A Bradford Book/MIT Press: Cambridge, MA/London, 2008), 375.

2. J. M. Callaghan and F. Kernic, "New Missions and Tasks for the 'Postmodern Military,'" in *Armed Forces and International Security: Global Trends and Issues*, ed. J. Callaghan and F. Kernic (New Brunswick, NJ and London: Transaction Publishers, 2003), 42.

3. D. Apgar, *Risk Intelligence: Learning to Manage What We Don't Know* (Boston: Harvard Business School Press, 2008), 3.

4. The literature on security risk assessment is both extensive and fast expanding. For broad discussions of security risk assessment, see B. E. Biringer, R. V. Matalucci, and S. L. O'Connor, *Security Risk Assessment and Management: A Professional Practice Guide for Protecting Buildings and Infrastructures* (New York: Wiley, 2007); J. F. Broder, *Risk Analysis and the Security Survey*, 3rd. ed. (Boston: Butterworth-Heinemann, 2006); Y. Y. Haimes, *Risk Modeling, Assessment, and Management*, 3rd. ed. (New York: Wiley, 2009); Kairab, S. *A Practical Guide to Security Assessments* (Boca Raton, FL: Auerbach Publications/Taylor & Francis, 2004); and K. Vellani, *Strategic Security Management: A Risk Assessment Guide for Decision Makers* (Amsterdam/Boston: Butterworth-Heinemann/Elsevier, 2007). Risk associated with the war on terror has been a particular focus (L. Amoore and M. de Goede, eds., *Risk and the War on Terror* (London: Routledge, 2008)), as has the global nature of threats in the twenty-first century (C. Abbott, P. Rogers, and J. Sloboda, *Beyond Terror: The Truth About the Real Threat to Our World* (London: Rider, 2006)). The most comprehensive overview with broad and very practically oriented coverage is probably provided by D. J. Landoll, *The Security Risk Assessment Handbook: A Complete Guide to Performing Security Risk Assessments* (Boca Raton, FL: Auerbach Publications/Taylor & Francis, 2005). The National Research Council has produced a critical but constructive report on bioterrorism. (National Academy Press, *Department of Homeland Security Bioterrorism Risk Assessment: A Call for Change* (Washington, DC: National Academy Press, 2008)). Not surprisingly given the geography of North America, a lot of attention has been given to the assessment of risk in coastal areas and harbors (e.g., see papers in I. Linkov, G. A. Kiker, and R. J. Wenning, eds., *Environmental Security in Harbors and Coastal Areas: Management Using Comparative Risk Assessment and Multi-Criteria Decision Analysis* (New York: Springer, 2007).

5. This phrase is from P. W. Singer, *Wired for War: The Robotics Revolution and Conflict in the 21st Century* (Harmondsworth, Middlesex, UK: Penguin HC, 2009). This is a highly engaging book on the changing face of war, as increasingly powerful robots, unmanned drones, and many other types of machinery become used in conflicts. The United States and other powerful countries are using this technology to fight wars, often against very poorly equipped third-world forces.

6. I am particularly thinking here of Gestalt psychologists, and their pioneering research on both perceptual organization and animal creativity (see

W. D. Ellis, *A Source Book of Gestalt Psychology* (London: Routledge and Kegan Paul, 1938). Through demonstrations on perception, such as by using the *Phi-Phenomenon*, and through animal research, such as studies showing that animals can demonstrate insight, Gestalt psychologists showed that the whole context has to be considered in order to best explain behavior.

7. J. J. Rousseau, *A Discourse on Inequality*, trans. M. Cranston (Harmondsworth, Middlesex, England: Penguin, 1754/1984).

8. The stag hunt and its wider implications have been extensively discussed by B. Skyrms (*The Stag Hunt and the Evolution of Social Structure* (Cambridge, UK: Cambridge University Press, 2004)).

9. These are discussed in the monumental treatise on human nature by D. Hume, *A Treatise on Human Nature* (Sioux Falls, SD: NuVision Publications, 1739/2008).

10. G. Hardin, "The Tragedy of the Commons," *Science* 162 (1968): 1243–1248.

11. The "tragedy of the commons" has resulted in closer attention being given to environmental policies and rights of ownership with respect to natural resources (for example, see discussions in D. W. Bromley, ed., *Making the Commons Work: Theory, Practice, and Policy* (San Francisco: ICS Press, 1992) and C. R. McManis, ed., *Biodiversity and the Law: Intellectual Property, Biotechnology, and Traditional Knowledge* (London: Earthscan, 2007).

12. For reviews of research on the prisoner's dilemma game during the height of the Cold War, see C. Nemeth, "A Critical Analysis of Research Utilizing the Prisoner's Dilemma Paradigm for the Study of Bargaining," in *Advances in Experimental Social Psychology*, vol. 6, 203–234, ed. L. Berkowitz (New York: Academic Press, 1972); A. Rapaport and A. M. Chammah, *Prisoner's Dilemma: A Study in Conflict and Cooperation* (Ann Arbor: University of Michigan Press, 1965).

13. The superior benefits of cooperation are also assumed in evolutionary theory (see J. J. Mansbridge, ed., *Beyond Self-Interest* (Chicago: University of Chicago Press, 1990).

14. For twenty-first century examples of the continued influence of the Prisoner's Dilemma Game, see R. Shiratori, K. Arai, and F. Kato, eds., *Gaming, Simulations, and Society: Research Scope and Perspective.* (New York: Springer, 2005). M. P. Marks, *The Prison as Metaphor: Re-examining International Relations* (New York: Peter Lang, 2004), offers a different way of using the prison as metaphor through which to view international relations.

15. J. G. Stoessinger, *Why Nations Go to War*, 10th ed. (Belmont, CA: Thomson Wadsworth, 2008), 293–294.

16. Examples of such 'illusions of control' are discussed in F. M. Moghaddam and C. Studer, "Cross-Cultural Psychology: The Frustrated Gadfly's Promises, Potentialities, and Failures," in *Handbook of Critical Psychology*, ed. D. Fox and I. Prillettensky (Newbury Park, CA: Sage Publications, 1997), 185–201 and refs.

17. I am thinking here particularly of work in the tradition of Sigmund Freud (1856–1939). Although the idea of the unconscious and irrationality had been discussed extensively before Freud (L.L. Whyte, *Unconscious before Freud* (New York: Basic Books, 1960)), it was through Freud's brilliant writings that

twentieth century humans gradually came to see themselves as conflicted and irrational. Of course, Freud has critics, particularly among those who present themselves as defenders of 'scientific psychology' and condemn Freud as 'unscientific'. For example, J. W. Kalat, *Introduction to Psychology*, 8th ed. (Belmont, CA: Thomson-Wadsworth, 2008) concludes that "Undeniably, Freud was a great pioneer in identifying new questions. The validity of his answers is less certain, however. He drew inferences from what his patients said and did without testing the validity of those inferences" (p. 537). In Freud's defense, it could be argued that Albert Einstein (1879–1955), perhaps the greatest scientist in modern times, developed theories without 'testing the validity of his inferences'. Einstein did not spend his time doing 'real' experiments, so presumably he is condemned as not being a "real" scientist.

18. I am thinking here particularly of experimental research on *implicit memory*, when a memory influences thoughts or actions without conscious awareness of the influence of the memory (for an experimental example, see D. A. Levy, C. E. L. Stark, and L. R. Squire, "Intact Conceptual Priming in the Absence of Declarative Memory," *Psychological Science* 15 (2004): 680–686; for a broader discussion, see D. L. Schacter, *Searching for Memory* (New York: Basic Books, 1996).

19. T. Riggs (2006), *Worldmark Encyclopedia of Religious Practices*, http://catalogue. nla.gov.av/Record/ 3127580. Thomas Riggs has edited a useful set of information about the variety of religious practices around the world. But there is also research exploring commonalities rather than differences across religions. For example, Harvey Whitehouse is leading an impressive international project to explain religion by reference to common features of religions, as well as their possible cognitive sources. See H. Whitehouse, *Explaining Religion*. Keynote paper presented at Inter-University Graduate Conference, London School of Economics and Political Science, London, 2009; H. Whitehouse and R. N. McCauley, eds., *Mind and Religion: Psychological and Cognitive Foundations of Religiosity* (Walnut Creek, CA: AltaMira Press, 2006).

20. P. Slovic, M. L. Finucane, E. Peters, and D. C. MacGregor, "Risk as Analysis and Risk as Feelings: Some Thought about Affect, Risk, and Rationality," *Risk Analysis* 24 (2004): 311–322.

21. G. Gigerenzer, "Dread Risk, September 11, and Fatal Traffic Accidents," *Psychological Science* 15 (2004): 286–287.

22. See the brief insightful discussion by M. M. Rothschild, "Terrorism and You: The Real Odds," *AEI-Brookings Joint Center: Policy Matters*, 1, no. 31 (2001): 1–2, which includes illuminating examples of how humans miscalculate risks, as well as C. R. Sunstein, "Terrorism and Probability Neglect," *Journal of Risk and Uncertainty* 26 (2003): 121–136.

23. W. Poortinga and N. F. Pidgeon, "Trust, the Asymmetry Principle, and the Role of Prior Beliefs," *Risk Analysis* 24 (2004): 1475–1486, have discussed the imbalance between the power of negative and positive information using the term *asymmetry principle*.

24. For a discussion of the experimental evidence supporting the idea of a negativity bias, see P. Rozin and E. B. Royzman, "Negativity Bias, Negativity

Dominance, and Contagion," *Personality and Social Psychology Review* 5 (2001): 296–320.

25. A good review of the seminal research on heuristics is found in D. Kahneman and A. Tversky, "On the Psychology of Prediction," *Psychological Review* 80 (1973): 237–251.

26. The confirmation bias was experimentally demonstrated about half a century ago by J. S. Bruner and M. C. Potter, "Interference in Visual Recognition," *Science* 144 (1964): 424–425.

27. Measures of the Authoritarian Personality were first developed by T. W. Adorno, E. Frenkel-Brunswik, D. J. Levinson, and B. W. Sanford, *The Authoritarian Personality* (New York: Harper & Row, 1950) and revised as the Right Wing Authoritarianism Scale by B. Altemeyer, *Right Wing Authoritarianism* (Winnipeg: University of Manitoba Press, 1981).

28. The modern personality measure of Machiavellianism was developed through research spearheaded by Richard Christie (1918–1992), and the items on this measure (see R. Christie and F. L. Geise, eds., *Studies in Machiavellianism* (New York: Academic Press, 1970), for details of the different versions of this scale) were derived through a process that began by using Niccolo Machiavelli's (1469–1527), *The Prince* (1513/1977), as the source.

29. The original Machiavellian intelligence hypothesis developed in the 1980s, and a second phase of research is reported in A. Whiten and R. A. Byrne, eds., *Machiavellian Intelligence II: Extensions and Evaluations* (Cambridge, UK: Cambridge University Press, 1997).

30. The term *ethnocentrism* was first introduced by William Sumner (1840–1910) in his book *Folkways* (Boston: Ginn, CA: Jossey-Bass, 1906), and the survey of ethnocentrism provided in 1971 by R. A. LeVine and D. T. Campbell, *Ethnocentrism: Theories of Conflict, Ethnic Attitudes, and Group Behavior* (New York: Wiley, 1971) is still very worth reading.

Chapter 3

1. The benefits of increasing specialization were highlighted by the economist Adam Smith (1723–1790), particularly in his monumental work *The Wealth of Nations* (New York: Prometheus Books, 1776/1991). Through divisions of labor, workers can be organized to be more productive. The benefits of specialization are most obvious in the organization of enormous factories in which each worker is responsible for a small task, and similarly in research centers where each researcher concentrates on a narrow problem. But increasing specialization is seldom critically questioned, and there is almost no attention given to the potential problems associated with the way in which specialization is taking place. For a more extensive discussion of the nature of specialization in the contemporary world, see F. M. Moghaddam, *The Specialized Society: The Plight of the Individual in an Age of Individualism*. New York: Praeger, 1997).

2. The broad field of human security is probably best reflected in the *Human Security Journal*. The sub-specialties within the broader field of security

studies are to some degree reflected in the specialized journals that are published, such as *Contemporary Security Policy, International Security, Journal of Military and Strategic Studies, Journal of Security Sector Management,* and *Human Security in Latin America, Security Dialogue.* A sub-specialty that looks at security from a peace perspective has also developed, as reflected in research published in journals such as *Journal of Peace Research, Journal of Conflict Resolution,* and *Peace Review.*

3. R. A. Mathew, *Resource Scarcity: Responding to the Security Challenge* (New York: International Peace Institute, 2008) provides a balanced overview of the ongoing debate about resource scarcity and security.

4. For example, as discussed by J. M. Coicaud and J. Jönsson, "From Foes to Bedfellows: Reconciling Security and Justice," *The Whitehead Journal of Diplomacy and International Relations* (Winter/Spring 2007): 21–32.

5. The idea that global poverty is an important factor in the national security of the United States was explicitly discussed in the 2002 *National Security Strategy of the United States* (Washington, DC: Government Printing Office).

6. For a basic overview of attachment research, see J. Cassidy and P. Shaver, eds., *Handbook of Attachment Theory and Research* (New York: Guildford Press, 1999); for explorations of attachment and relationships see W. Koops, J. B. Hoeksma, and D. C. Van den Boom, eds., *Development of Interaction and Attachment: Traditional and Non-traditional Approaches* (Amsterdam: North-Holland/Elsevier, 1997) and E. Waters and E. M. Cummings, "A Secure Base from Which to Explore Close Relationships," *Child Development* 71 (2000): 164–172.

7. The research on temperament has been spearheaded by Jerome Kagan; see J. Kagan, N. Snidman, D. Arcus, and J. S. Reznick, *Galen's Prophecy: Temperament in Human Nature* (New York: Basic Books, 1994).

8. We can trace a clear line of thinking from Charles Darwin, to Konrad Lorenz, to John Bowlby, and on to modern researchers focusing on the functional basis of attachment in humans and many other species. See Chapter 11 in F. M. Moghaddam, *Great Ideas in Psychology: A Cultural and Historical Introduction* (Oxford: Oneworld, 2005).

9. Eckhard H. Hess, *Imprinting: Early Experience and the Developmental Psychobiology of Attachment* (New York: D. Van Nostrand Reinhold, 1973) provides an excellent discussion of research by Lorenz (who wrote the foreword) and others on imprinting.

10. See H. F. Harlow, M. K. Harlow, and S. J. Soumi, "From Thought to Therapy: Lessons from a Primate Laboratory, *American Scientist* 59 (1971): 538–549. My friend Rom Harré, *Pavlov's Dogs and Schrödinger's Cat: Scenes from the Living Laboratory* (Oxford, UK: Oxford University Press, 2009, pp. 160–171) has written most insightfully, and critically, about Harlow.

11. See J. Bowlby, *Attachment and Loss.* Vol. 1, *Attachment* (New York: Basic Books, 1969); *Attachment and Loss.* Vol. 2, *Separation: Anxiety and Anger* (New York: Basic Books, 1973); *Attachment and Loss.* Vol. 3, *Loss: Sadness and Depression* (New York: Basic Books, 1980).

12. M. D. S. Ainsworth's *Infancy in Uganda* (Baltimore: Johns Hopkins University Press, 1967) pioneering research was conducted in Uganda.

13. There have been a number of challenges to the cultural validity of the strange situation research methodology. See K. Takahashi, "Are the Key Assumptions of the 'Strange Situation' Procedure Universal?," *Human Development* 33 (1990): 23–30. Even in the West, with two-career families becoming the "middle class norm," the concept of a single caretaker seems less appropriate.

14. See S. J. Suomi, "Behavioral Inhibition and Impulsive Aggressiveness: Insights from Studies with Rhesus Monkeys," in *Child Psychology: A Handbook of Contemporary Issues*, ed. L. Balter and C. S. Tamis-Lemonda, 510–525 (Philadelphia: Taylor & Francis, 1999).

15. This assertion is typically discussed in relation to case studies provided by clinicians, but there is also support from empirical studies that look at long-term trends in attachment; for example, see studies reported in K. E. Grossman, K. Grossman, and E. Waters, eds., *Attachment from Infancy to Adulthood: The Major Longitudinal Studies* (New York: Guildford Press, 2005).

16. See the discussion of "interobjectivity" and "intersubjectivity" in F. M. Moghaddam, "Interobjectivity: The Collective Roots of Individual Consciousness and Social Identity," in *Individuality and the Group: Advances in Social Identity*, ed. T. Postmes and J. Jetten, 155–174 (London: Sage, 2006).

17. Social comparison theory was formalized in its original form by L. Festinger, "A Theory of Social Comparison Processes," *Human Relations* 7 (1954): 117–140.

18. See the seminal papers by Maslow edited by R. J. Lowry, *Dominance, Self-Esteem, and Self-Actualization: Germinal Papers of A. H. Maslow* (Monterey, CA: Brooks/Cole, 1973).

19. C. P. Alderfer, *Existence, Relatedness, and Growth; Human Needs in Organizational Settings* (New York: Free Press, 1972).

20. M. Sherif, *The Psychology of Group Norms* (New York: Harper, 1936).

21. S. Asch, "Studies of Independence and Conformity: A Minority of One against a Unanimous Majority," *Psychological Monographs* 70, no. 9, (1956): 416.

22. See the papers in S. Moscovici, G. Mugny, and E. Van Avermaet, eds., *Perspectives on Minority Influence* (Cambridge, UK: Cambridge University Press, 1985).

23. As an example of the literature on the social construction of news, see P. C. Washburn, *The Social Construction of International News: We're Talking about Them, They're Talking about Us* (Westport, CT: Praeger, 2002).

24. Crime provides the classic example of how a social problem can be manufactured and manipulated for political purposes. See the readings in G. W. Potter and V. E. Kappeler, *Constructing Crime: Perspectives on Making News and Social Problems* (Long Grove, IL: Waveland Press, 2006).

25. Resource mobilization theory is an example of a materialist theory that assumes psychological processes are shaped by material forces (for example, see T. D. McCarthy and M. Wolfson, "Resource Mobilization by Local Social Movement Organizations: Agency, Strategy, and Organization in the Movement against Drunk Driving," *American Sociological Review* 61 (1996): 1070–1088).

26. In this discussion we should acknowledge the complex relationship between culture, biology, and weight (B. Dolan, "Cross-cultural Aspects of

Anorexia Nervosa and Bulimia: A Review," *Journal of American Academy of Child and Adolescent Psychiatry* 37 (1994): 802–809; E. Ravussin, M. E. Valencia, J. Esparza, P. H. Bennett, and L. O. Schulz, "Effects of a Traditional Lifestyle on Obesity in Pima Indians," *Diabetics Care* 17 (1994): 1067–1074).

27. M. C. Libicki, *Conquest in Cyberspace: National Security and Information Warfare* (Cambridge, U.K: Cambridge University Press, 2007), provides a dry but generally well-developed discussion of issues in the rapidly evolving field of cyber security. For a wider set of perspectives, see the readings in L. J. Janczewski and A. M. Colarik, *Cyber Warfare and Cyber Terrorism* (Hershey, PA: IGI Global, 2007).

28. M. A. Vatis, "Cyber Attacks: Protecting America's Security against Digital Attacks," in *Countering Terrorism: Dimensions of Preparedness*, ed. A. D. Howitt and R. L. Pangi, 219–249 (Cambridge, MA: MIT Press, 2003) points out that ". . . the line between state-sponsored information warfare and attacks by foreign civilians who oppose U.S. policy is not always easy to draw . . ." (p. 227).

29. G. Hardin, "The Tragedy of the Commons," *Science* 162 (1968): 1243–1248.

30. T. R. Malthus, *Essay on the Principle of Population as It Affects the Future Improvement of Society* (London: J. M. Dent., 1983).

31. See G. Hardin, "Extension of 'the Tragedy of the Commons,'" *Science* 280 (1998): 682–683, for a succinct discussion of how his concern with population growth led to his exploration of the "tragedy of the commons."

32. Of course, international trade is not the only factor impacting wages; technological innovations are also a major influence. See readings in R. C. Feenstra, *The Impact of International Trade on Wages* (Chicago: University of Chicago Press, 2000).

33. See discussions in F. Field, *China, India, and the United States: Competition for Energy Resources* (Abu Dhabi, United Arab Emirates: Emirates Center for Strategic Studies and Research, 2008).

34. David Sirota, *The Uprising: An Unauthorized Tour of the Populist Revolt Scaring Wall Street and Washington* (New York: Crown Publishers, 2008), provides a populist account of the revolt.

35. This is first discussed in F. M. Moghaddam, *The Individual and Society: A Cultural Integration* (New York: Worth, 2002).

Chapter 4

1. See R. L. Kugler, *Policy Analysis in National Security Affairs: New Methods for a New Era* (Washington, DC: National Defense University Press, 2006), for a reassessment of national security in the twenty-first century, with a broader conception of security that encompasses economic and political development. The broader view of security is reflected in teaching about security at a number of academic centers, such as at Canada's Simon Fraser University (see http:www.humansecuritygateway.info). There is also excellent teaching material

available through the Canadian Consortium on Human Security (see http://
www.humansecurity.info/#/teachinghumansecurity/4527270214). The idea that
global poverty is a security risk for the United States and other Western societies is directly reflected in the *Global Poverty Report* made public following the
G8 Okinawa Summit in 2000, as well as the 2002 *National Security Strategy of the
United States* (Washington, DC: Government Printing Office). http://www.adb
.org/documents/reports/global_poverty/2000/98_2000.pdf.

2. This criticism is applicable to the way security is discussed in the land-
mark 1994 United Nations Development Program's *Human Development Report*
(Retrieved Dec. 9, 2008, at http://hdr.undp.org/en/reports/global/hdr1994/
chapters) as well as to the Commission on Human Security's follow-up report
Human Security Now: Protecting and Empowering People (New York: United
Nations Publications, 2003). This broader view of human security has also been
explored in relation to conflict prevention. See D. H. Deudney and R. A.
Matthew, *Contested Grounds: Security and Conflict in the New Environmental Poli-
tics* (New York: State University of New York Press, 1999); C. L. Sriram and
Z. Nielsen, *Exploring Subregional Conflict: Opportunities for Conflict Prevention*
(Boulder, CO: Lynne Rienner Publishers, 2004).

3. The distinction between military and non-military factors is justified.
Although social capital and other "soft" factors are associated with military
strength, their impact on security is independent of the military.

4. This line of argument is directly influenced by the great Russian
researcher Lev Vygotsky, "All the higher functions originate in actual relationships between individuals" (*Mind in Society*, Cambridge, MA: Harvard University Press, 1978, p. 57).

5. Among the studies of societies that have disintegrated to an extent that
even particularized trust evaporated, Colin Turnbull's (*The Mountain People*,
New York: Simon & Schuster, 1972) case study of the Ik is particularly compelling. The Ik were a traditional hunting-and-gathering society who, because of
the creation of modern nation states and rigid national boundaries, became confined to one location in northern Uganda, near the border with Kenya. Deprived
of their traditional hunting-and-gathering life patterns, and unable to adapt to
the inhospitable land to which they were now confined, the Ik society fell apart
at the seams. The physical decline, "People crawled rather than walked—the
very young and the very old all crawled" (p. 222) was accompanied by a moral
decline, "The lack of any sense of moral responsibility toward each other, the
lack of any sense of belonging to, needing or wanting each other, showed up
daily and most clearly in what otherwise would have passed for familial relationships" (p. 218). Trust disappeared from even family relationships, and
family members failed to help one another and even stole food from other
starving family members.

6. See discussions in M. E. Warren, *Democracy & Trust* (Cambridge, UK:
Cambridge University Press, 1999).

7. It is in this regard that we can better understand the wider function of
torture carried out by government agencies: torture is adopted not so much to
acquire information, but to instill fear in populations. See F. M. Moghaddam,

"Interrogation Policy and American Psychology in Global Context," *Journal of Peace Psychology* 13 (2007): 437–443. Some governments are not unhappy for it to be known that their agents torture captured "enemies," because such knowledge can intimidate potential opposition movements, at home and abroad.

8. The term *commonsense justice* rather than *subjective justice* has sometimes been used as to distinguish "subjective" versus "objective" (black letter) aspects of law, but I prefer not to use this term because subjective justice is often far removed from common sense.

9. There has been a long tradition of research on human rights, with some attention given to the psychology of human rights (for an early empirical study, see F. M. Moghaddam and V. Vuksanovic, "Attitudes and Behavior toward Human Rights across Different Contexts: The Role of Right-Wing Authoritarianism, Political Ideology, and Religiosity," *International Journal of Psychology* 25 (1990): 455–474. However, just as there is no well-known "declaration of human duties," there is scant research on duties. An attempt was made to redress this imbalance and give more attention to duties by gathering available psychological research on both rights and duties, the resulting publication being N. Finkel and F. M. Moghaddam, eds., *The Psychology of Rights and Duties: Empirical Contributions and Normative Commentaries* (Washington, DC: American Psychological Association Press, 2004).

10. See T. R. Tyler and Y. J. Huo, *Trust in the Law* (New York: Russell Sage Foundation, 2002).

11. S. C. Wright, D. M. Taylor, and F. M. Moghaddam, "Responding to Membership in a Disadvantaged Group: From Acceptance to Collective Protest," *Journal of Personality and Social Psychology* 58 (1990): 994–1003.

12. Probably the best discussion of false consciousness and intergroup relations can be found in M. G. Billig, *Social Psychology and Intergroup Relations* (London: Academic Press, 1976).

13. This calculation was presented by the Nobel Prize winning economist Paul Krugman, (2006).

14. B. Ehrenreich, *Nickel and Dimed: On (Not) Getting on in America* (New York: Henry Holt, 2002), has received well deserved positive critical attention.

15. These statistics are part of a discussion about "executive pay" at a time when the United States federal government had to use billions of tax-payer dollars to prop up the private business sector in America (D. S. Hilzenrath, "Executive Pay," *The Washington Post* (Dec. 21, 2008): F1, F4.). Even during the worst economic downturn since the great depression about eighty years before, there was little relationship between executive pay and executive performance as reflected by company profits. A summary of world wealth is given by J. Berlin, "Millionaires' Club," *National Geographic* (November 2008), "... the population of those with a million U.S. dollars in assets, not including home value, rose most last year in ... India (up 23%) ... China (20%) ... Brazil (19%) and ... Russia (14%). They're joining the U.S. (The most millionaires total), Switzerland (most per capita), North America (per continent)" (unnumbered page).

16. The debate as to whether people are "ideological" in a consistent and important sense (see M. P. Fiorina, S. J. Abrams, and J. C. Pope, *Culture War? The*

Myth of a Polarized America, 2nd ed. (New York: Longman, 2006); J. T. Jost, "The End of the End of Ideology," *American Psychologist* 61 (2006): 651–670) has focused too much on ideology as an intra-personal characteristic associated with supposedly universal personality traits (see F. M. Moghaddam, *Great Ideas in Psychology: A Cultural and Historical Introduction* (Oxford, UK: Oneworld, 2005, Ch. 13). In this discussion, I am concerned with ideology as a social, collectively shared phenomenon.

17. I have no doubt that the monarchy in Iran would have lasted longer, and the chances for a transition to some form of open society would have improved, if (1) the Shah and his advisors had been more competent, and (2) American policies in the 1970s had been less shaped by the need to defeat communism at all costs, even at the cost of supporting Islamic fundamentalists to fight the communists in the Near and Middle East region. The long-term cost of American support for Islamic fundamentalism as a tactic to fight communism in the 1970s has not yet become fully clear, but what is clear is that the cost is extraordinarily high.

18. Typical of the traditional approach is a popular book by R. Brooks and S. Goldstein, *The Power of Resilience* (New York: McGraw Hill, 2004), a kind of self help for individuals to become more resilient. There have been a lot of these individual focused "cookbooks." A few authors have taken an interest in a more collective approach to resilience, such as in the family setting (F. Walsh, *Strengthening Family Resilience*, 2nd ed. (New York: The Guildford Press, 2006)) and at work (L. Rai, *Effectiveness in Workforce Development Collaboration—The Role of Leadership in Engendering Cooperative Capability, Collective Vision, and Collaborative Resilience* (Germany: VDM Verlag Dr. Mueller e.k., 2008)).

19. This is named after the then U.S. secretary of state George Marshall. Starting around 1947, The Marshall Plan involved substantial U.S. economic investment in countries such as France and Germany, and in some ways prepared the ground for the modern European Union. See readings in J. Agnew and J. N. Entrikin, *The Marshall Plan Today: Model and Metaphor* (London: Routledge, 2004).

20. See S. A. Carless and C. De-Paola, "The Measurement of Cohesion in Work Teams," *Small Group Research* 31 (2000): 71–88.

21. K. L. Dion, "Group Cohesion: From 'Field of Forces' to Multidimensional Construct," *Group Dynamics* 4, (2000): 7–26, has provided an insightful and broad discussion of the changes in thinking in research on cohesiveness.

22. See S. M. Gully, D. J. Devine, and D. Whitney, "A Meta-analysis of Cohesion and Performance: Effects of Level of Analysis and Task Interdependence," *Small Group Research* 26 (1995): 497–520.

23. The concept of "superordinate goals" was central to the intergroup research of the highly creative Turkish-American researcher Muzafer Sherif (1966).

24. As a general rule, out-group threat is associated with greater in-group cohesion. See K. L. Dion, "Intergroup Conflict and Intragroup Cohesiveness," in *The Social Psychology of Intergroup Relations* (211–224), W. G. Austin and S. Worchel, eds. (Pacific Grove, CA: Brooks/Cole, 1979). The Freudian model of

intergroup conflict gives central place to the idea that perceived threats from dissimilar out-groups help to nurture loving relationships within the in-group. See Chapter 3 in F. M. Moghaddam, *Multiculturalism and Intergroup Relations: Psychological Implications for Democracy in Global Context* (Washington, DC: American Psychological Association Press, 2008).

25. I. L. Janis, *Groupthink*, 2nd ed. (Boston: Houghton Mifflin, 1982) and *Crucial Decisions: Leadership in Policymaking and Crisis Management* (New York: Free Press, 1989) has done the most important pioneering work on groupthink.

26. The account provided by Plato (c.428–c.348 BC) of the trial, conviction, and death of Socrates (469–399 BC), provides an example of how altruism can be interpreted differently by different individuals. As Plato describes the events, friends and followers of Socrates put forward different plans for saving the master, who is accused of corrupting the minds of the young in Athens, and condemned to death. Socrates is to die in captivity by drinking poison; but there is time and opportunity for him to escape abroad. But Socrates refuses to flee, saying, "Where a man has once taken up his stand, either because it seems best to him or in obedience to his orders, there I believe he is bound to remain and face the danger, taking no account of death or anything else before dishonor." From the perspective of Socrates, his action is altruistic with respect to the larger humanity and the pursuit of truth, "When I leave this court I shall go away condemned by you to death, but they [my accusers] will go away convicted by Truth herself of depravity and wickedness. And they accept their sentence as I accept mine. No doubt it was bound to be so, and I think that the result is fair enough" (Plato, *The Last Days of Socrates*, trans. H. Tredennick (Baltimore, MD: Penguin Classics, 1959), p.73).

27. R. Dawkins (*The Selfish Gene*, 2nd ed. (Oxford, UK: Oxford University Press, 1989).

28. For further critical discussion of evolutionary accounts of human behavior, see F. M. Moghaddam, *Great Ideas in Psychology: A Cultural and Historical Introduction*. Oxford, UK: Oneworld, 2005, Ch. 19).

29. See particularly Chapter 2 in F. M. Moghaddam, *The Individual and Society: A Cultural Integration* (New York: Worth, 2002).

30. For example, see the readings in Y. Baumeister, *Self in Social Psychology* (New York: Psychology Press, 1999).

31. M. I. Handel, *Masters of War: Classical Strategic Thought*, 3rd ed. (London: Frank Cass, 2003), p. xviii.

32. J. D. Sachs, "The Strategic Significance of Global Inequality," *Environmental Change and Security Program (ECSP) Report* 9 (2003), p. 27.

33. P. Roberts, *The End of Oil: On the Edge of a Perilous New World* (New York: Houghton 2005), p. 248.

Part II

1. P. R. Ehrlich and A. H. Ehrlich, *The Dominant Animal: Human Evolution and the Environment* (Washington, DC: Island Press, 2008).

2. D. W. Orr, "The Ecology of Giving and Consuming," in *Consuming Desires: Consumption, Culture, and the Pursuit of Happiness*, ed. R. Rosenblatt, 137–154 (Washington, DC: Island Press, 1999).

3. "The Toxins Trickle Downward," *The Economist* (March 14–20, 2009): 62–63.

4. For a more extensive treatment, see the discussion of the "micro/macro universal law" of change, in F. M. Moghaddam, *The Individual and Society: A Cultural Integration*. New York: Worth, 2002.

Chapter 5

1. I. Shah, *The Pleasantries of the Incredible Mulla Nasrudin* (New York: Penguin, 1968), p. 82.

2. Many countries of the Near East and Middle East claim Mulla Nasrudin as their own (including Turkey, Iran, and Afghanistan), and the same stories about Nasrudin are told in the different languages of the region.

3. W. Whitman, *Leaves of Grass* (New York: Signet Classic, 1955), p. 89.

4. The first time the Shah had to flee was in 1953, when a coup orchestrated by the American Central Intelligence Agency (CIA) and the British Secret Intelligence Service (SIS) went wrong at first. The coup eventually succeeded in ousting the only democratically elected head of government in the history of Iran, Mohammad Mossadegh (1882–1967), and reinstated the Shah as dictator-monarch. Mossadegh's main "sin" was that he nationalized the Iranian oil industry, against the interests of British and American oil companies.

5. These propositions derive from social identity theory (H. Tajfel and J. C. Turner, "The Social Identity Theory of Intergroup Behavior," in *Psychology of Intergroup Relations*, ed. S. Worchel and W. G. Austin, 7–24 (Chicago: Nelson-Hall, 1986), which has stimulated hundreds of studies. See also Moghaddam, F. M. (2008), *Multiculturalism and Intergroup Relations: Psychological Implications for Democracy in Global Context*. (Washington, DC: American Psychological Association Press).

6. Shakespeare, W. (1996). *Hamlet* (ed. J. B. Spencer). London, UK: Penguin.

7. J. Swift, *Gulliver's Travels* (Boston: Houghton Mifflin, 1726/1960), p. 38.

8. Ibid., p. 39.

9. Ibid., pp. 39–40.

10. L. Tolstoy, *War and Peace*, trans. R. Edmonds, vol. 1. (Harmondsworth, UK.: Penguin, 1865-1868), p. 604.

11. Since the 1990s there has been a marked shift toward a more Vygotskian interpretation of human development with less emphasis on the independent individual treated as a biological entity. See F. M. Moghaddam, *Great Ideas in Psychology: A Cultural and Historical Introduction*, Ch. 10 (Oxford, UK: Oneworld, 2005). The influence of environmental conditions on human development is receiving greater attention from developmental scientists. See J. P. Shonkoff and D. A. Phillips, eds., *From Neurons to Neighborhoods: The Science of Early Childhood Development* (Washington, DC: National Academy Press, 2000).

12. The field of environmental psychology evolved from the late 1960s to explore the impact of place and the built environment on our cognition and social relationships. See P. A. Bell, T. E. Greene, J. D. Fisher, and A. Baum, *Environmental Psychology*, 5th ed. (Hillsdale, NJ: Lawrence Erlbaum, 2005), for an overview. In more recent years the power of place has been explored in relation to globalization trends, with H. de Blij, *The Power of Place: Geography, Destiny, and Globalization's Rough Landscape* (New York: Oxford University Press, 2008) arguing persuasively that despite all the talk about globalization and the world being "flat," where a person is born continues to play an important role in their future paths and behavior.

13. D. Belt, "Fast Lane to the Future: A New Superhighway Linking Its Four Major Cities Is Bringing Old and New India into Jarring Proximity," *National Geographic* (Oct. 2008): 78.

14. The most impressive research on this has been conducted by the British epidemiologist Michael Marmot, *The Status Syndrome: How Social Standing Affects Our Health and Longevity* (New York: Times Books/Henry Holt, 2004).

15. For discussions of the sex trade as part of the global economy, see K. Farr, *Sex Trafficking: The Global Market in Women and Children* (New York: Worth, 2004) and K. Siddharth, *Sex Trafficking: Inside the Business of Modern Slavery* (New York: Columbia University Press, 2008).

16. J. Schwartz, "Vocal Minority Insists It Was All Smoke and Mirrors," *The New York Times* (July 13, 2009): D8.

17. A. K. Cronin, "Cyber-mobilization: The New *Levée en Masse*," *Parameters* (Summer 2006): 77.

18. Homer-Dixon, T. (2006). *The Upside of Down: Catastrophe, Creativity, and the Renewal of Civilization.* Washington, DC: Island Press.

19. Quoted in M. Slackman, "Emirates See Fiscal Crisis as Chance to Save Culture," *The New York Times* (Nov 12, 2008): A5.

20. Ibid.

Chapter 6

1. Freud is the most influential thinker in the irrationalist tradition, arguing that 'becoming civilized' involves being socialized to repress certain basic instincts, so that the "civilized person" has lost certain "natural" forms of enjoyment, "The repressive activity of civilization brings it about that primary possibilities of enjoyment, which have . . . been repudiated by the censorship in us, are lost to us." (S. Freud, *Jokes and Their Relation to the Unconscious*, in *The Standard Edition of the Complete Psychological Works of Sigmund Freud*, ed. and trans. J. Strachey, vol. 8 (London: Hogarth Press, 1960, original work published 1905), p. 101). An example of a twenty-first century irrationalist model is Terror Management Theory (T. Pyszczynski, S. Solomon, and J. Greenberg, *In the Wake of 9/11: The Psychology of Terror* (Washington, DC: American Psychological Association Press, 2004).

2. Researchers in this camp used to work under the label "sociobiologists," but the label became unfashionable, in part because it took on politically incorrect connotations, and most of the research following the "genes cause behavior" line now come under the title "evolutionary psychology" (see J. A. Palmer and L. K. Palmer, *Evolutionary Psychology: The Ultimate Origins of Human Behavior* (Boston: Allyn & Unwin, 2002), for an overview).

3. I am thinking here of traditional cognitive science, which has dominated our view of human behavior since the 1950s, but has foundational flaws. See R. Harré, *Cognitive Science: A Philosophical Introduction* (London and Thousand Oaks, CA: Sage, 2002).

4. For an example of research in this tradition, see T. R. Tyler and Y. Huo, *Trust in the Law* (New York: Russell Sage Foundation, 2002).

5. These theories are reviewed in Moghaddam, F. M. (2008). *Multiculturalism and Intergroup Relations: Psychological Implications for Democracy in Global Context.* Washington, DC: American Psychological Association Press.

6. This research is discussed in M. Sherif, *Group Conflict and Cooperation: Their Social Psychology* (London: Routledge & Kegan Paul, 1966).

7. This realist view about the causal link between competition for scarce resources and conflict is clearly reflected in the more recent "green" literature on the environment; for example, see Jacqueline Vaughn, *Conflicts over Natural Resources: A Reference Handbook* (Santa-Barbara, CA: ABC-CLIO, 2007).

8. D. Seckler and U. Amarasinghe, "Major Problems in the Global Water-Food Nexus," in *Perspectives in World Food and Agriculture,* ed. C. G. Scanes and J. A. Miranowski (Ames, IA: Iowa State Press, 2004).

9. A lot of useful information about water use in the United States can be found on an Environmental Protection Agency (EPA) Web site, http://www.epa.gov/watersense/pubs/index.htm (Retrieved June 12, 2009).

10. The competition for scarce non-renewable resources suggests there is a limit to growth, but there is disagreement about when this limit is reached (for some assessments, see readings in D. Pirages and K. Cousins, *From Resource Scarcity to Ecological Security: Exploring New Limits to Growth* (Cambridge, MA: MIT Press, 2005).

11. The policies of both world and regional powers in the Near and Middle East are very much shaped by the value of oil and gas reserves in the region (see readings in L. C. Brown, ed., *Diplomacy in the Middle East: The International Relations of Regional and Outside Powers* (London: I. B. Tauris, 2001).

12. Saint Sir T. More, *Utopia* (Cambridge, UK, and New York: Cambridge University Press, 1516/1988).

13. K. Marx, "The Eighteenth Brumaire of Louis Bonaparte," in *Collected Works of Karl Marx and Frederick Engels,* vol. 11, 99–197 (London: Lawrence and Wishart, 1979, original work published 1852); K. Marx and F. Engels, *Communist Manifesto* (New York: Pantheon, 1967, original work published 1848).

14. Classic elite theory is best represented in the work of V. Pareto, *The Mind and Society: A Treatise on General Sociology,* 4 vols. (New York: Dover, 1935). A version of elite theory more compatible with democracy is presented by G. Mosca, *The Ruling Class* (New York: McGraw Hill, 1939).

15. J. Sidanius, F. Pratto, C. van Laar, and S. Levin, "Social Dominance Theory: Its Agenda and Method," *Political Psychology* 25 (2004): 845–880.

16. J. T. Jost, M. R. Banaji, and B. A. Nosek, "A Decade of System Justification Theory: Accumulated Evidence for Conscious and Unconscious Bolstering of the Status Quo," *Political Psychology* 25 (2004): 881–919.

17. S. C. Wright, D. M. Taylor, and F. M. Moghaddam, "Responding to Membership in a Disadvantaged Group: From Acceptance to Collective Protest," *Journal of Personality and Social Psychology* 58 (1990): 994–1003.

18. For example, see F. Devine, *Social Class in America and Britain* (Edinburgh: University of Edinburgh Press, 1997).

19. "The Toxins Trickle Downward," *The Economist* (March 14–20, 2009): 62–63.

20. D. Cobble, "Historical Perspectives on Representing Nonstandard Workers," in *Nonstandard Work,* 291–312, ed. F. Carré, M. A. Ferber, L. Golden, and S. A. Herzenberg (Ithaca, NY: Cornell University Press, 2000).

21. For further discussions of the growth of nonstandard work, see the discussions in F. Carré, M. A. Ferber, L. Golden, and S. A. Herzenberg, eds., *Nonstandard Work* (Ithaca, NY: Cornell University Press, 2000).

22. This is the title of an excellent book by A. Ross, *Nice Work If You Can Get It: Life and Labor in Precarious Times* (New York: New York University Press, 2009), discussing the new labor market and the spread of nonstandard work.

23. Alex Ehrlich of the Swiss bank UBS, quoted on the front page (p. A1) of *The New York Times,* Thurs. Oct. 2, 2008.

24. "World on the Edge," *The Economist* (Oct. 4–10, 2008): 11–12.

25. N. Kulish, "Crisis Jolts Poland, and Other Go-Go Markets," *The New York Times* (October 27, 2008): 1.

26. P. Krugman, "Falling Wage Syndrome," *The New York Times* (May 4, 2009): A23.

Chapter 7

1. This issue is thoughtfully discussed by J. Fox, "World Separation of Religion and State in the 21st Century," *Comparative Political Studies* 39 (2006): 537.

2. See B. Altemeyer, "The Decline of Organized Religion in Western Civilization," *International Journal for the Psychology of Religion* 14 (2004): 77–89, for a discussion of the decline in religion in Western societies.

3. J. Fox, *Ethnoreligious Conflict in the Late Twentieth Century: A General Theory* (Lanham, MD: Lexington Books, 2002).

4. P. L. Berger, "Secularism in Retreat," *The National Interest* 46 (1996/1997): 3.

5. These apparently competing trends are reflected in discussions about religion and conflict. For example, see R. S. Appleby, *The Ambivalence of the Sacred: Religion, Violence, and Reconciliation,* Carnegie Commission on Preventing Deadly Conflict Series (Lanham, MD: Rowman & Littlefield, 2000); D. Little, ed., *Peacemakers in Action: Profiles of Religion in Conflict Resolution* (Cambridge, UK: Cambridge University Press, 2007); and P. Mojzes, ed., *Religion and the War in Bosnia* (Atlanta, GA: Scholars Press, 1998).

6. B. Hunsberger and L. M. Jackson, "Religion, Meaning, and Prejudice," *Journal of Social Issues* 61 (2005): 807–826.

7. L. M. Jackson and B. Hunsberger, "An Intergroup Perspective on Religion and Prejudice," *Journal for the Scientific Study of Religion* 38 (1999): 509–523.

8. See the readings in T. Banchoff, ed., *Democracy and the New Religious Pluralism* (Oxford, UK: Oxford University Press, 2007), pp. 3–16.

9. C. Kimball, *When Religion Becomes Evil* (San Francisco: HarperCollins, 2002).

10. D. G. Myers, *The Pursuit of Happiness* (New York: Avon, 1993), provides an excellent exploration of happiness and points out the role of religion in reported happiness.

11. S. Dein and K. M. Loewenthal, "Holy Healing: The Growth of Religious and Spiritual Therapies," *Mental Health, Religion & Culture* 1 (1998): 85–89.

12. S. Sembhi and S. Dein, "The Use of Traditional Healers by Asian Psychiatric Patients in the UK: A Pilot Study," *Mental Health, Religion & Culture* 1 (1998): 127–133, discuss the example of Asian psychiatric patients in the United Kingdom using traditional healers.

13. For example, see R. F. Baumeister, "Religion and Psychology: Introduction to the Special Issue," *Psychological Inquiry* 13 (2002): 165–267; and P. C. Hill and K. I. Pargament, "Advances in the Conceptualization and Measurement of Religion and Spirituality," *American Psychologist* 58 (2003): 64–74.

14. Robert Wright, *The Evolution of God* (New York: Little, Brown, 2009) has described the evolution of our ideas about God.

15. I. Silberman (2005), "Religion as a Meaning System: Implications for the New Millennium." *Journal of Social Issues,* 61, 641-664.

16. For example, see the discussions in T. R. Sarbin, ed., *Narrative Psychology: The Storied Nature of Human Conduct* (New York: Praeger, 1986).

17. J. F. Haught, *Science & Religion: From Conflict to Conversation* (New York: Paulist Press, 1995), p. 203.

18. F. Close, *Nothing: A Very Short Introduction* (New York: Oxford University Press, 2009).

19. C. W. M. Hart, A. R. Pilling, and J. C. Goodale, *The Tiwi of Northern Australia* (Belmont, CA: Wadsworth, 2001), p. 17.

20. R. F. Fortune, *Sorcerers of Dobu* (Prospect Heights, IL: Waveland Press, 1989 (originally published 1932), p.238).

21. N. Chagnon, *Yanomamo*, 5th ed. (New York: Harcourt Brace, 1997), p. 104.

22. Ibid.

23. See particularly Chapter 11 in C. Benson, *The Cultural Psychology of the Self: Place, Morality and Art in Human Worlds* (London: Routledge, 2001).

24. M. Waddell, *Stories from the Bible: Old Testament Stories Retold* (New York: Ticknor & Fields, 1993), p. 8.

25. Grimm's fairy tales have been published in almost countless editions and in numerous languages around the world. A very affordable Barnes & Noble edition was published in 2003: *Grimm's Fairy Tales* (Barnes & Noble Classics Series), ed. E. Dalton (New York: Barnes & Noble Books, 2003).

26. F. M. Moghaddam, R. Harré, and N. Lee, eds., *Global Conflict Resolution through Positioning Analysis* (New York: Springer, 2008).

27. M. Bekoff, *Wild Justice and Fair Play: Cooperation, Forgiveness, and Morality in Animals* (Chicago: University of Chicago Press, 2005).

28. J. R. Seul "'Ours Is the Way of God': Religion, Identity, and Intergroup Conflict," *Journal of Peace Research* 36 (1999): 558.

29. F. M. Moghaddam, *Multiculturalism and Intergroup Relations: Psychological Implications for Democracy in Global Context* (Washington, DC: American Psychological Association Press, 2008).

30. See F. M. Moghaddam, *Multiculturalism and Intergroup Relations: Psychological Implications for Democracy in Global Context* (Westport CT: Praeger Security International, 2008, pp. 31-32).

31. For example, see J. M. Nelson, *Psychology, Religion, and Spirituality* (New York: Springer, 2009).

32. S. Y. Mitchem and E. M. Townes, eds., *Faith, Health, and Healing in African American Life* (Westport, CT: Praeger, 2008).

33. F. M. Moghaddam (*The Individual and Society: A Cultural Integration* (New York: Worth, 2002)).

34. M. A. Vasquez, A. L. Peterson, and P. J. Williams, eds., *Christianity, Social Change, and Globalization in the Americas* (Piscataway, NJ: Rutgers University Press, 2001).

35. Moghaddam, F. M. (2006), *How Globalization Spurs Terrorism: The Lopsided Benefits of "One World" and Why That Fuels Violence* (Westport, CT: Praeger Security International).

Chapter 8

1. For a historical and international review of torture, see D. Rejali, *Torture and Democracy* (Princeton, NY: Princeton University Press, 2007). A more focused discussion of torture carried out under successive U.S. government administrations is provided by M. Otterman, *American Torture: From the Cold War to Abu Ghraib and beyond* (Carlton, Victoria, Australia: Melbourne University Press, 2007), and under the George W. Bush administration specifically by P. Sands, *Torture Team: Rumsfeld's Memo and the Betrayal of American Values* (New York: Palgrave Macmillan, 2008).

2. I have previously provided a formal definition of terrorism as "politically motivated violence, perpetrated by individuals, groups, or state-sponsored agents, intended to bring about feelings of terror and helplessness in a population in order to influence decision-making and to change behavior" (F. M. Moghaddam, *From the Terrorists' Point of View: What They Experience and Why They Come to Destroy* (Westport, CT: Praeger Security International, 2006), p. 9.) This definition also fits torture.

3. The readings in A. F. Lang, Jr. and A. Russell Beattie, eds., *War, Torture, and Terrorism: Rethinking the Rules of International Security* (London: Routledge, 2009), reflect some of the attention being given to the common security challenges posed by twenty-first century torture and terrorism.

4. The "ticking bomb" scenario has received a great deal of critical attention, such as in Y. Ginbar, *Why Not Torture Terrorists? Moral, Practical, and Legal*

Aspects of the "Ticking Bomb" Justification (New York: Oxford University Press, 2008).

5. The controversial legal scholar Alan Dershowitz, *Why Terrorism Works: Understanding the Threat, Responding to the Challenge* (New Haven, CT: Yale University Press, 2002), is the most prominent person making this argument, putting forward the case that (1) torture is justified under certain extraordinary "ticking bomb" scenario circumstances and (2) it is better to make torture legal under certain extraordinary circumstances, because then it can be monitored and controlled.

6. Mirko Bagaric and Julie Clarke, *Torture: When the Unthinkable Is Morally Permissible* (Albany, NY: State University of New York Press, 2007), set out the case for torture in a straightforward, some would say radical, manner. Particularly see Chapters 5, 6, and 7, in which they argue that torture is under certain conditions a "humane" practice, that it is effective, and that it is not antidemocratic.

7. A question included in surveys by the Pew Research Center for the People & the Press since 2004 is the following: "Do you think the use of harsh interrogation techniques, including torture, has ever saved American lives since the September 11 (2001) terrorist attacks on the World Trade Center and the Pentagon?" Almost half of the American population has responded "yes" to this question. However, it is not clear how many of these Americans were persuaded to say "yes" as a result of government "propaganda" programs.

8. I am thinking in particular of failure of the American press to report objectively during the weapons of mass destruction fiasco leading to the U.S.-led invasion of Iraq. It is extraordinary that during the pre-war propaganda build up by the George W. Bush administration, so little critical attention was given by the American press to the claim that Iraq had amassed weapons of mass destruction.

9. P. Sands, *Torture Team: Rumsfeld's Memo and the Betrayal of American Values* (New York: Palgrave Macmillan, 2008).

10. B. Lincoln, *Religion, Empire and Torture: A Case of Achaemenian Persia, with a Postscript on Abu Ghraib* (Chicago: University of Chicago Press, 2007), provides an analysis of the use of torture by Achaemenian Persia, linking his study to twenty-first century American experiences in dealing with terror suspects.

11. See particularly Chapter 1 in F. M. Moghaddam, *From the Terrorists' Point of View: What They Experience and Why They Come to Destroy* (Westport, CT: Praeger Security International, 2006).

12. For example, see Chapter 10 in M. Bagaric and J. Clarke, *Torture: When the Unthinkable Is Morally Permissible* (Albany, NY: State University of New York Press, 2007). They conclude that as far as torture is concerned, "the ends justify the means."

13. R. Baraheni, *The Crowned Cannibals: Writings on Repression in Iran* (New York: Vintage Books, 1977), p. 133.

14. Particularly after 2006, the leadership of the American Psychological Association came under increasing pressure to change its official position on the issue of torture, and to explicitly ban the participation of its members in any

"enhanced interrogation techniques" that do not meet the international standards of what constitutes torture.

15. This is the title of a highly insightful book by Dexter Filkins, *The Forever War* (New York: Alfred A. Knopf, 2008), exploring the folly of the U.S. launching an endless "war on terror."

16. S. Freud, "Group Psychology and the Analysis of the Ego," in *The Standard Edition of the Complete Psychological Works of Sigmund Freud*, ed. and trans. J. Strachey, vol. 18, 67–143, (London: Hogarth Press; (1921/1955; original work published 1921).

17. J. Dollard, L. Doob, N. Miller, O. Mowrer, and R. Sears, *Frustration and Aggression* (New Haven, CT: Yale University Press, 1939).

18. For an indication of the new direction of research, see N. Miller, W. C. Pederson, M. Earlywine, and V. E. Pollock, "A Theoretical Model of Triggered Displaced Aggression," *Personality and Social Psychology Review* 7 (2003): 75–97.

19. E. Stover and E. O. Nightingale, "Introduction," in *The Breaking of Bodies and Bones: Torture, Psychiatric Abuse, and the Health Professions,* ed. E. Stover and E. O. Nightingale (New York: W. H. Freeman, 1985), p. 7.

20. J. M. Darley and T. S. Pittman, "The Psychology of Compensatory and Retributive Justice," *Personality and Social Psychology Review* 7 (2003): 324–336, explore this aspect of retributive justice. See also K. M. Carlsmith and J. M. Darley, "Psychological Aspects of Retributive Justice," in *Advances in Experimental Social Psychology*, ed. M. P. Zanna, vol. 40, 193–236 (San Diego: Elsevier, 2008).

21. P. Liberman, "An Eye for an Eye: Public Support for War against Evildoers," *International Organization* 60 (2006): 687–722.

22. K. M. Carlsmith and A. M. Sood, "The Fine Line between Interrogation and Retribution," *Journal of Experimental Social Psychology* 45 (2009): 191–196.

23. K. M. Carlsmith, "The Roles of Retribution and Utility in Determining Punishment," *Journal of Experimental Social Psychology* 42 (2006): 437–451.

24. The modern version of this theory was developed by M. J. Lerner, *The Belief in a Just World: A Fundamental Delusion* (New York: Plenum Press, 1980). See C. L. Hafer and L. Bègue, "Experimental Research on Just-World Theory: Problems, Developments, and Future Challenges," *Psychological Bulletin* 131 (2005): 128–167, for more recent developments.

25. L. E. Fletcher and E. Stover, *Guantánamo and Its Aftermath: U.S. Detention and Interrogation Practices and Their Impact on Former Detainees* (University of California, Berkeley: Human Rights Center and International Human Rights Law Clinic, 2008), p. 44.

26. The pioneering research on authoritarians was carried out following the Second World War (T. W. Adorno, E. Frenkel-Brunswik, D. J. Levinson, and B. W. Sanford, *The Authoritarian Personality* (New York: Harper & Row, 1950). The more recent research has been spearheaded by Bob Altemeyer, "Reducing Prejudice in Right-Wing Authoritarians," in *The Psychology of Prejudice: The Ontario Symposium*, ed. M. P. Zanna and J. M. Olson, Vol. 7, 131–148 (Hillsdale, NJ: Lawrence Erlbaum, 1994).

27. B. Crossette, "Voice: Sri Lanka, the Destruction of South Asia's Most Developed Society," *Journal of Aggression, Maltreatment & Trauma* 9 (2004): 229.

For a more in-depth assessment of the conflict in Sri Lanka, see A. Bandarage *The Separatist Conflict in Sri Lanka: Terrorism, Ethnicity, Political Economy* (London: Routledge, 2009).

28. In contexts such as Sri Lanka, where terrorism is being used by a power minority in their fight for independence, some would claim that I am misusing the term *terrorists* to describe *freedom fighters*. I reject this criticism. It is not the end goal that determines whether or not a bomb attack is a terrorist attack or not; just because a bomb attack is part of a fight for independence does not mean it qualifies as an act of a freedom fighter rather than a terrorist. Terrorism is characterized by such things as the target and immediate goal; it is politically motivated violence, very often targeted at civilians, and intended to bring about feelings of terror and helplessness among a people in order to influence decision-making and to change behavior. (See F. M. Moghaddam, 2006, p. 9, *From the Terrorist Point of View: What They Experience and Why They Come to Destroy,* Westport, CT: Praeger Security International).

29. P. R. Ehrlich and A. H. Ehrlich, *The Dominant Animal: Human Evolution and the Environment* (Washington, DC: Island Press, 2008), p. 8.

30. F. M. Moghaddam, *From the Terrorist Point of View: What They Experience and Why They Come to Destroy* (Westport, CT: Praeger Security International, 2006).

31. L. Cavalli-Sforza, P. Menozzi, and A. Piazza, *The History and Geography of Human Genes* (Princeton, NJ: Princeton University Press, 1994).

32. S. Wells, *The Journey of Man: A Genetic Odyssey* (Princeton, NJ: Princeton University Press, 2002).

33. C. Darwin, *The Origin of Species by Means of Natural Selection or the Preservation of Favored Races in the Struggle for Life* (New York: The Modern Library, 1993 (original work published 1859)), pp. 385–386.

34. M. S. Rodriguez and A. T. Grafton, *Migration in History: Human Migration in Comparative Perspective* (Rochester, NY: Rochester University Press), 2007.

35. P. R. Ehrlich, *Human Natures: Genes, Cultures, and the Human Prospect* (Washington, DC: Island Press, 2000).

36. See discussions in R. M. Miller, ed., *Germans in America: Retrospect and Prospect* (Philadelphia: The German Society of Philadelphia, 1984).

37. R. E. Park, *Race and Culture* (Glencoe, IL: Free Press, 1950).

38. D. Crystal, *Language Death* (Cambridge, UK: Cambridge University Press, 2000; A. Dalby, *Language in Danger: The Loss of Linguistic Diversity and the Threat to Our Future* (New York: Columbia University Press, 2003).

39. F. M. Moghaddam, *From the Terrorist Point of View: What They Experience and Why They Come to Destroy* (Westport, CT: Praeger Security International, 2006).

Chapter 9

1. See E. D. Weitz, *A Century of Genocide: Utopias of Race and Nation* (Princeton, NJ: Princeton University Press, 2003).

2. F. M. Moghaddam, *How Globalization Spurs Terrorism* (Westport, CT: Praeger Security International, 2008).

3. For example, P. R. Ehrlich, *Human Natures: Genes, Cultures, and the Human Prospect* (Washington, DC: Island Press, 2000).

4. For example, I. Deutscher, *Accommodating Diversity: National Policies That Prevent Ethnic Conflict* (Lanham, MD: Lexington Books, 2002).

5. For example, Walzer, M. (1997), *On Toleration* (New Haven, CT: Yale University Press).

6. See I. Cuellar and F. A. Paniagua, *Handbook of Multicultural Mental Health: Assessment and Treatment of Diverse Populations* (San Diego: Academic Press, 2000); L. A. Suzuki, J. G. Ponterotto, and P. J. Meller, eds., *Handbook of Multicultural Assessment: Clinical, Psychological, and Educational Applications*, 2nd ed. (San Francisco: Jossey-Bass, 2001).

7. See C. A. Grant and J. L. Lei, eds., *Global Constructions of Multicultural Education: Theories and Reality* (Mahwah, NJ: Lawrence Erlbaum, 2001); C. A. McGee Banks and J. A. Banks, *Multicultural Education*, 6th ed. (John Wiley & Sons, 2008).

8. F. M. Moghaddam (2008), *Multiculturalism and Intergroup Relations: Psychological Implications for Democracy in Global Context* (Washington, DC: American Psychological Association Press, 2008).

9. W. E. Lambert and D. M. Taylor, *Coping with Cultural and Racial Diversity in Urban America* (New York: Praeger, 1990); C. Taylor, "The Politics of Recognition," in *Multiculturalism and "the Politics of Recognition,"* ed. A. Guttman, 25–73 (Princeton, NJ: Princeton University Press, 1992).

10. "Omni" (Latin origin) means all, and the term *omniculturalism* indicates "cultural characteristics shared by everyone."

11. M. Sherif, *Group Conflict and Cooperation: Their Social Psychology* (London: Routledge & Kegan Paul, 1966).

12. For examples, see S. L. Gaertner and J. F. Dovidio, *Reducing Intergroup Bias: The Common Ingroup Identity Model* (Philadelphia: Psychology Press, 2000); J. A. Richeson and R. J. Nussbaum, "The Impact of Multiculturalism versus Color-Blindness on Racial Bias," *Journal of Experimental Social Psychology* 40 (2004): 417–423.

13. I. Zangwill, *The Melting Pot: Drama in Four Acts* (New York: Macmillan, 1909), p. 37.

14. Moghaddam (2008, p. 132).

15. Of course, Zangwill (*The Melting Pot,* 1909) only mentions "The races of Europe" (p. 37), excluding people of African and Asian descent, among others.

16. The most prominent representative of this groups is R. E. Park, *Race and Culture* (Glencoe, IL: Free Press, 1950).

17. See R. Alba and V. Nee, "Rethinking Assimilation Theory for a New Era of Immigration," *International Migration Review* 31 (1997): 826–874, for arguments and evidence in favor of assimilation in the modern era.

18. R. Putnam, *Bowling Alone: The Collapse and Revival of American Community* (New York: Simon & Schuster, 2000).

19. F. M. Moghaddam, *Multiculturalism and Intergroup Relations: Psychological Implications for Democracy in Global Context* (Washington, DC: American Psychological Association Press, 2008).

20. C. Paraskevopoulos, P. Getimis, and N. Rees, *Adapting to EU Multi-level Governance: Regional and Environmental Policies in Cohesion and CEE Countries* (Aldershot, England; Burlington, VT: Ashgate, 2006).

21. W. G. Allport *The Nature of Prejudice* (Cambridge, MA: Addison-Wesley, 1954).

22. Tropp, L. R. and Pettigrew, T. F. (2005). "Relationships Between Intergroup Content and Prejudice Among Minority and Majority Status Groups." *Psychological Science*, 16, 951-957.

23. T. F. Pettigrew and L. R. Tropp, "Does Outgroup Contact Reduce Prejudice? Recent Meta-analytic Findings," in *Reducing Prejudice and Discrimination: Social Psychological Perspectives*, ed. S. Oskamp, 93–114 (Mahwah, NJ: Erlbaum, 2000); F. Pettigrew and L. R. Tropp, "A Meta-analytic Test of Intergroup Contact Theory," *Journal of Personality and Social Psychology* 90 (2006): 751–783.

24. R. B. Zajonc, "Attitudinal Effects of Mere Exposure," *Journal of Personality and Social Psychology* 9 (2, Pt. 2) (1968): 1–27.

25. For an example of this research, see A. Eller and D. Abrams, "'Gringos' in Mexico: Cross-sectional and Longitudinal Effects of School-Promoted Contact in Intergroup Bias," *Group Processes & Intergroup Relations* 6 (2003): 55–75.

26. For a more in-depth discussion of catastrophic evolution, see F. M. Moghaddam, "Catastrophic Evolution, Culture, and Diversity Management Policy," *Culture & Psychology* 12 (2006): 415-434.

27. From among numerous examples, see L. Ryan, *The Aboriginal Tasmanians*, 2nd ed. (St. Leonards, Australia: Allen & Unwin, 1996), regarding the case of Tasmanians.

28. For research on the relationship between similarity and attraction, see D. Byrne, *The Attraction Paradigm* (New York: Academic Press, 1971); E. Berscheid and H. T. Reis. "Attraction and Close Relationships," in *The Handbook of Social Psychology*, ed. D. T. Gilbert, S. T. Fiske, and G. Lindzey, Vol. 2, 4th ed., 193–281, (New York: McGraw-Hill, 1998).

29. R. A. Neimeyer and K. A. Mitchell, "Similarity and Attraction: A Longitudinal Study," *Journal of Social and Personality Relationships* 5 (1988): 131–148.

30. One of the few studies that directly tested the similarity-attraction hypothesis in a multicultural context at the intergroup level is L. Osbeck, F. M. Moghaddam, and S. Perreault, "Similarity and Attraction among Majority and Minority Groups in a Multicultural Context," *International Journal of Intercultural Relations* 219 (1997): 113–123.

31. S. Freud, "Civilization and Its Discontents," in *The Standard Edition of the Complete Psychological Works of Sigmund Freud*, ed. and trans. J. Strachey, Vol. 21, 64–145 (London: Hogarth Press, 1961), p. 114. Original work published 1930.

32. This research was pioneered by Henri Tajfel, Michael Billig, John Turner, and others (H. Tajfel, ed., *Differentiation between Social Groups* (London: Academic Press, 1978); H. Tajfel, C. Flament, M. Billig, and R. F. Bundy, "Social Categorization and Intergroup Behaviour," *European Journal of Social Psychology* 1 (1971): 149–177.

33. W. J. Wilson and R. P. Taub, *There Goes the Neighborhood: Racial, Ethnic, and Class Tensions in Four Chicago Neighborhoods and Their Meaning for America* (New York: Knopf, 2006).

34. C. Krauthammer, "In Plain English: Let's Make It Official," *Time* (June 12, 2006): 112.

35. J. D. Stephens, "Capitalist Development and Democracy: Empirical Research on the Social Origins of Democracy," in *The Idea of Democracy*, ed. D. Copp, J. Hampton, and J. E. Roemer, 409–446 (New York: Cambridge University Press, 1993); D. Welsh, "Domestic Politics and Ethnic Conflict," in *Ethnic Conflict and International Security*, ed. M. E. Brown, 43–60 (Princeton, NJ: Princeton University Press, 1993).

36. D. L. Horowitz, "Democracy in Divided Societies," *Journal of Democracy* 4 (1993): 18–38.

37. See M. S. Fish and R. S. Brooks, "Does Diversity Hurt Democracy? *Journal of Democracy* 15 (2004): 154–166.

38. E. D. Hirsch, Jr., *Cultural Literacy: What Every American Needs to Know* (New York: Vintage Books, 1988).

39. S. J. Ceci and P. B. Papierno, "The Rhetoric and Reality of Gap Closing: When the 'Have-Nots' Gain But the 'Haves' Gain Even More," *American Psychologist* 60 (2005): 149–160.

40. M. H. Bornstein and R. H. Bradley, *Socioeconomic Status, Parenting, and Child Development* (Mahwah, NJ: Erlbaum, 2003).

41. See F. M. Moghaddam, *How Globalization Spurs Terrorism* (Westport, CT: Praeger Security International, 2008), pp. 41–43, for the United States context.

42. N. Glazer and D. P. Moynihan, *Beyond the Melting Pot*, 2nd ed. (Cambridge, MA: MIT Press, 1970).

43. J. W. Berry, R. Kalin, and D. M. Taylor, *Multiculturalism and Ethnic Attitudes in Canada* (Ottawa, Ontario, Canada: Supply and Services Canada, 1977).

44. For example, see W. Tseng, *Culture and Psychopathology: A Guide to Clinical Assessment* (New York: Routledge, 1997).

45. R. Mahalingam and C. McCarthy, *Multicultural Curriculum: New Directions for Social Theory, Practice, and Policy* (New York: Routledge, 2000).

46. J. R. Logan, W. Zhang, and R. D. Alba, "Immigrant Enclaves and Ethnic Communities in New York and Los Angeles," *American Sociological Review* 67 (2002): 299–322.

47. Multiculturalism has been supported by researchers arguing it to be superior on moral and ethical groups (e.g., B. J. Fowers and B. J. Davidov, "The Virtue of Multiculturalism: Personal Transformation, Character, and Openness to the Other," *American Psychologist* 61 (2006): 581–594.

48. P. E. Trudeau, "Statement by the Prime Minister in the House of Commons, October 8, 1971," in *Multiculturalism in Canada: The Challenge of Diversity* (Scarborough, Ontario, Canada: Nelson Canada, 1971/1992), p. 281. (Original work published 1971).

49. See M. Cole, S. R. Cole, and C. Lightfoot, *The Development of Children*. 4th ed. (New York: Worth, 2004).

50. For example, see J. R. Bowen (*Why the French Don't Like Headscarves* (Princeton, NJ: Princeton University Press, 2006).

51. W. E. Lambert and D. M. Taylor, *Coping with Cultural and Racial Diversity in Urban America* (New York: Praeger, 1990); C. Negy, T. L. Shreve, B. J. Jensen, and N. Uddin, "Ethnic Identity, Self-Esteem, and Ethnocentrism: A Study of

Social Identity versus Multicultural Theory of Development," *Cultural Diversity and Ethnic Minority Psychology* 9 (2003): 333–344; M. Verkuyten, "Ethnic Group Identification and Group Evaluation among Minority and Majority Groups: Testing the Multiculturalism Hypothesis," *Journal of Personality and Social Psychology 88* (2005): 121–138.

52. L. Wang *Discrimination by Default: How Racism Becomes Routine.* (New York: New York University Press, 2006).

53. J. Wrench, *Diversity Management and Discrimination: Immigrants and Ethnic Minorities in the EU* (Aldershot, England: Ashgate, 2007).

54. F. M. Moghaddam and D. M. Taylor, "The Meaning of Multiculturalism for Visible Minority Immigrant Women," *Canadian Journal of Behavioural Science* 19 (1987): 121–136.

55. W. E. Lambert and D. M. Taylor, *Coping with Cultural and Racial Diversity.*

56. P. E. Trudeau, "Statement by the Prime Minister," p. 281.

57. In line with W. E. Lambert, L. Mermegis and D. M. Taylor, "Greek Canadians' Attitudes toward Own Group and Other Canadian Ethnic Groups: A Test of the Multiculturalism Hypothesis," *Canadian Journal of Behavioral Science* 18 (1986): 35–51; M. Verkuyten, "Ethnic Group Identification," among others.

58. For example, W. G. Allport, *The Nature of Prejudice* (Cambridge, MA: Addison-Wesley, 1954).

59. For example, M. B. Brewer, "The Psychology of Prejudice: Ingroup Love or Outgroup Hate?" *Journal of Social Issues* 55 (1999): 429–444.

60. Going back to W. G. Sumner, *Folkways* (Boston: Ginn. CA: Jossey-Bass, 1906) and S. Freud, "Group Psychology and the Analysis of the Ego," in *The Standard Edition of the Complete Psychological Works of Sigmund Freud,* ed. and trans. J. Strachey, Vol. 18, 67–143. (London: Hogarth Press, 1955). (Original work published 1921.)

61. H. Tajfel and J. C. Turner, "The Social Identity Theory of Intergroup Behavior, in *Psychology of Intergroup Relations,* ed. S. Worchel and W. G. Austin, 7–24 (Chicago: Nelson-Hall, 1986).

62. For example, see S. Hinkle and R. Brown, "Intergroup Comparisons and Social Identity: Some Links and Lacunae," in *Social Identity Theory: Constructive and Critical Advances*, ed. D. Abrams and M. Hogg, 48–70 (London: Harvester Whatsheaf, 1990); and the alternative views of J. C. Turner and K. J. Reynolds, "The Social Identity Perspective in Intergroup Relations: Theories, Themes, and Controversies," in ed. M. B. Brewer and M. Hewstone, *Self And Social Identity,* 259–277 (Oxford, England: Blackwell, 2004).

63. See reading in Y. Baumeister, *Self in Social Psychology* (New York: Psychology Press, 1999).

64. C. Negy, et al., "Ethnic Identity, Self-Esteem, and Ethnocentrism"; M. Verkuyten, "Ethnic Group Identification."

65. H. Tajfel, *Differentiation between Social Groups* (London: Academic Press, 1978); N. Lee, E. Lessem, and F. M. Moghaddam, "Standing Out and Blending in: Differentiation and Conflict," in *Global Conflict Resolution through Positioning Analysis,* ed. F. M. Moghaddam, R. Harré, and N. Lee, 113–131 (New York: Springer, 2008).

66. H. Tajfel, C. Flament, M. Billig, and R. F. Bundy, "Social Categorization and Intergroup Behaviour," *European Journal of Social Psychology* 1 (1971): 149–177.

67. For discussions see D. E. Brown, *Human Universals* (Philadelphia: Temple University Press, 1991); F. M. Moghaddam, *Social Psychology: Exploring Universals in Social Behavior* (New York: Freeman, 1998); A. Norenzayan and S. J. Heine, "Psychological Universals: What Are They, and How Can We Know?" *Psychological Bulletin* 131 (2005): 763–784.

68. See critical discussions by F. M. Moghaddam and C. Studer, "Cross-cultural Psychology: The Frustrated Gadfly's Promises, Potentialities, and Failures," in *Handbook of Critical Psychology,* ed. D. Fox and I. Prillettensky, 185–201 and references (Newbury Park, CA: Sage Publications, 1997); R. Shweder, "Cultural Psychology: What Is It?" in *Cultural Psychology: Essays on Comparative Human Development*, ed. J. W. Stigler, R. A. Shweder, and G. Herdt, 1–43 (Cambridge, MA: Cambridge University Press, 1990).

69. S. Dehaene, V. Izard, P. Pica, and E. Spelke, E., "Core Knowledge of Geometry in an Amazonian Indigene Group," *Science* 311 (January 20, 2006): 381–384.

70. Heine, S. J. and Renshaw, K. (2002), "Interjudge Agreement, Self-enhancement, and Liking: Cross-cultural Divergences." *Personality and Social Psychology Bulletin, 28*, 578-587; l. Osbeck, F. M. Moghaddam, and S. Perreault, "Similarity and Attraction among Majority and Minority Groups in a Multicultural Context," *International Journal of Intercultural Relations* 21 (1997): 113–123.

71. R. B. Zajonc, "Social Facilitation," *Science* 149 (1965): 269–274.

72. F. M. Moghaddam (2008), *Multiculturalism and Intergroup Relations: Psychological Implications for Democracy in Global Context* (Washington, DC: American Psychological Association Press, 2008).

73. S. J. Heine, *Cultural Psychology* (New York: Norton, 2008), presents a highly insightful discussion of possible universals.

74. F. M. Moghaddam (2008), *Multiculturalism and Intergroup Relations: Psychological Implications for Democracy in Global Context* (Washington, DC: American Psychological Association Press, 2008).

75. J. S. Adams, "Toward an Understanding of Inequity," *Journal of Abnormal and Social Psychology* 67 (1963): 422–436; G. C. Homans, *Social Behavior: Its Elementary Forms* (New York: Harcourt, Brace & World, 1961); D. M. Messick and K. S. Cook, eds., *Equity Theory* (New York: Praeger, 1983); E. Walster, G. E. Walster and E. Berscheid, *Equity: Theory and Research* (Boston: Allyn & Bacon, 1978).

76. M. J. Lerner, *The Belief in a Just World: A Fundamental Delusion* (New York: Plenum Press, 1980).

77. C. L. Hafer and L. Bègue, "Experimental Research on Just-World Theory: Problems, Developments, and Future Challenges," *Psychological Bulletin* 131 (2005): 128–167.

78. D. Grossman *On Killing: The Psychological Cost of Learning to Kill in War and Society* (New York: Little, Brown, 1995).

79. D. M. Messick and K. S. Cook, eds. *Equity Theory* (New York: Praeger, 1983).

80. J. T. Jost and M. R. Banaji, "The Role of Stereotypes in System Justification and the Production of False Consciousness," *British Journal of Social Psychology* 33 (1994): 1–27.

81. S. Milgram, *Obedience to Authority: An Experimental View* (New York: Harper & Row, 1974).

82. See P. Zimbardo, *The Lucifer Effect: Understanding How Good People Turn Evil* (New York: Random House, 2007).

83. F. M. Moghaddam, *The Individual and Society: A Cultural Integration* (New York: Worth, 2002).

84. See readings in M. D. Barrett, ed., *Children's Single-Word Speech* (Chichester, England: Wiley, 1985); D. Rutter and K. Durkin, "Turn Taking in Mother-Infant Interaction: An Examination of Vocalization and Gaze," *Developmental Psychology* 23 (1987): 54–61.

85. N. Reissland and T. Stephenson, "Turn-taking in Early Vocal Interaction: A Comparison of Premature and Term Infants' Vocal Interaction with Their Mothers," *Child: Care, Health and Development* 2 (1999): 447–456; H. S. Ross, R. E. Filyer, S. P. Lollis, M. Perlman, and J. L. Martin, "Administering Justice in the Family," *Journal of Family Psychology* 8 (1994): 254–273.

86. R. Ellickson, *Order without Law: How Neighbors Settle Disputes* (Boston: Harvard University Press, 2005).

87. E. A. Lind and T. R. Tyler, *The Social Psychology of Procedural Justice* (New York: Plenum Press, 1988), pp. 222–230.

88. For example, T. R. Tyler and Y. J. Huo, *Trust in the Law* (New York: Russell Sage Foundation, 2002).

89. R. Putnam, *Making Democracy Work: Civic Traditions in Modern Italy* (Princeton, NJ: Princeton University Press, 1993).

90. R. Putnam, *Bowling Alone: The Collapse and Revival of American Community* (New York: Simon & Schuster, 2000).

91. F. M. Moghaddam, *The Specialized Society: The Plight of the Individual in an Age of Individualism* (New York: Praeger, 1997).

92. T. R. Tyler and Y. J. Huo, *Trust in the Law* (New York: Russell Sage Foundation, 2002).

93. R. A. Teixeira, *The Disappearing American Voter* (Washington, DC: Brookings Institute, 1992).

94. M. Bekoff (*Wild Justice and Fair Play: Cooperation, Forgiveness, and Morality in Animals* (Chicago: University of Chicago Press, 2005).

95. F. B. M. De Waal, *Good Natured: The Origins of Right and Wrong in Humans and Other Animals.* (Cambridge, MA: Harvard University Press, 1996); M. D. Hauser, M. K. Chen, F. Chen, and E. Chuang Give unto others: Genetically unrelated cotton-top tamarin monkeys preferentially give food to those who altruistically give food back," *Proceedings of the Royal Society of London*, B 270 (2003): 2363–2370.

96. S. F. Brosnan and F. B. M. de Waal, "Monkeys Reject Unequal Pay," *Nature* 425 (2003): 297–299.

97. D. J. Langford, S. E. Crager, Z. Shehzad, S. B. Smith, S. G. Sotocinal, J. S. Levenstadt, et al., "Social Modulation of Pain as Evidence of Empathy in Mice," *Science* 312 (June 30, 2006): 1967–1970.

98. M. Bekoff, C. Allen, and G. M. Burghardt, eds. *The Cognitive Animal* (Cambridge, MA: MIT Press, 2002).

99. As argued by M. D. Hauser, *Moral Minds: How Nature Designed Our Universal Sense of Right and Wrong* (New York: HarperCollins, 2006), for example, but also see the arguments against this idea in W. Sinnott-Armstrong, ed., *Moral Psychology.* Vol. 1. *The Evolution of Morality: Adaptations and Innateness* (Cambridge, MA: MIT Press, 2008).

100. For example, K. Lorenz, *On Aggression*, trans. M. Wilson (New York: Harcourt, Brace & World, 1966).

101. See O. Curry, ''The Conflict-Resolution Theory of Virtue,'' in *Moral Psychology.* Vol. 1. *The Evolution of Morality: Adaptations and Innateness,* ed. W. Sinnott-Armstrong, 251–261 (Cambridge, MA: MIT Press, 2008), for a more recent analysis using similar arguments.

102. For example, A. Dershowitz, *Rights from Wrongs: A Secular Theory of the Origin of Rights* (New York: Basic Books, 2004).

103. N. Lee, E. Lessem, and F. M. Moghaddam, ''Standing Out and Blending in: Differentiation and Conflict,'' in *Global Conflict Resolution through Positioning Analysis*, ed. F. M. Moghaddam, R. Harré, and N. Lee, 113–131 (New York: Springer, 2008).

104. F. M Moghaddam, *How Globalization Spurs Terrorism: The Lopsided Benefits of ''One World'' and Why That Fuels Violence* (Westport, CT: Praeger Security International, 2006). F. M. Moghaddam, *Multiculturalism and Intergroup Relations: Psychological Implications for Democracy in Global Context* (Washington, DC: American Psychological Association Press, 2008).

105. H. Tajfel and J. C. Turner, ''An Integrative Theory of Intergroup Conflict,'' in *The Social Psychology of Intergroup Relations*, ed. W. G. Austin and S. Worchel (Monterey, CA: Brooks/Cole,1979).

106. See discussions in T. Postmes and J. Jetten, eds., *Individuality and the Group: Advances in Social Identity* (London: Sage, 2007).

107. M. B. Brewer and S. Roccas, ''Individual Values, Social Identity, and Optimal Distinctiveness,'' in *Individual Self, Relational Self, Collective Self*, ed. C. Sedikides and M. B. Brewer, 219–237 (Philadelphia: Psychology Press, 2001); and see Lee, et al., ''Standing Out and Blending In.''

108. J. P. Shonkoff and D. A. Phillips, eds. *From Neurons to Neighborhoods: The Science of Early Childhood Development* (Washington, DC: National Academy Press, 2000).

References

Abbott, C., P. Rogers, and J. Sloboda. 2006. *Global responses to global threats: Sustainable security for the twenty-first century.* Oxford: Oxford Research Group.

Abbott, C., P. Rogers, and J. Sloboda. 2007. *Beyond Terror: The Truth About the Real Threat to Our World.* London: Rider.

Adams, J. S. 1963. Toward an understanding of inequity. *Journal of Abnormal and Social Psychology* 67: 422–436.

Adorno, T. W., E. Frenkel-Brunswik, D. J. Levinson, and B. W. Sanford. 1950. *The authoritarian personality.* New York: Harper & Row.

Agnew, J., and J. N. Entrikin, eds. 2004. *The Marshall Plan today: Model and metaphor.* London: Routledge.

Aid, M. 2009. *The secret sentinel.* New York: Bloomsbury Press.

Ainsworth, M. D. S. 1967. *Infancy in Uganda.* Baltimore: Johns Hopkins University Press.

Alba, R., and V. Nee. 1997. Rethinking assimilation theory for a new era of immigration. *International Migration Review* 31: 826–874.

Alderfer, C. P. 1972. *Existence, relatedness, and growth; human needs in organizational settings.* New York: Free Press.

Allport, W. G. 1954. *The nature of prejudice.* Cambridge, MA: Addison-Wesley.

Altemeyer, B. 1981. *Right wing authoritarianism.* Winnipeg: University of Manitoba Press.

Altemeyer, B. 1994. Reducing prejudice in right-wing authoritarians. In *The psychology of prejudice: The Ontario Symposium,* ed. M. P. Zanna and J. M. Olson, Vol. 7, 131–148. Hillsdale, NJ: Lawrence Erlbaum.

Altemeyer, B. 2004. The decline of organized religion in Western civilization. *International Journal for the Psychology of Religion* 14: 77–89.

Amoore, L., and M. de Goede, eds. 2008. *Risk and the war on terror.* London: Routledge.

Apgar, D. 2008. *Risk intelligence: Learning to manage what we don't know.* Boston: Harvard Business School Press.

Appleby, R. S. 2000. *The ambivalence of the sacred: religion, violence, and reconciliation.* Carnegie Commission on Preventing Deadly Conflict Series. Lanham, MD: Rowman & Littlefield.

As newspapers struggle, news is cut and the focus turns local. 2008, July 21. *The New York Times,* P.C6

Asch, S. 1956. Studies of independence and conformity: A minority of one against a unanimous majority. *Psychological Monographs* 70 (9), (No, 416).

Bagaric, M., and J. Clarke. 2007. *Torture: When the unthinkable is morally permissible.* Albany, NY: State University of New York Press.

Baldwin, D. 1997. The concept of security. *Review of International Studies* 23: 5–26.

Banchoff, T., ed. 2007. *Democracy and the new religious pluralism,* 3–16. Oxford, UK: Oxford University Press.

Bandarage, A. 2009. *The separatist conflict in Sri Lanka: Terrorism, ethnicity, political economy.* London: Routledge.

Baraheni, R. 1977. *The crowned cannibals: Writings on repression in Iran.* New York: Vintage Books.

Barrett, M. D., ed. 1985. *Childrens single-word speech.* Chichester, England: Wiley.

Baumeister, R. F. 2002. Religion and psychology: Introduction to the special issue. *Psychological Inquiry* 13: 165–267.

Baumeister, Y. 1999. *Self in social psychology.* New York: Psychology Press.

Bekoff, M. 2005. *Wild justice and fair play: Cooperation, forgiveness, and morality in animals.* Chicago: University of Chicago Press.

Bekoff, M., C. Allen, and G. M. Burghardt, eds. 2002. *The cognitive animal.* Cambridge, MA: MIT Press.

Bell, P. A., T. E. Greene, J. D. Fisher, and A. Baum. 2005. Environmental psychology. 5th ed. Hillsdale, NJ: Lawrence Erlbaum.

Belt, D. 2008. Fast lane to the future: A new superhighway linking its four major cities is bringing old and new India into jarring proximity. *National Geographic* (October): 72–99.

Benson, C. 2001. *The cultural psychology of the self: Place, morality and art in human worlds.* London: Routledge.

Berger, P. L. 1996/1997. Secularism in retreat. *The National Interest* 46: 3–12.

Berlin, J. (2008). Millionaires' club. *National Geographic* (November).

Berry, J. W., R. Kalin, and D. M. Taylor. 1977. *Multiculturalism and ethnic attitudes in Canada.* Ottawa, Ontario, Canada: Supply and Services Canada.

Berscheid, E., and H. T. Reis. 1998. Attraction and close relationships. In *The handbook of social psychology,* ed. D. T Gilbert, S. T. Fiske, and G. Lindzey, Vol. 2, 4th ed., 193–281. New York: McGraw-Hill.

Billig, M. G. 1976. *Social psychology and intergroup relations.* London: Academic Press.

Biringer, B. E., R. V. Matalucci, and S. L. O'Connor. 2007. *Security risk assessment and management: A professional practice guide for protecting buildings and infrastructures.* New York: Wiley.

Bornstein, M. H., and R. H. Bradley. 2003. *Socioeconomic status, parenting, and child development.* Mahwah, NJ: Lawrence Erlbaum.

Bowen, J. R. 2006. *Why the French don't like headscarves*. Princeton, NJ: Princeton University Press.

Bowlby, J. 1969. *Attachment and loss: Volume 1. Attachment*. New York: Basic Books.

Bowlby, J. 1973. *Attachment and loss: Volume 2. Separation: Anxiety and anger*. New York: Basic Books.

Bowlby, J. 1980. *Attachment and loss: Volume 3. Loss: Sadness and depression*. New York: Basic Books.

Brewer, M. B. 1999. The psychology of prejudice: Ingroup love or outgroup hate? *Journal of Social Issues* 55: 429–444.

Brewer, M. B., and S. Roccas. 2001. Individual values, social identity, and optimal distinctiveness. In *Individual self, relational self, collective self*, ed. C. Sedikides and M. B. Brewer, 219–237. Philadelphia: Psychology Press.

Broder, J. F. 2006. *Risk analysis and the security survey*. 3rd ed. Boston: Butterworth-Heinemann.

Bromley, D. W., eds. 1992. *Making the commons work: Theory, practice, and policy*. San Francisco: ICS Press.

Brooks, R., and S. Goldstein. 2004. *The power of resilience*. New York: McGraw Hill.

Brosnan, S. F., and F. B. M. de Waal. 2003. Monkeys reject unequal pay. *Nature* 425: 297–299.

Brown, D. E. 1991. *Human universals*. Philadelphia: Temple University Press.

Brown, L. C., ed. 2001. *Diplomacy in the Middle East: The international relations of regional and outside powers*. London: I. B. Tauris.

Bruner, J. S., and M. C. Potter. 1964. Interference in visual recognition. *Science* 144: 424–425.

Byrne, D. 1971. *The attraction paradigm*. New York: Academic Press.

Callaghan, J. M., and F. Kernic. 2003. New missions and tasks for the "postmodern military." In *Armed forces and international security: Global trends and issues*, ed. J. Callaghan and F. Kernic, 41–43. New Brunswick, NJ and London, UK: Transaction Publishers.

Campbell, D. 1998. *Writing security: United States foreign policy and the politics of identity*. Minneapolis, MN: University of Minnesota Press.

Carless, S. A., and C. De-Paola. 2000. The measurement of cohesion in work teams. *Small Group Research* 31: 71–88.

Carlsmith, K. M. 2006. The roles of retribution and utility in determining punishment. *Journal of Experimental Social Psychology* 42: 437–451.

Carlsmith, K. M., and J. M. Darley. 2008. Psychological aspects of retributive justice. In *Advances in experimental social psychology*, ed. M. P. Zanna, Vol. 40, 193–236. San Diego: Elsevier.

Carlsmith, K. M., and A. M. Sood. 2009. The fine line between interrogation and retribution. *Journal of Experimental Social Psychology* 45: 191–196.

Carré, F., M. A. Ferber, L. Golden, and S. A. Herzenberg, eds. 2000, *Nonstandard work*. Ithaca, NY: Cornell University Press.

Cassidy, J., and P. Shaver, ed. 1999. *Handbook of attachment theory and research*. New York: Guildford Press.

Cavalli-Sforza, L., P. Menozzi, and A. Piazza. 1994. *The history and geography of human genes.* Princeton, NJ: Princeton University Press.

Ceci, S. J., and P. B. Papierno. 2005. The rhetoric and reality of gap closing: When the ''have-nots'' gain but the ''haves'' gain even more. *American Psychologist* 60: 149–160.

Chagnon, N. 1997. *Yanomamo.* 5th ed. New York: Harcourt Brace.

Christie, R., and F. L. Geise, eds. 1970. *Studies in Machiavellianism.* New York: Academic Press.

Close, F. 2009. *Nothing: A very short introduction.* New York: Oxford University Press.

Cobble, D. 2000. Historical perspectives on representing nonstandard workers. In *Nonstandard work,* ed. F. Carré, M. A. Ferber, L. Golden, and S. A. Herzenberg, 291–312. Ithaca, NY: Cornell University Press.

Coicaud, J. M., and J. Jönsson. 2007. From foes to bedfellows: Reconciling security and justice. *The Whitehead Journal of Diplomacy and International Relations* (Winter/Spring): 21–32.

Cole, M., S. R. Cole, and C. Lightfoot. 2004. *The development of children.* 4th ed. New York: Worth.

Collins, A., ed. 2007. *Contemporary security studies.* Oxford, UK: Oxford University Press.

Commission on Human Security. 2003. *Human security now: Protecting and empowering people.* New York: United Nations Publications.

Cronin, A. K. 2006. Cyber-mobilization: The new *levée en masse. Parameters* (Summer): 77–87.

Crossette, B. 2004. ''Voice: Sri Lanka, the destruction of South Asia's most developed society.'' *Journal of Aggression, Maltreatment & Trauma* 9: 229–231.

Croxton, D. 1999. *Peacemaking in early Europe: Cardinal Mazarin and the Congress of Westphalia, 1643–1648.* London: Associated University Presses.

Crystal, D. 2000. *Language death.* Cambridge, UK: Cambridge University Press.

Cuellar, I., and F. A. Paniagua, eds. 2000. *Handbook of multicultural mental health: Assessment and treatment of diverse populations.* San Diego: Academic Press.

Curry, O. 2008. The conflict-resolution theory of virtue. In *Moral psychology. Vol. 1. The evolution of morality: Adaptations and innateness,* ed. W. Sinnott-Armstrong, 251–261. Cambridge, MA: MIT Press.

Dalby, A. 2003. *Language in danger: The loss of linguistic diversity and the threat to our future.* New York: Columbia University Press.

Darley, J. M., and T. S. Pittman. 2003. The psychology of compensatory and retributive justice. *Personality and Social Psychology Review* 7, 324–336.

Darwin, C. (1993). *The origin of species by means of natural selection or the preservation of favored races in the struggle for life.* New York: The Modern Library. (Original work published 1859.)

Dawkins, R. 1989. *The selfish gene.* 2nd ed. Oxford, UK: Oxford University Press.

De Blij, H. 2008. *The power of place: Geography, destiny, and globalization's rough landscape.* New York: Oxford University Press.

Dehaene, S., V. Izard, P. Pica, and E. Spelke. 2006. Core knowledge of geometry in an Amazonian Indigene group. *Science* 311 (January 20): 381–384.

Dein, S., and K. M. Loewenthal. 1998. Holy healing: The growth of religious and spiritual therapies. *Mental Health, Religion & Culture* 1: 85–89.

Delpeuch, F., B. Maire, E. Monnier, and M. Holdsworth. (2009). *Globesity: A planet out of control?* London: Earthspan Publications.

Dershowitz, A. 2002. *Why terrorism works: Understanding the threat, responding to the challenge.* New Haven, CT: Yale University Press.

Dershowitz, A. 2004. *Rights from wrongs: A secular theory of the origin of rights.* New York: Basic Books.

Deudney, D. H., and R. A. Matthew, eds. 1999. *Contested grounds: Security and conflict in the new environmental politics.* Albany, NY: State University of New York Press.

Deutscher, I. 2002. *Accommodating diversity: National policies that prevent ethnic conflict.* Lanham, MD: Lexington Books.

Devine, F. 1977. *Social class in America and Britain.* Edinburgh: University of Edinburgh Press.

De Waal, F. B. M. 1996. *Good natured: The origins of right and wrong in humans and other animals.* Cambridge, MA: Harvard University Press.

Dion, K. L. 1979. Intergroup conflict and intragroup cohesiveness. In *The social psychology of intergroup relations,* ed. W. G. Austin and S. Worchel, 211–224. Pacific Grove, CA: Brooks/Cole.

Dion, K. L. 2000. Group cohesion: From "field of forces" to multidimensional construct. *Group Dynamics* 4: 7–26.

Dolan, B. 1994. Cross-cultural aspects of anorexia nervosa and bulimia: A review. *Journal of American Academy of Child and Adolescent Psychiatry* 37: 802–809.

Dollard, J., L. Doob, N. Miller, O. Mowrer, and R. Sears. 1939. *Frustration and aggression.* New Haven, CT: Yale University Press.

Donne, J. 1623/1975. *Devotions upon emergent occasions.* Ed. A. Raspa. Montreal: McGill University Press.

Ehrenreich, B. 2002. *Nickel and dimed: On (not) getting on in America.* New York: Henry Holt.

Ehrlich, P. R. 2000. *Human natures: Genes, cultures, and the human prospect.* Washington, DC: Island Press.

Ehrlich, P. R., and A. H. Ehrlich. 2004. *One with Nineveh: Politics, consumption and the human future.* Washington, DC: Island Press.

Ehrlich, P. R., and A. H. Ehrlich. 2008. *The dominant animal: Human evolution and the environment.* Washington, DC: Island Press.

Eller, A., and D. Abrams. 2003. "Gringos" in Mexico: Cross-sectional and longitudinal effects of school-promoted contact in intergroup bias. *Group Processes & Intergroup Relations* 6: 55–75.

Ellickson, R. 2005. *Order without law: How neighbors settle disputes.* Boston: Harvard University Press.

Ellis, W. D. 1938. *A source book of Gestalt psychology.* London: Routledge and Kegan Paul.

Farr, K. 2004. *Sex trafficking: The global market in women and children.* New York: Worth.

Feenstra, R. C., ed. 2000. *The impact of international trade on wages.* Chicago: University of Chicago Press.

Ferraro, V. 2003. Globalizing weakness: Is global poverty a threat to the interests of states? *Environmental Change and Security Program (ECSP) Report* 9: 12–19.

Festinger, L. 1954. A theory of social comparison processes. *Human Relations* 7: 117–140.

Field, F., ed. 2008. *China, India, and the United States: Competition for energy resources.* Abu Dhabi, United Arab Emirates: Emirates Center for Strategic Studies and Research.

Filkins, D. 2008. *The forever war.* New York: Alfred A. Knopf.

Finkel, N., and F. M. Moghaddam, eds. 2004. *The psychology of rights and duties: Empirical contributions and normative commentaries.* Washington, DC: American Psychological Association Press.

Fiorina, M. P., S. J. Abrams, and J. C. Pope. 2006. *Culture war? The myth of a polarized America.* 2nd ed. New York: Longman.

Fish, M. S., and R. S. Brooks. 2004. Does diversity hurt democracy? *Journal of Democracy* 15: 154–166.

Fletcher, L. E., and E. Stove. 2008. *Guantánamo and its aftermath: U.S. detention and interrogation practices and their impact on former detainees.* University of California, Berkeley: Human Rights Center and International Human Rights Law Clinic.

Fortune, R. F. 1989. *Sorcerers of Dobu.* Prospect Heights, Ill: Waveland Press. (Originally published 1932.)

Fowers, B. J., and B. J. Davidov. 2006. The virtue of multiculturalism: Personal transformation, character, and openness to the other. *American Psychologist* 61: 581–594.

Fox, J. 2002. *Ethnoreligious conflict in the late twentieth century: A general theory.* Lanham, MD: Lexington Books.

Fox, J. 2006. World separation of religion and state in the twenty-first century. *Comparative Political Studies* 39: 537–569.

Freud, S. (1900–1901). The interpretation of dreams (second part). In *The standard edition of the complete psychological works of Sigmund Freud,* ed. and trans. J. Strachey, Vol. 5. London: Hogarth Press. (Original work published 1953.)

Freud, S. 1955. Group psychology and the analysis of the ego. In *The standard edition of the complete psychological works of Sigmund Freud,* ed. and trans. J. Strachey, Vol. 18, 67–143. London: Hogarth Press. (Original work published 1921.)

Freud, S. 1960. Jokes and their relation to the unconscious. In *The standard edition of the complete psychological works of Sigmund Freud,* ed. and trans. J. Strachey, Vol. 8, 9–236. London: Hogarth Press. (Original work published 1905.)

Freud, S. 1961. Civilization and its discontents. In *The standard edition of the complete psychological works of Sigmund Freud,* ed. and trans. J. Strachey, Vol. 21, 64–145. London: Hogarth Press. (Original work published 1930.)

Gaertner, S. L., and J. F. Dovidio. 2000. *Reducing intergroup bias: The common ingroup identity model.* Philadelphia: Psychology Press.

Gigerenzer, G. 2004. Dread risk, September 11, and fatal traffic accidents. *Psychological Science* 15: 286–287.

Ginbar, Y. 2008. *Why not torture terrorists? Moral, practical, and legal aspects of the "ticking bomb" justification*. New York: Oxford University Press.

Glazer, N., and D. P. Moynihan. 1970. *Beyond the melting pot*. 2nd ed. Cambridge, MA: MIT Press.

Grant, C. A., and J. L. Lei, eds. 2001. *Global constructions of multicultural education: Theories and reality*. Mahwah, NJ: Lawrence Erlbaum.

Grimm, J., W. Grimm, L. E. Grimm. 2003. *Grimm's Fairy Tales* (Barnes & Noble Classics Series), ed. E. Dalton. New York: Barnes & Noble Books.

Grossman, D. 1995. *On killing: The psychological cost of learning to kill in war and society*. New York: Little, Brown.

Grossman, K. E., K. Krossman, and E. Waters, eds. 2005. *Attachment from infancy to adulthood: The major longitudinal studies*. New York: Guildford Press.

Gully, S. M., D. J. Devine, and D. Whitney. 1995. A meta-analysis of cohesion and performance: Effects of level of analysis and task interdependence. *Small Group Research* 26: 497–520.

Hafer, C. L., and L. Bégue. 2005. Experimental research on just-world theory: Problems, developments, and future challenges. *Psychological Bulletin* 131: 128–167.

Haimes, Y. Y. 2009. *Risk modeling, assessment, and management*. 3rd ed. New York: Wiley.

Handel, M. I. 2003. *Masters of war: Classical strategic thought*. 3rd ed. London: Frank Cass.

Hardin, G. 1968. The tragedy of the commons. *Science* 162: 1243–1248.

Hardin, G. 1998. Extension of "the tragedy of the commons." *Science* 280: 682–683.

Harlow, H. F., M. K. Harlow, and S. J. Soumi. 1971. From thought to therapy: Lessons from a primate laboratory. *American Scientist* 59: 538–549.

Harré, R. 2002. *Cognitive science: A philosophical introduction*. London & Thousand Oaks, CA: Sage.

Harré, R. 2009. *Pavlov's dogs and Schrödinger's cat: Scenes from the living laboratory*. Oxford, UK: Oxford University Press.

Hart, C. W. M., A. R. Pilling, and J. C. Goodale. 2001. *The Tiwi of northern Australia*. Belmont, CA: Wadsworth.

Haught, J. F. 1995. *Science & religion: From conflict to conversation*. New York: Paulist Press.

Hauser, M. D. 2006. *Moral minds: How nature designed our universal sense of right and wrong*. New York: HarperCollins.

Hauser, M. D., M. K. Chen, F. Chen, and E. Chuang. 2003. Give unto others: Genetically unrelated cotton-top tamarin monkeys preferentially give food to those who altruistically give food back. *Proceedings of the Royal Society of London* B 270: 2363–2370.

Heine, S. J. 2008. *Cultural psychology*. New York: Norton.

Heine, S. J., and Renshaw, K. 2002. "Interjudge Agreement, Self-enhancement, and Liking: Cross-cultural Divergences." *Personality and Social Psychology Bulletin, 28*, 578–587.

Hess, E. H. 1973. *Imprinting: early experience and the developmental psychobiology of attachment.* New York: D. Van Nostrand Reinhold.

Hiatt, F. 2007. "The Vanishing Foreign Correspondent." *The Washington Post*, Jan. 29, p. A15.

Hill, P. C., and K. I. Pargament. 2003. Advances in the conceptualization and measurement of religion and spirituality. *American Psychologist* 58: 64–74.

Hilzenrath, D. S. 2008, December 21. Executive pay. *The Washington Post*, F1, F4.

Hinkle, S., and R. Brown. 1990. Intergroup comparisons and social identity: Some links and lacunae. In *Social identity theory: Constructive and critical advances*, ed. D. Abrams and M. Hogg, 48–70. London: Harvester Whatsheaf.

Hirsch, E. D. Jr. 1988. *Cultural literacy: What every American needs to know.* New York: Vintage Books.

Homans, G. C. 1961. *Social behavior: Its elementary forms.* New York: Harcourt, Brace & World.

Homer-Dixon, T. 2006. *The Upside of Down: Catastrophe, Creativity, and the Renewal of Civilization.* Washington, DC: Island Press.

Horowitz, D. L. 1993. Democracy in divided societies. *Journal of Democracy* 4: 18–38.

Hume, D. 1739/2008. *A treatise on human nature.* Sioux Falls, SD: NuVision Publications.

Hunsberger, B., and L. M. Jackson. 2005. Religion, meaning, and prejudice. *Journal of Social Issues* 61: 807–826.

Jackson, L. M., and B. Hunsberger. 1999. An intergroup perspective on religion and prejudice. *Journal for the Scientific Study of Religion* 38: 509–523.

Janczewski, L. J., and A. M. Colarik, eds. 2007. *Cyber warfare and cyber terrorism.* Hershey, PA: IGI Global.

Janis, I. L. 1982. *Groupthink.* 2nd ed. Boston: Houghton Mifflin.

Janis, I. L. 1989. *Crucial decisions: Leadership in policymaking and crisis management.* New York: Free Press.

Jost, J. T. 2006. The end of the end of ideology. *American Psychologist* 61: 651–670.

Jost, J. T., and M. R. Banaji. 1994. The role of stereotypes in system justification and the production of false consciousness. *British Journal of Social Psychology* 33: 1–27.

Jost, J. T., M. R. Banaji, and B. A. Nosek. 2004. A decade of system justification theory: Accumulated evidence for conscious and unconscious bolstering of the status quo. *Political Psychology* 25: 881–919.

Kagan, J., N. Snidman, D. Arcus, and J. S. Reznick. 1994. *Galen's prophecy: Temperament in human nature.* New York: Basic Books.

Kahneman, D., and A. Tversky. 1973. On the psychology of prediction. *Psychological Review* 80: 237–251.

Kairab, S. 2004. *A practical guide to security assessments.* Boca Raton, FL: Auerbach Publications/Taylor & Francis.

Kalat, J. W. 2008. *Introduction to psychology.* 8th ed. Belmont, CA: Thomson-Wadsworth.

Kimball, C. 2002. *When religion becomes evil.* San Francisco, CA: HarperCollins Publishers.

Koops, W., J. B. Hoeksma, and D. C. Van den Boom, eds. 1997. *Development of interaction and attachment: Traditional and non-traditional approaches.* Amsterdam: North-Holland/Elsevier.

Krauthammer, C. 2006. In plain English: Let's make it official. *Time* (June 12): 112.

Krugman, P. 2009, May 4. Falling wage syndrome. *The New York Times*, A23.

Kugler, R. L. 2006. *Policy analysis in national security affairs: New methods for a new era.* Washington, DC: National Defense University Press.

Kulish, N. 2008, October 27. Crisis jolts Poland, and other Go-Go markets. *The New York Times.*

Lambert, W. E., L. Mermegis, and D. M. Taylor. 1986. "Greek Canadians attitudes toward own group and other Canadian ethnic groups: A test of the multiculturalism hypothesis." *Canadian Journal of Behavioral Science* 18: 35–51.

Lambert, W. E., and D. M. Taylor. 1990. *Coping with cultural and racial diversity in urban America.* New York: Praeger.

Landoll, D. J. 2005. *The security risk assessment handbook: A complete guide to performing security risk assessments.* Boca Raton, FL: Auerbach Publications/ Taylor & Francis.

Lang, A. F. Jr., and A. Russell Beattie, eds. 2009. War, torture, and terrorism: Rethinking the rules of international security. London: Routledge.

Langford, D. J., S. E. Crager, Z. Shehzad, S. B. Smith, S. G. Sotocinal, J. S. Levenstadt, et al. 2006. Social modulation of pain as evidence of empathy in mice. *Science* 312 (June 30): 1967–1970.

Lee, N., E. Lessem, and F. M. Moghaddam. 2008. Standing out and blending in: Differentiation and conflict. In *Global conflict resolution through positioning analysis*, ed. F. M. Moghaddam, R. Harré, and N. Lee, 113–131. New York: Springer.

Lerner, M. J. 1980. *The belief in a just world: A fundamental delusion.* New York: Plenum Press.

LeVine, R. A., and D. T. Campbell. 1971. *Ethnocentrism: Theories of conflict, ethnic attitudes, and group behavior.* New York: Wiley.

Levy, D. A., C. E. L. Stark, and L. R. Squire. 2004. Intact conceptual priming in the absence of declarative memory. *Psychological Science* 15: 680–686.

Liberman, P. 2006. An eye for an eye: Public support for war against evildoers. *International Organization* 60: 687–722.

Libicki, M. C. 2007. *Conquest in cyberspace: National security and information warfare.* Cambridge, UK: Cambridge University Press.

Lincoln, B. 2007. *Religion, empire and torture: A case of Achaemenian Persia, with a postscript on Abu Ghraib.* Chicago: University of Chicago Press.

Lind, E. A., and T. R. Tyler. 1988. *The social psychology of procedural justice.* New York: Plenum Press.

Linkov, I., G. A. Kiker, and R. J. Wenning, eds. 2007. *Environmental security in harbors and coastal areas: Management using comparative risk assessment and multi-criteria decision analysis.* New York: Springer.

Little, D., ed. 2007. *Peacemakers in Action: Profiles of Religion in Conflict Resolution*. Cambridge: Cambridge University Press.

Logan, J. R., W. Zhang, R. D. Alba. 2002. Immigrant enclaves and ethnic communities in New York and Los Angeles. *American Sociological Review* 67: 299–322.

Lorenz, K. 1966. *On aggression*, trans. M. Wilson. New York: Harcourt, Brace & World.

Lowry, R. J., ed. 1973. *Dominance, self-esteem, and self-actualization: Germinal papers of A. H. Maslow*. Monterey, CA: Brooks/Cole.

Machiavelli, N. 1977. *The Prince*, trans. and ed. R. M. Adams. New York: Norton. (First published 1513.)

Mahalingam, R., and C. McCarthy. 2000. *Multicultural curriculum: New directions for social theory, practice, and policy*. New York: Routledge.

Malthus, T. R. 1983. *Essay on the principle of population as it affects the future improvement of society*. London: J. M. Dent.

Mansbridge, J. J., ed. 1990. *Beyond self-interest*. Chicago: University of Chicago Press.

Marks, M. P. 2004. *The prison as metaphor: Re-examining international relations*. New York: Peter Lang.

Marmot, M. G. 2004. *The status syndrome: How social standing affects our health and longevity*. New York: Times Books/Henry Holt.

Marx, K. 1979. The eighteenth brumaire of Louis Bonaparte. In *Collected works of Karl Marx and Frederick Engels*, Vol. 11, 99–197. London: Lawrence and Wishart. (Original work published 1852.)

Marx, K., and F. Engels. 1967. *Communist manifesto*. New York: Pantheon. (Original work published 1848.)

Mathew, R. A. 2008. *Resource scarcity: Responding to the security challenge*. International Peace Institute.

McCarthy, T. D., and M. Wolfson. 1996. Resource mobilization by local social movement organizations: Agency, strategy, and organization in the movement against drunk driving. *American Sociological Review* 61: 1070–1088.

McGee Banks, C. A., and J. A. Banks. 2008. *Multicultural education*. 6th ed. New York: John Wiley & Sons.

McMahon, R. J. 2003. *The cold war: A very short introduction*. Oxford, UK: Oxford University Press.

McManis, C. R., ed. 2007. *Biodiversity and the law: Intellectual property, biotechnology, and traditional knowledge*. London: Earthscan.

Messick, D. M., and K. S. Cook, eds. 1983. *Equity theory*. New York: Praeger.

Midlarsky, M. I. 1989. *Handbook of war studies*. Boston: Unwin Hyman.

Milgram, S. 1974. *Obedience to authority: An experimental view*. New York: Harper & Row.

Miller, N., W. C. Pederson, M. Earlywine, and V. E. Pollock. 2003. A theoretical model of triggered displaced aggression. *Personality and Social Psychology Review* 7: 75–97.

Miller, R. M., ed. 1984. *Germans in America: Retrospect and prospect*. Philadelphia: The German Society of Philadelphia.

Mitchem, S. Y., and E. M. Townes, eds. 2008. *Faith, health, and healing in African American life*. Westport, CT: Praeger.

Moghaddam, F. M. 1997. *The specialized society: The plight of the individual in an age of individualism*. New York: Praeger.

Moghaddam, F. M. 1998. *Social psychology: Exploring universals in social behavior*. New York: Freeman.

Moghaddam, F. M. 2002. *The individual and society: A cultural integration*. New York: Worth.

Moghaddam, F. M. 2005. *Great ideas in psychology: A cultural and historical introduction*. Oxford, UK: Oneworld.

Moghaddam, F. M. 2006. *From the terrorists' point of view: What they experience and why they come to destroy*. Westport, CT: Praeger Security International.

Moghaddam, F. M. 2006. Interobjectivity: The collective roots of individual consciousness and social identity. In *Individuality and the group: Advances in social identity*, ed. T. Postmes and J. Jetten, 155–174. London: Sage.

Moghaddam, F. M. 2006. Catastrophic evolution, culture, and diversity management policy. *Culture & Psychology* 12: 415–434.

Moghaddam, F. M. 2007. Interrogation policy and American psychology in global context. *Journal of Peace Psychology* 13: 437–443.

Moghaddam, F. M. (2008a). *How globalization spurs terrorism*. Westport, CT: Praeger Security International.

Moghaddam, F. M. (2008b). *Multiculturalism and intergroup relations: Psychological implications for democracy in global context*. Washington, DC: American Psychological Association Press.

Moghaddam, F. M., R. Harré, and N. Lee, eds. 2008. *Global conflict resolution through positioning analysis*. New York: Springer.

Moghaddam, F. M., and C. Studer. 1997. Cross-cultural psychology: The frustrated gadflys promises, potentialities, and failures. In *Handbook of Critical Psychology*, ed. D. Fox and I. Prillettensky, 185–201 and refs. Newbury Park: Sage Publications.

Moghaddam, F. M., and D. M. Taylor. 1987. The meaning of multiculturalism for visible minority immigrant women. *Canadian Journal of Behavioural Science* 19: 121–136.

Moghaddam, F. M., and V. Vuksanivic. 1990. Attitudes and behavior toward human rights across different contexts: The role of right-wing authoritarianism, political ideology, and religiosity. *International Journal of Psychology* 25: 455–474.

Mojzes, P., ed. 1998. *Religion and the war in Bosnia*. Atlanta: Scholars Press.

More, T. Sir, Saint. 1988. *Utopia*. Cambridge, UK, & New York: Cambridge University Press.

Mosca, G. 1939. *The ruling class*. New York: McGraw Hill.

Moscovici, S., G. Mugny, and E. Van Avermaet, eds. 1985. *Perspectives on minority influence*. Cambridge, UK: Cambridge University Press.

Murray, O. 1998. Introduction. In, *The Greeks and Greek civilization*, J. Burckhardt, xi-xliv. New York: HarperCollins.

Myers, D. G. 1993. *The pursuit of happiness*. New York: Avon.

Myers, N., and J. Kent. 2004. *The new consumers.* Washington, DC: Island Press.

National Academy Press. 2008. *Department of Homeland Security Bioterrorism Risk Assessment: A call for change.* Washington, DC: National Academy Press.

National Research Council. 2003. *Countering agricultural bioterrorism.* Washington, DC: The National Academies Press.

The National Security Strategy of the United States (NSS). 2002. Washington, DC: Government Printing Office.

Negy, C., T. L. Shreve, B. J. Jensen, and N. Uddin. 2003. Ethnic identity, self-esteem, and ethnocentrism: A study of social identity versus multicultural theory of development. *Cultural Diversity and Ethnic Minority Psychology* 9: 333–344.

Neimeyer, R. A., and K. A. Mitchell. 1988. Similarity and attraction: A longitudinal study. *Journal of Social and Personality Relationships* 5: 131–148.

Nelson, J. M. 2009. *Psychology, religion, and spirituality.* New York: Springer.

Nemeth, C. 1972. A critical analysis of research utilizing the Prisoner's Dilemma paradigm for the study of bargaining. In *Advances in experimental social psychology*, ed. L. Berkowitz, Vol. 6, 203–234. New York: Academic Press.

Norenzayan, A., and S. J. Heine. 2005. Psychological universals: What are they, and how can we know? *Psychological Bulletin* 131: 763–784.

O'Hanlon, M. E. 2005. Defence Strategy for the Post-Saddam Era. Washington, DC: Brookings Institute Press.

Orr, D. W. 1999. The ecology of giving and consuming. In *Consuming desires: Consumption, culture, and the pursuit of happiness*, ed. R. Rosenblatt, 137–154. Washington, DC: Island Press.

Osbeck, L., F. M. Moghaddam, and S. Perreault. 1997. Similarity and attraction among majority and minority groups in a multicultural context. *International Journal of Intercultural Relations* 21: 113–123.

Otterman, M. 2007. *American torture: From the Cold War to Abu Ghraib and beyond.* Carlton, Victoria, Australia: Melbourne University Press.

Palmer, J. A., and L. K. Palmer, L. 2002. *Evolutionary psychology: The ultimate origins of human behavior.* Boston: Allyn & Unwin.

Paraskevopoulos, C., P. Getimis, N. Rees, eds. 2006. *Adapting to EU multi-level governance: Regional and environmental policies in cohesion and CEE countries.* Aldershot, England; Burlington, VT: Ashgate.

Pareto, V. 1935. The mind and society: A treatise on general sociology. 4 vols. New York: Dover.

Park, R. E. 1950. *Race and culture.* Glencoe, IL: Free Press.

Pettigrew, T. F., and L. R. Tropp. 2000. Does outgroup contact reduce prejudice? Recent meta-analytic findings. In *Reducing prejudice and discrimination: Social psychological perspectives*, ed. S. Oskamp, 93–114. Mahwah, NJ: Lawrence Erlbaum.

Pettigrew, T. F., and L. R. Tropp. 2006. A meta-analytic test of intergroup contact theory. *Journal of Personality and Social Psychology* 90: 751–783.

Pirages, D., and K. Cousins, eds. 2005. *From resource scarcity to ecological security: Exploring new limits to growth.* Cambridge, MA: MIT Press.

Plato. 1959. *The last days of Socrates.* Trans. H. Tredennick. Baltimore, MD: Penguin Classics.

Poortinga, W., and N. F. Pidgeon. 2004. Trust, the asymmetry principle, and the role of prior beliefs. *Risk Analysis* 24: 1475–1486.

Postmes, T., and J. Jetten, eds. 2007. *Individuality and the group: Advances in social identity.* London: Sage.

Potter, G. W., and V. E. Kappeler, eds. 2006. *Constructing crime: Perspectives on making news and social problems.* Long Grove, IL: Waveland Press.

Prinz, J. J. 2008. Is morality innate? In *Moral psychology*, ed. E. Sinnott-Armstrong, Vol. 1, 367–406. Cambridge, MA/London: A Bradford Book/MIT Press.

Putnam, R. 1993. *Making democracy work: Civic traditions in modern Italy.* Princeton, NJ: Princeton University Press.

Putnam, R. 2000. *Bowling alone: The collapse and revival of American community.* New York: Simon & Schuster.

Pyszczynski, T., S. Solomon, and J. Greenberg. 2004. *In the wake of 9/11: The psychology of terror.* Washington, DC: American Psychological Association Press.

Rai, L. 2008. *Effectiveness in workforce development collaboration—The role of leadership in engendering cooperative capability, collective vision, and collaborative resilience.* Germany: VDM Verlag Dr. Mueller e.k.

Rapaport, A., and A. M. Chammah. 1965. *Prisoners dilemma: A study in conflict and cooperation.* Ann Arbor: University of Michigan Press.

Ravussin, E., M. E. Valencia, J. Esparza, P. H. Bennett, and L. O. Schulz. 1994. Effects of a traditional lifestyle on obesity in Pima Indians. *Diabetics Care* 17: 1067–1074.

Reissland, N., and T. Stephenson. 1999. Turn-taking in early vocal interaction: A comparison of premature and term infants' vocal interaction with their mothers. *Child: Care, Health and Development* 2: 447–456.

Rejali, D. 2007. *Torture and democracy.* Princeton, NY: Princeton University Press.

Richeson, J. A., and R. J. Nussbaum. 2004. The impact of multiculturalism versus color-blindness on racial bias. *Journal of Experimental Social Psychology* 40: 417–423.

Riggs, T. 2006. *Worldmark Encyclopedia of Religious Practices* (2006) http://catalogue.nla.gov.av/Record/3127580.

Roberts, P. 2005. *The end of oil: On the edge of a perilous new world.* New York: Houghton Mifflin.

Rodriguez, M. S., and A. T. Grafton, eds. 2007. *Migration in history: Human migration in comparative perspective.* Rochester, NY: Rochester University Press.

Ross, A. 2009. *Nice work if you can get it: Life and labor in precarious times.* New York: New York University Press.

Ross, H. S., R. E. Filyer, S. P. Lollis, M. Perlman, and J. L. Martin. 1994. Administering justice in the family. *Journal of Family Psychology* 8: 254–273.

Rothschild, M. M. 2001. Terrorism and you: The real odds. *AEI-Brookings Joint Center: Policy Matters* 1 (31): 1–2.

Rousseau, J. J. 1754/1984. *A discourse on inequality.* Trans. M. Cranston. Harmondsworth, Middlesex, England: Penguin.

Rozen, P., and E. B. Royzman. 2001. Negativity bias, negativity dominance, and contagion. *Personality and Social Psychology Review* 5: 296–320.

Rutter, D., and K. Durkin. 1987. Turn taking in mother-infant interaction: An examination of vocalization and gaze. *Developmental Psychology* 23: 54–61.

Ryan, L. 1996. *The Aboriginal Tasmanians.* 2nd ed. St. Leonards, Australia: Allen & Unwin.

Sachs, J. D. 2003. The strategic significance of global inequality. *Environmental Change and Security Program (ECSP) Report* (9), 27–35.

Sagan, S. 1994. The perils of proliferation: Organization theory, deterrence theory, and the spread of nuclear weapons. *International Security* 18: 66–107.

Sands, P. 2008. *Torture team: Rumsfelds memo and the betrayal of American values.* New York: Palgrave Macmillan.

Sarbin, T. R., ed. 1986. *Narrative psychology: The storied nature of human conduct.* New York: Praeger.

Schacter, D. L. 1996. *Searching for memory.* New York: Basic Books.

Schwartz, J. 2009, July 13. Vocal minority insists it was all smoke and mirrors. *The New York Times,* D8.

Seckler, D., and U. Amarasinghe. 2004. Major problems in the global water-food nexus. In *Perspectives in world food and agriculture 2004,* ed. C. G. Scanes and J. A. Miranowski. Ames, IA: Iowa State Press.

Sembhi, S., and S. Dein. 1998. The use of traditional healers by Asian psychiatric patients in the UK: A pilot study. *Mental Health, Religion & Culture* 1: 127–133.

Seul, J. R. 1999. "Ours is the way of God": Religion, identity, and intergroup conflict. *Journal of Peace Research* 36: 553–569.

Shah, I. 1968. *The pleasantries of the incredible Mulla Nasrudin.* New York: Penguin.

Shambaugh, D. 1996. Containment or engagement? Calculating Beijings responses. *International Security* 19: 149–209.

Sherif, M. 1936. *The psychology of group norms.* New York: Harper.

Sherif, M. 1966. *Group conflict and cooperation: Their social psychology.* London: Routledge & Kegan Paul.

Shiratori, R., K. Arai, and F. Kato, eds. 2005. *Gaming, simulations, and society: Research scope and perspective.* New York: Springer.

Shonkoff, J. P., and D. A. Phillips, D., eds. 2000. *From neurons to neighborhoods: The science of early childhood development.* Washington, DC: National Academy Press.

Shweder, R. 1990. Cultural psychology: What is it? In *Cultural psychology: Essays on comparative human development,* ed. J. W. Stigler, R. A. Shweder, and G. Herdt, 1–43. Cambridge, UK: Cambridge University Press.

Sidanius, J., F. Pratto, C. van Laar, and S. Levin. 2004. Social dominance theory: Its agenda and method. *Political Psychology* 25: 845–880.

Siddharth, K. 2008. *Sex trafficking: Inside the business of modern slavery.* New York: Columbia University Press.

Silberman, I. 2005. Religion as a Meaning System: Implications for the New Millennium. *Journal of Social Issues, 61,* 641–664.

Singer, P. W. 2009. *Wired for war: The robotics revolution and conflict in the twenty-first century.* Harmondsworth, Middlesex, UK: Penguin HC.

Sinnott-Armstrong, W., ed. 2008. *Moral psychology. Vol. 1. The evolution of morality: Adaptations and innateness.* Cambridge, MA: MIT Press.

Sirota, D. 2008. *The uprising: An unauthorized tour of the populist revolt scaring Wall Street and Washington.* New York: Crown Publishers.

Skyrms, B. 2004. *The stag hunt and the evolution of social structure.* Cambridge, UK: Cambridge University Press.

Slackman, M. 2008, Nov 12. Emirates see fiscal crisis as chance to save culture. *The New York Times*, A5.

Slovic, P., M. L. Finucane, E. Peters, and D. C. MacGregor. 2004. Risk as analysis and risk as feelings: Some thought about affect, risk, and rationality. *Risk Analysis* 24: 311–322.

Smith, A. 1776/1991. *The wealth of nations.* New York: Prometheus Books.

Sriram, C. L., and Z. Nielsen, eds. 2004. *Exploring subregional conflict: Opportunities for conflict prevention.* Boulder, CO: Lynne Rienner Publishers.

Stephens, J. D. 1993. Capitalist development and democracy: Empirical research on the social origins of democracy. In *The idea of democracy*, ed. D. Copp, J. Hampton, and J. E. Roemer, 409–446. New York: Cambridge University Press.

Stoessinger, J. G. 2008. *Why nations go to war.* 10th ed. Belmont, CA: Thomson Wadsworth.

Stover, E., and E. O. Nightingale. 1985. Introduction. In *The breaking of bodies and bones: Torture, psychiatric abuse, and the health professions*, ed. E. Stover and E. O. Nightingale, 1–26. New York: W. H. Freeman.

Sumner, W. G. 1906. *Folkways.* Boston: Ginn. CA: Jossey-Bass.

Sunstein, C. R. 2003. Terrorism and probability neglect. *Journal of Risk and Uncertainty* 26: 121–136.

Suomi, S. J. 1999. Behavioral inhibition and impulsive aggressiveness: Insights from studies with Rhesus monkeys. In *Child psychology: A handbook of contemporary issues*, ed. L. Balter and C. S. Tamis-Lemonda, 510–525. Philadelphia: Taylor & Francis.

Suzuki, L. A., J. G. Ponterotto, and P. J. Meller, eds. 2001. *Handbook of multicultural assessment: Clinical, psychological, and educational applications.* 2nd ed. San Francisco: Jossey-Bass.

Swift, J. 1726/1960. *Gulliver's travels.* Boston: Houghton Mifflin.

Tajfel, H., ed. 1978. *Differentiation between social groups.* London: Academic Press.

Tajfel, H., C. Flament, M. Billig, and R. F. Bundy. 1971. Social categorization and intergroup behaviour. *European Journal of Social Psychology* 1: 149–177.

Tajfel H., and J. C. Turner, 1979. An Integrative Theory of Intergroup Conflict. In *The Social Psychology of Intergroup Relations*, eds. W. G. Austink and S. Worchel, 33–47. Monterey, CA: Brooks/Cole.

Tajfel, H., and J. C. Turner, 1986. The social identity theory of intergroup behavior. In *Psychology of intergroup relations*, ed. S. Worchel and W. G. Austin, 7–24. Chicago: Nelson-Hall.

Takahashi, K. 1990. Are the key assumptions of the "strange situation" procedure universal? *Human Development* 33: 23–30.

Taylor, C. 1992. The politics of recognition. In *Multiculturalism and "the politics of recognition,"* ed. A. Guttman, 25–73. Princeton, NJ: Princeton University Press.

Teixeira, R. A. 1992. *The disappearing American voter.* Washington, DC: Brookings Institute.

Thucydides. 1951. *The Peloponnesian war.* Trans. J. H. Finley, Jr. New York: The Modern Library.

Tolstoy, L. (1865–1868). *War and peace.* 2 vols. Trans. R. Edmonds. Harmondsworth, UK: Penguin.

The toxins trickle downward. 2009. *The Economist* (March 14–20): 62–63.

Trudeau, P. E. 1992. Statement by the Prime Minister in the House of Commons, October 8, 1971. In *Multiculturalism in Canada: The challenge of diversity,* 281–283. Scarborough, Ontario, Canada: Nelson Canada. (Original work published 1971.)

Tseng, W. 1997. *Culture and psychopathology: A guide to clinical assessment.* New York: Routledge.

Turnbull, C. M. 1972. *The mountain people.* New York: Simon & Schuster.

Turner, J. C., and K. J. Reynolds. 2004. The social identity perspective in intergroup relations: Theories, themes, and controversies. In *Self and social identity,* ed. M. B. Brewer and M. Hewstone, 259–277. Oxford, England: Blackwell.

Tyler, T. R., and Y. J. Huo. 2002. *Trust in the law.* New York: Russell Sage Foundation.

United Nations Development Program. 1994. Human development report. Retrieved Dec. 9, 2008, at http://hdr.undp.org/en/reports/global/hdr1994/chapters.

Vasquez, M. A., A. L. Peterson, and P. J. Williams, eds. 2001. *Christianity, social change, and globalization in the Americas.* Piscataway, NJ: Rutgers University Press.

Vatis, M. A. 2003. Cyber attacks: Protecting America's security against digital attacks. In *Countering terrorism: Dimensions of preparedness,* ed. A. D. Howitt and R. L. Pangi, 219–249. Cambridge, MA: MIT Press.

Vaughn, J. 2007. *Conflicts over natural resources: A reference handbook.* Santa Barbara, CA: ABC-CLIO.

Vellani, K. 2007. *Strategic security management: A risk assessment guide for decision makers.* Amsterdam/Boston: Butterworth-Heinemann/Elsevier.

Verkuyten, M. 2005. Ethnic group identification and group evaluation among minority and majority groups: Testing the multiculturalism hypothesis. *Journal of Personality and Social Psychology* 88: 121–138.

Vygotsky, L. 1978. *Mind in society.* Cambridge, MA: Harvard University Press.

Waddell, M. 1993. *Stories from the Bible: Old Testament stories retold.* New York: Ticknor & Fields.

Walsh, F. 2006. *Strengthening family resilience.* 2nd ed. New York: The Guildford Press.

Walster, E., G. E. Walster, and E. Berscheid. 1978. *Equity: Theory and research.* Boston: Allyn & Bacon.

Walzer, M. 1997. *On Toleration.* New Haven, CT: Yale University Press.

Walzer, M. 2006. *Just and unjust wars*. 4th ed. New York: Basic Books.

Wang, L. 2006. *Discrimination by default: How racism becomes routine*. New York: New York University Press.

Warren, M. E., ed. 1999. *Democracy & trust*. Cambridge, UK: Cambridge University Press.

Washburn, P. C. 2002. *The social construction of international news: We're talking about them, they're talking about us*. Westport, CT: Praeger.

Waters, E., and E. M. Cummings. 2000. A secure base from which to explore close relationships, *Child Development* 71: 164–172. Political preferences. *Psychological Science* 19: 448–455.

Weissberg, M. 2003. *Conceptualizing human security. Swords and Ploughshares: A Journal of International Affairs* XIII: 3–11.

Weitz, E. D. 2003. *A century of genocide: Utopias of race and nation*. Princeton, NJ: Princeton University Press.

Wells, S. 2002. *The journey of man: A genetic odyssey*. Princeton, NJ: Princeton University Press.

Welsh, D. 1993. Domestic politics and ethnic conflict. In *Ethnic conflict and international security*, ed. M. E. Brown, 43–60. Princeton, NJ: Princeton University Press.

Whitehouse, H. 2009. *Explaining religion*. Keynote paper presented at Inter-University Graduate Conference, London School of Economics and Political Science, London.

Whitehouse, H., and R. N. McCauley, eds. 2006. *Mind and religion: Psychological and cognitive foundations of religiosity*. Walnut Creek, CA: AltaMira Press.

Whiten, A., and R. A. Byrne, eds. 1997. *Machiavellian intelligence II: Extensions and evaluations*. Cambridge, UK: Cambridge University Press.

Whitman, W. 1955. *Leaves of grass*. New York: Signet Classic.

Whyte, L. L. 1960. *Unconscious before Freud*. New York: Basic Books.

Wilson, W. J., and R. P. Taub. 2006. *There goes the neighborhood: Racial, ethnic, and class tensions in four Chicago neighborhoods and their meaning for America*. New York: Knopf.

Wrench, J. 2007. *Diversity management and discrimination: Immigrants and ethnic minorities in the EU*. Aldershot, England: Ashgate.

Wright, R. 2009. *The evolution of God*. New York: Little, Brown.

Wright, S. C., D. M. Taylor, and F. M. Moghaddam. 1990. Responding to membership in a disadvantaged group: From acceptance to collective protest. *Journal of Personality and Social Psychology* 58: 994–1003.

Zajonc, R. B. 1965. Social facilitation. *Science* 149: 269–274.

Zajonc, R. B. 1968. Attitudinal effects of mere exposure. *Journal of Personality and Social Psychology*, 9 (2, Pt. 2): 1–27.

Zangwill, I. 1909. *The melting pot: Drama in four acts*. New York: Macmillan.

Zimbardo, P. 2007. *The Lucifer effect: Understanding how good people turn evil*. New York: Random House.

Name Index

Subject Index

About the Author

FATHALI M. MOGHADDAM is Director of the Conflict Resolution Program, Department of Government, and Professor, Department of Psychology, Georgetown University, Washington, D.C., and Senior Fellow at the Stanford Center on Policy, Education, and Research on Terrorism. Dr. Moghaddam was born in Iran, educated in England, and worked for the United Nations and for McGill University, before joining Georgetown University in 1990. He returned to Iran in 1979 and was researching there during the hostage taking crisis and the early years of the Iran-Iraq war. Dr. Moghaddam has conducted experimental and field research on intergroup relations in numerous cultural contexts and has received awards for his publications on conflict, justice, and culture. His most recent books include *Multiculturalism and Intergroup Relations: Implications for Democracy in Global Context* (2008), *How Globalization Spurs Terrorism* (2008), and *Global Conflict Resolution Through Positioning Analysis* (2008, with Rom Harré and Naomi Lee).